THE ANATOMY OF
AIRCRAFT

Ninety years of development from the Wright Flyer to the B-2 "Stealth" Bomber

THE ANATOMY OF
AIRCRAFT

Ninety years of development from the Wright Flyer to the B-2 "Stealth" Bomber

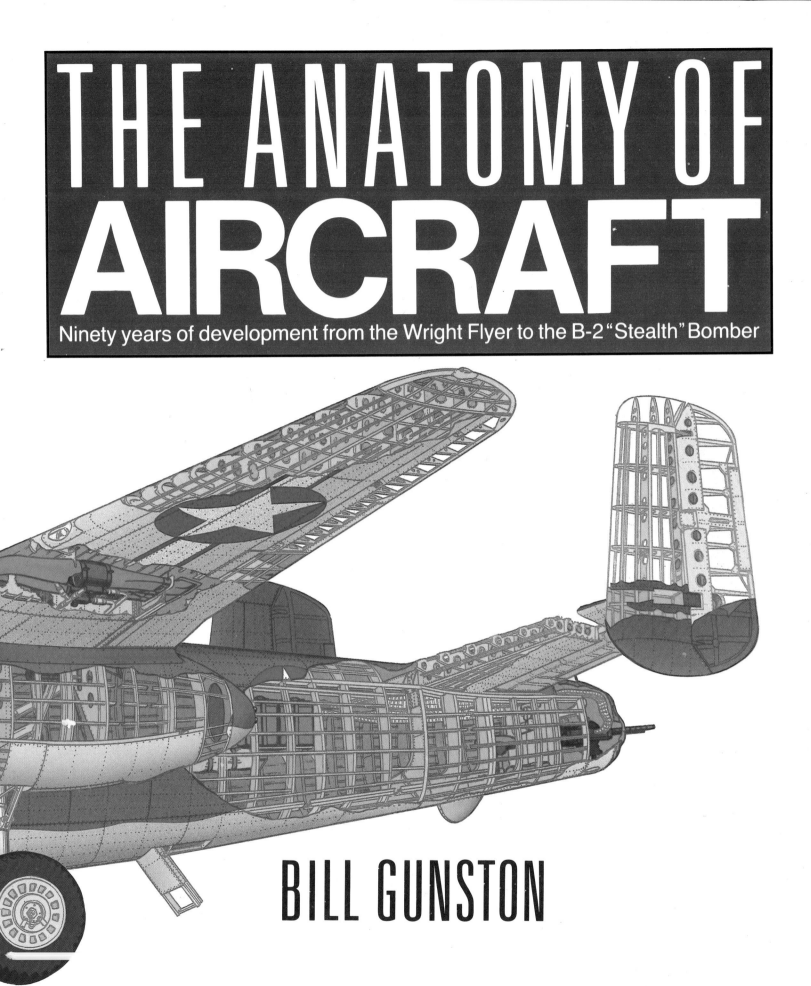

BILL GUNSTON

Longmeadow Press

First edition published 1988
This 1990 edition is published by
Longmeadow Press
201 High Ridge Road
Stamford, Connecticut 06904

Designed by Derek Avery

ISBN 0-681-40714-X

Printed in Italy

0 9 8 7 6 5 4 3

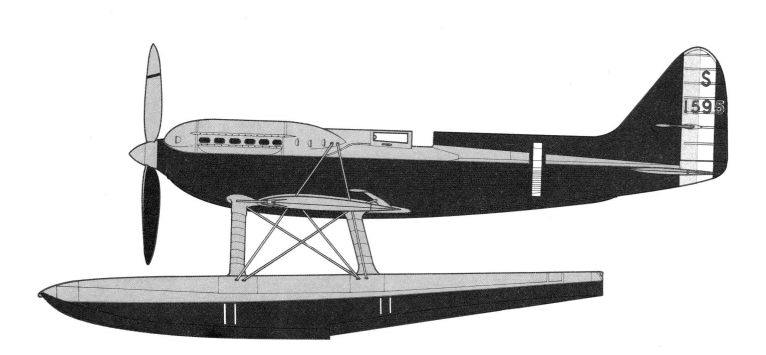

CONTENTS

Like most of Man's inventions, aircraft have not stayed the same but have developed continually. In a non-stop process triggered by competition, and the spur of warfare, aircraft have been made bigger, faster, longer-ranged, more capacious, more reliable, higher-flying, and, not least, safer. Perhaps more than any other human creations, they have changed visibly.

They have also diversified. Though in ancient times men who wanted to fly tried to copy the birds, the first type of aircraft actually to work was the balloon, which happened by chance and has virtually no parallel in nature. Men first rose into the sky by balloon in 1783. Only 20 years later Sir George Cayley described in detail how an aeroplane (North America = airplane) should be built, but such an invention was beyond the state of the art at that time. In 1852 a long and rather streamlined balloon spluttered round the sky driven by a small propeller; this was the first dirigible (French for 'steerable'), later called an airship. By 1895 the German Lilienthal was jumping off hills learning how to control his gliders; he was the first pilot. At last, in 1903 the Wright brothers, by attacking the problem methodically, built a controllable powered aeroplane.

This was not quite the end of diversification. In 1908 inventors built helicopters, but these proved difficult to tame and the successful helicopter dates from 1936 (some would say 1939). A little earlier, the Spaniard Juan de la Cierva invented and perfected the autogyro.

This book looks inside an important selection of aircraft to see how the breed has developed. Almost all are aeroplanes, in all shapes and sizes, though there are also an autogyro and a helicopter. Among the older types are a float seaplane racer and a flying-boat airliner. Most of the aircraft included are military, because to most readers warplanes are more interesting than those which merely serve mankind in useful ways!

AERODYNAMICS

Aerodynamics, the study of fluids (such as air) in motion, is the science underlying the design of all aircraft that move through the air. Knowledge of it is needed for several reasons. The air flowing round a wing is made to give lift, to raise an aeroplane into the air against the pull of gravity. Air flowing over hinged control surfaces generates forces that steer the aircraft in any direction. Streamlining is needed in modern aircraft to enable high speeds to be reached. Aerodynamic knowledge governs the design of propellers, helicopter rotors and the insides of jet engines.

It is difficult for us today to comprehend how little was known at the turn of the present century. The Wright brothers, seeking a sound foundation for the design of their aeroplane, soon found that virtually all existing 'knowledge' was suspect. They had to do their own research. They built one of the world's first wind tunnels, to blow air past small models, investigate how they behaved and measure the forces.

At that time almost the only things known for sure in aerodynamic design were that a smooth streamlined shape offered less drag (air resistance) than a severe box-like shape, and that an inclined plane (a flat plate held at a small angle, leading edge uppermost) could be made to generate lift. But the lift from an inclined plane shaped like a plank, with a rectangular cross-section, was not very great. The air flowing over the bluff leading edge would (it was later discovered) swirl away in huge eddies, causing drag rather than lift. So one of the first tasks of the pioneer aviators was to find the best cross-section for a wing. This shape, called an aerofoil, is quite distinctive, with an upward curved front rising to a highest point a short way back from the leading edge and then smoothly falling away down to the sharp trailing edge. For structural reasons, the wire-braced wings of early aircraft were only an inch or two deep, and often had no covering on the underside at all. By the 1920s a typical bomber or transport wing had a flat underside and a huge arched top, the thickest part being at about 25 per cent chord (one quarter of the way back from the leading edge). Fighters and racers had wings that were similar but thinner.

Early aircraft were often biplanes, as explained in the next section, 'Structures'. Biplane wings tended to be thin, and the first unbraced monoplanes had very thick wings in order to make the wings strong enough. With better structural knowledge it became possible to make monoplane wings much thinner. By 1940 the fastest aircraft had wings of so-called laminar-flow profile. The thickest part moved back from around 25 to about 40 per cent chord, and the underside began to bulge outwards almost as much as the top. Jet propulsion opened the way to undreamed-of increases in speed, and this called for thinner wings and new plan-forms. Most important was the swept wing, the wings leaning backwards like an arrowhead. This had the effect of making the wing appear even thinner, and enabled aircraft to fly much nearer to the speed of sound before sharp increases in drag made further gain in speed impossible. Another wing shape at this time was the delta, a triangle flying point-first, which was easy to make and had quite low drag even at supersonic speed. The speed of sound is called Mach 1; a Boeing 747 and other jetliners fly at about Mach 0·8 (at high altitude this is about 0·8 × 660mph or 528mph); the supersonic Concorde flies at Mach 2, or 1,320mph. Concorde has a special form of delta called a Gothic slender delta, very large in chord and small in span and with a graceful curved leading edge.

One of the basic qualities of an aeroplane is its L/D, or lift-drag ratio. Normally the lift has to equal the weight, so the designer tries to minimise drag. But there are complicating factors. For best range (distance flown) a wing needs to have a very high aspect ratio. This is a measure of the slenderness of a wing, and is numerically equal to the square of the span divided by the area. For a simple rectangular wing it is span divided by chord. The highest aspect ratios, ranging up to fantastic slender structures with aspect ratio of more than 37, are seen on championship sailplanes. Most aeroplanes have aspect ratio around 7, although the aspect ratio of Concorde's wing is only 1·7. At the speed of other aircraft, this would be disastrously inefficient, but at Mach 2 it is the best shape. No aerodynamics can do anything about the complete change in flow as Mach 1 is exceeded. Shockwaves form on the nose, leading edges and on any projecting part, such as the engine inlets. Drag increases tremendously. Thus, while L/D for a typical subsonic jetliner is about 16, Concorde does well to achieve L/D of about 8. Even this poor figure is twice what was thought possible 40 years ago!

When few aircraft exceeded 100mph, streamlining did not matter. Biplanes held together by struts and wires were as good as 'clean' monoplanes. But as aircraft got faster, the shape and aerodynamic design became overwhelmingly important. Engines, previously stuck out in the open, became enclosed in tight-fitting cowlings which actually converted what had been drag into useful thrust. Landing gears were carried on struts with a streamlined teardrop section, and streamlined spats enclosed the wheels. Then, with what to us seems remarkable reluctance, designers began making the whole landing gear retract inside the wing, engine nacelles or fuselage. Early retractable gears were complex, clumsy, weak, heavy and expensive; and because pilots were unused to them, they often forgot to lower the wheels before landing. The Spitfire and Bf 109 of the mid-1930s were two pioneers of neat, retractable landing gear.

The new breed of streamlined monoplanes in the 1930s naturally had far less drag than their clumsy predecessors, and when the pilot closed the throttle they hardly slowed down. Diving at the small grass airfields, they went even faster, and arriving over the desired touchdown point they just 'floated' right across the field. The answer was to fit the wing with flaps, large surfaces hinged down or extended on curved tracks from below the rear of the wing. Partly down, the flaps added lift and only a little drag, and were useful on takeoff. Fully depressed, they added a huge amount of drag, and made landing slower and safer. In a nutshell, they made a small wing behave like a large one, but in cruising flight the small wing had much less drag.

Britain had pioneered flaps in 1914 and retractable gear in 1920, but failed to use them. Another 1920 invention, however, was used straight away. Trying to make a wing lift too much at too low a speed, or trying to pull out of a dive too suddenly or make too sharp a turn, all cause the smooth airflow over the wing to break down. The air swirls away in useless eddies in what is called a stall, and the aircraft is likely to drop like a stone. Fitting a long thin auxiliary wing along the top of the leading edge can force the air not to break away but continue to give lift. The slender strip, called a slat, is pulled open by the extra lift on it, and it is the slot, the narrow gap between the slat and the wing, that prevents the stall by guiding the air.

Any useful aircraft must be controllable. Lilienthal did it by shifting his body-weight. Soon this was considered crude and part of aviation's prehistoric era – yet today thousands of hang-gliding enthusiasts do just that! The Wright brothers were the pioneers of the controllable aeroplane, but the scheme they used was eventually discontinued. To roll the aircraft into a correctly banked turn they warped (twisted) the wings, by pulling up the trailing

Below:
Exact scale models are used in wind tunnels to simulate the aerodynamic forces to be experienced by the full size aircraft.

edge of the wings on one side of the machine and pulling down on the other. This was quite acceptable with primitive structures, but, as aircraft design matured, it was realised a better answer was to cut out the outer part of the wing trailing edge and hinge it to the rest of the wing. Called ailerons, these surfaces are normally easy to move and work in opposition: whichever aileron is pushed down causes that wing to rise, and vice versa. The rudder is simple, acting like that of a boat. Usually it hardly needs to be used, but in an aeroplane with engines spread along the wings, failure of an outer engine causes a powerful yawing (slewing) effect which the pilot has to counteract with harsh use of the rudder, in order to keep straight. To dive and climb, the Wrights used foreplanes, resembling miniature biplane wings pivoted at the front of the aircraft to make the nose rise or fall. By 1909, Blériot's scheme of having a pivoted tailplane or elevators (in the USA a tailplane is called a stabilizer) had become almost universal and stayed that way until about 1950. New jet designs then introduced alternative ideas. Deltas were fitted with trailing-edge controls called elevons, combining the duties of elevators and ailerons. Tailplanes themselves were pivoted, and driven by powerful hydraulic rams, separate elevators no longer being needed. Flaperons were invented to act as both ailerons and flaps. Spoilers, hinged above the wing, began to replace ailerons, enabling high-lift flaps to be extended right to the wing tips. Powered tailplanes, used for diving and climbing in place of elevators, were then made to work in opposite directions to roll the aircraft, being renamed tailerons. Perhaps most exciting of all, the wings were attached by pivots so that sweep angle could be adjusted by the pilot: full span for takeoff and landing, a little sweep for subsonic cruise, a little more for combat, and maximum sweep – the wings being folded back so acutely they are hardly seen – for a dash at low level at maximum supersonic speed.

STRUCTURES

Naturally, the earliest aircraft were made from materials that were handy, readily available and reasonably light, such as spruce, bamboo, piano wire and fabric, the latter being brushed with varnish or other liquid to make it taut and waterproof. Small metal fittings, usually of brass or steel, were used at the joints, and to anchor the all-important wires that braced the whole apparatus. Wires were life or death. If one broke, it often meant the death of the aviator. One pioneer pilot, asked how he checked that all his bracing wires were correct, answered, 'Simple! I take a canary with me on board, and if it escapes I know a wire is loose!'.

By 1916 the leading edge of the wing and the front half of the fuselage were often skinned in veneer or plywood, glued and then pinned in place. By 1920 some wings were made wholly of wood, though hinged control surfaces stayed fabric-covered, even on many all-metal aircraft of the 1930s. Even more radical was a type of construction introduced in World War I by Fokker, among others, which until well into the 1950s was still common on lightplanes because of its simplicity and cheapness. The fuselage, often together with the fin, was assembled by welding together accurately cut (and sometimes curved) pieces of steel tube. If everything was joined in an accurate frame, called a jig, then every fuselage was the same as the others. The result was a tough and cheap structure which could be covered in fabric or used as the basis for a more streamlined shape filled out by light wood 'formers' over which fabric or veneer could be attached.

All the Fokker warplanes and airliners of the 1920s had welded-tube fuselages and wooden wings. The only firm that could rival Fokker was Junkers of Germany, who were pioneers of light alloys, such as Duralumin, made by adding a little copper and other elements to aluminium to make it harder and stronger. These were in many ways better than any other materials, for they were strong, non-corrosive and light enough to be used for the skin as well as the underlying airframe. Their main drawback was high cost, and many firms, including almost all British ones, stuck to traditional materials because change was difficult and initially expensive. Even Junkers decided to roll the light-alloy skin sheets through ridged rollers so that they came out corrugated. Such sheet is much more rigid than thin flat sheet, and though it was heavier (because for a 1,000-sq ft surface a corrugated sheet contains much more than 1,000sq ft of metal), it seemed a good idea. Junkers thought the air would naturally flow past along the corrugations, and it was not until the 1940s that it was realized the air invariably flowed diagonally across them, and that the corrugations caused high drag. Junkers gave up using corrugated skin just before World War II.

Britain and some other countries failed to think ahead in aircraft structures. Wood was unsuitable for the tropics and so the RAF and other customers asked for metal instead, but all that was done was to replace the wooden parts by metal – steel or aluminium – with fabric covering. It was left to the Germans and Americans to devise all-metal 'stressed-skin' construction, which by 1940 had become almost universal. In effect it was a translation into metal of so-called 'monocoque' structures used in a very few aircraft before World War I. Monocoque means single-shell. Instead of building a strong skeleton and then covering it with fabric or other light sheet, the strength was made in the skin itself, as in the claw of a lobster. The early monocoque machines were made of sheet after sheet of thin veneer, often of tulip wood, wrapped round to the correct shape and glued in place until the whole structure was strong, beautifully streamlined and completely hollow inside. This marvellous method was unusual because it was very expensive to make and difficult to repair.

The breakthrough came when tulip-wood veneer was replaced by mass-produced sheets of Duralumin. At a stroke this opened the way not only to aircraft that were simple and cheap but also to monoplanes that needed no struts or wires and so, if they had powerful engines, could fly at high speeds. A refinement which gave a smooth external surface was flush riveting; instead of the rivets having projecting heads, they were countersunk into the skin so that after the aircraft was painted it was difficult (if it was well made) to see a single rivet or skin joint.

By the 1950s, aircraft had become impressively powerful and heavy. Wings were no longer made by wrapping thin strips and angle-sections round to construct ribs extending from leading edge to trailing edge. Instead there was a main wing box, as the structural heart of the wing, with light leading and trailing sections. The wing box consisted of a front spar, a rear spar and very strong upper and lower skins, all massively built to bear loads far heavier than any other part of the aircraft. The spars were made up of long vertical Duralumin walls, from wing-tip to wing-tip, with extra-strong edges (called booms) above and below. Most booms were T-section above and an inverted T below, the stem of the T being riveted or bolted to the vertical wall (called the web). The heavy skins, curved in giant machines to the exact profile of the wing, were attached to the cross-member of each T. In jet bombers and airliners, the skins were so thick they were attached by precision-drilled bolts with countersunk heads.

Integral construction came in at this time. Instead of stiffening a skin by adding rows of angle-sections all over it, the skin was sculptured by starting with a massive thick slab and then cutting away at it with colossal machine tools, often weighing many hundreds of tons. Light alloys can be cut at high speed, and a giant skin mill pours out bright metal chips at the rate of truckloads each minute. Eventually the panel may be not much thicker than heavy cardboard, but immensely stiff and strong because of the closely spaced ribs on the back, each perhaps several inches high. Usually the machined panel is then lightly 'chem-milled' by etching it in a bath of acid to remove the slightest scratch or tool mark. Until after 1950, nobody bothered about such things; then, following crashes of Britain's Comet jet airliners, it was realized that fatigue, caused by repeated applications of quite normal loads, can make strong structures crack apart. The slightest crack, scratch or sharp corner can start a fatigue crack, and every modern aircraft is designed to fly thousands of hours – perhaps representing a 40-year active life – without cracks appearing.

We are familiar with 'tear along the perforations', so it can be seen that the designer would rather not drill too many holes. Most aircraft have thousands of rivets in close-spaced rows, but after World War II Britain led the way in replacing many rivets by bonding – in effect, a form of glueing, but with metal. Most metal bonding is done under heat and pressure, but the joints are as strong as the metal. A more familiar form of bonding is welding, where abutting metal surfaces are actually melted together. Spot welding, done at high speed by accurate machines, is often used to attach skin panels. Various forms of bonding are also used to make 'sandwich' panels consisting of two metal sheets kept a short distance (say, an inch) apart by a light interior. In World War II the sandwich core

was usually balsa, a wood much lighter than cork, but today the core is usually a honeycomb, like that made by bees, assembled under computer control from strips of metal so thin they are virtually foil. Other cores are expanded polystyrene and similar 'foamed-in-place' low-density plastics. Sandwich panels are smooth, strong and rigid, but unbelievably light.

Naturally, the invention of plastics led aircraft designers to see if they could be used to make air vehicles. In 1950, experiments were done with Durestos, using millions of fine asbestos fibres bonded with adhesive in high-pressure moulds. Glass-fibre was used increasingly for such things as radomes enclosing radar aerials (which have to be transparent to radio waves), wing-tips, tailcones and smooth curved fairings, but most GRP (glass reinforced plastics) parts are too flexible to bear the main loads. The big breakthrough came in 1966 with the invention – again, mainly in Britain – of CFRP (carbon-fibre reinforced plastics). Also known as graphite fibres, these particular ones are made by cooking spun fibres, such as polyacrilonitrile, in a white-hot furnace. The resulting black threads are much finer than human hairs, but fantastically strong. Bonded together in millions with resin adhesives, they can be used to make black rods, strips, sheets and even complete wings or tails. Changing from a riveted aluminium structure to a CFRP one typically cuts weight by half, eliminates fatigue problems and, usually, also cuts costs because the finished part is all one piece.

Today CFRP is used in partnership with even newer structures. Materials made of extremely strong fibres joined by adhesive to form a solid mass are called 'composite' structures. They can be cunningly tailored so that the fibres are aligned along the directions of the applied loads. For example, a CFRP wing would have most of its fibres arranged transversely, running from root to tip, rather than across the wing from front to back. Newest of the fibres used in aircraft composite structures is Kevlar, called an 'arachnoid' fibre because of its similarity to spider-web. Even traditional metals are fighting back, and the latest airliners have major wing skins of aluminium-lithium alloy which can bear heavier loads whilst weighing less. By using CFRP, thin aluminium, Styrofoam plastics, fine wires and Mylar transparent film covering, it is possible to make safe, man-powered aircraft with a span greater than Concorde yet weighing less than 60lb!

PROPULSION

Though 19th-Century experimenters used steam, compressed air and electricity, the only engines important in aviation have been of the internal-combustion type, burning petroleum fuels. On the other hand, more than any other of man's vehicles, aircraft engines have diversified into totally different classes.

At first virtually all engines were of the Otto-cycle species of four-stroke piston engines (as used in cars), burning petrol (North America, gasoline). A very few aircraft were powered by diesel engines (as used in heavy goods trucks and trains), but the saving in fuel was outweighed by the diesel's massive weight, cost and other problems. In the 1930s a few pioneers worked on methods of jet propulsion that would overcome the limitation of aircraft speed of around 500mph imposed by propellers. Some worked on rockets, and it was a rocket burning liquid oxygen and ethyl alcohol that first drove an aircraft faster than sound in 1947. Most worked on turbojets, which are gas turbines whose sole purpose is to pump out a high-speed jet of hot gas. Yet another new engine species appeared in the 1950s and, after 30 years of 'almost', seems likely at last to sweep away reciprocating piston engines. This is the RC (rotating-combustion) engine.

From the start, Otto-type engines came in different forms. The Wright brothers used a row of four cylinders, with primitive cooling by surrounding jackets of water. Other builders increased power by using more cylinders, many pioneer aviators using the Antoinette V-8 engine, with eight cylinders in two rows angled like a V. In 1909 the world of aviation was excited by the Gnome, a radically different rotary engine. Machined from steel, and shining like a jewel, it had seven or nine cylinders arranged like spokes of a wheel. Strangely, they were air-cooled, with fins. Stranger still, the crankshaft was fixed to the aircraft and the engine buzzed round with the propeller!

Rotaries were important in World War I, powering the Sopwith Camel, for example, but by 1920 they had given way to the static radial, in which it is the crankshaft that spins round inside a fixed engine. For the next 30 years there were arguments over air and water cooling. Some air-cooled engines were of the in-line type, a famous example being the Gipsy series which powered the 1934 Comet racer. Most lightplanes today have air-cooled engines with four or six opposed cylinders, as fitted to the Saab Supporter. Most air-cooled engines have been radials, usually with one or two rows each of seven or nine cylinders. The F4U Corsair fighter, for example, had an engine in the 2,000hp class with two rows each of nine 'pots'. Even here there was scope for variation, as when the British Bristol company pioneered the use of sleeve valves (as in the engines of the Short G-class flying boat).

Proponents of the rival water-cooled engines could claim more power for a given frontal area, and by the mid-1920s improved installations made these engines look much more streamlined. A comparison between the S.6B and the contemporary Hawk III will show why a water-cooled engine was picked for the racer. On the other hand, practical military or airline machines could not dissipate surplus heat through radiators all over the surface, as did the S.6B, and water radiators caused extra weight, drag and vulnerability. Moreover, the shortness of the air-cooled radial improved fighter manoeuvrability, and these engines worked much better in extremely cold or hot climates. It was a ding-dong battle. By World War II, most people thought the streamlined in-line or V engines had

won, but they were wrong. Properly installed air-cooled radials took over in fighters and airliners, until replaced by jets.

A gas turbine can, of course, be geared down to drive a propeller, the resulting engine being a turboprop. These burn less fuel than turbojets, and are also quieter, but they are unable to fly aircraft faster than 500mph. Today, engine and propeller makers are trying to develop new kinds of 'propfan' engines that will bring efficiency and lower noise to speeds up to 600mph. Meanwhile, turbojets themselves have been improved out of all recognition. Starting as noisy, fuel-hungry engines for fighters, they have been developed as quiet fuel-efficient turbofan engines, such as fitted to the Airbus 300B. Handling a colossal airflow, enough to fill a cathedal each second, the fan on the front may be 8ft across and develop nearly all the thrust. It is driven by a relatively small 'core engine', almost like that which drives the propeller gearbox in a turboprop. Jet engines (turbojets or turbofans) for supersonic aircraft are usually boosted by an afterburner, a large jetpipe in which, for takeoff or full-throttle flight, extra fuel is burned. Many, including almost all airline engines, have reversers which blow the jet forwards after landing, to slow the aircraft quickly and save wear and tear on the brakes; reversers are especially useful on icy runways.

Reversers are a simple way of 'vectoring' (pointing in different directions) the jet from an engine in order to push the aircraft in the direction needed. In the most sophisticated form, seen in the Harrier and Sea Harrier, the thrust can be directed diagonally forwards for braking, downwards for lift and rearwards for normal flight. The Harrier has a unique engine with four nozzles, two discharging air from the fan and two hot gas from the turbine. All nozzles can be vectored together, driven by gears from a motor running on compressed air from the engine. With the four nozzles pointing down, opening the throttle lifts the aircraft straight off the ground (which can be a small platform on a ship). The Harrier was the first VTOL (vertical takeoff and landing) jet to go into combat service. The nozzles can also be rotated at near supersonic speed (Viffing, from Vectoring In Forward Flight), allowing the Harrier to make previously-impossible flight manoeuvres and prove a dangerous adversary in air combat.

Below:
British Aerospace's Harrier T.52 demonstrator showing off its vectored thrust, carrying out a short rolling landing.

SYSTEMS

The first aircraft had no systems except a few wires to operate the flight controls, and a pipe joining the fuel tank to the engine. Gradually, as aircraft became more complicated, so their systems became more diverse and widespread. Today airframes are merely the structures needed to hold together the myriad complex systems that give the aircraft its capability, and which often cost far more than the simple body in which they are installed. There is a parallel with our own bodies, whose 'systems' are incredibly complicated compared with the mere skeleton/skin structure in which they are packed!

The first aircraft system was for fuel. At first there was just a tank, filled by hand through a cap, with feed by gravity to the carburettor on the engine. Today most military or commercial aircraft do not have separate fuel tanks, though crashproof flexible cells or bags are still found in lightplanes and some helicopters. Instead the fuel is housed in integral tankage formed by the main wing box or sections of fuselage, which are sealed to prevent the slightest leak. The A-4 Skyhawk of 1954 showed a new approach in that the fuselage rode on an integral tank which happened to be shaped like a wing, with slats and flaps added at front and rear. With increasing system capacity, pressure-fuelling became necessary, the whole aircraft being replenished at rates exceeding two tons per minute from a single high-pressure coupling.

This in turn opened the way to improved inflight refuelling. Britain, the US Navy and some other countries adopted the probe/drogue method, the supply tanker trailing a hose with a funnel-shaped drogue on the end, into which the receiver aircraft inserted its probe (which is often retractable). The valves in the drogue and probe are automatically opened on proper connection. The USAF adopted a 'Flying Boom' method, in which a rigid telescopic pipe on the tanker is steered by a tanker boom operator into a socket on top of the receiver.

Electric systems began with a few wires supplying current from a DC battery to a radio and to navigation lights, red on the left wing-tip, green on the right and white at the tail. To keep the battery charged, there was usually a tiny generator driven by a windmill in the airstream. By the 1930s the more powerful engines drove DC generators feeding circuits of rapidly growing complexity. Today, even lightplanes have electrics much more complicated than the average house. Big aircraft have literally thousands of electrical items on board. The main power is generated by AC alternators putting out scores of kilowatts. Raw AC is used to heat windscreens, propellers, air inlets, leading edges, instrument sensors and many other items to prevent ice forming. The avionics (aviation electronics) are supplied with AC at precisely 400 Hertz (400 cycles per second), while DC is supplied from transformer rectifier units. At least one generator will be driven by a separate APU (auxiliary power unit), usually driven by a small gas turbine, to provide ground power without running the main engines (which the APU can also start, by supplying electric power or compressed air).

Most of the main power functions aboard today's aircraft are usually hydraulic. Special non-inflammable oil fills hundreds or thousands of pipes which, when needed, can be pressurized to very high pressure, typically 3,000 or 4,000lb/ sq in. Thus, a piston with a diameter of 3in could exert a force of 14 tons. Each engine will drive at least one hydraulic pump, and the total horsepower of the system may be hundreds or even thousands. The hydraulic power is divided into several totally separate systems, arranged so that faults in one system cannot have any effect on the others; thus, power is always available for the vital services, of which the most essential are the flight controls. Complex electro-hydraulic power units, sensitive to what the pilot wants the aircraft to do, drive the spoilers, ailerons, tailplane or tailerons, rudder and airbrakes. The biggest power input of all may be needed to drive the flaps and landing gear retraction. Other circuits drive nosewheel steering, and anything from cargo doors to windscreen wipers. Back in World War II, hydraulics also operated gun turrets and bomb doors.

The ECS (environmental control system) covers anything that affects comfort of the humans on board. In early aircraft there might be just a muff around the exhaust pipe to feed warm air to one point in the cockpit or cabin, other parts being freezing. Today the whole interior is probably pressurized by a complex system energized by the main engines, or by separate compressors, to maintain interior pressure near that at sea level. Air is warmed (or cooled in a refrigeration circuit), and dried or humidified, to give the most comfortable internal conditions. Emergency oxygen is stored as high-pressure gas or as liquid, and in the very newest aircraft there is an Obogs (On-board oxygen generation system).

To prevent ice forming, the leading edges of the wings may be heated electrically as already mentioned, or by hot air from the engines, or generated in special heaters. For slower aircraft, a more economical method is to use pneumatic boots, each made up of several long flat rubber strips. These are alternately inflated with compressed air and then deflated, forcing ice to break off and be blown away. Even helicopter rotor blades and propellers are today protected against ice forming.

Left:
The "Glass Cockpit" of a modern airliner. Most of the old style instruments have now been replaced by more versatile, cathode ray tube displays.

WRIGHT FLYER

Orville and Wilbur Wright's first powered machine, the Flyer — a name they subsequently gave to all of their powered machines — was built during the summer of 1903. In September it was delivered to the Kill Devil Hills where the brothers found their base camp in a state of disrepair. However, a 1902 glider that they had built was there, although very badly damaged. They repaired this to be able to practise on, giving it a new double rear rudder like the one on the new Flyer. There then followed weeks of intensive preparations, practice gliding and many minor but frustrating setbacks. Mechanical breakages, repairs, replacements and adjustments of various kinds delayed the final completion of the Flyer until 12 December.

Unfavourable weather then postponed the inaugural flight until the morning of the fourteenth when the brothers summoned as witnesses their friends from the nearby Kill Devil Lifesaving Station. They then carried their machine to the end of the starting rail. Flyer I, which had waited patiently for its first trial, was a biplane with a 40ft (12m) wingspan. The aircraft had a wing area of 510 sq ft (48 sq m) and a camber of approximately 1 in 20, which was supported on two long skids. The 12 horsepower engine drove two pusher propellers by means of cycle-chains, one of which was crossed to produce counter-rotation.

The aircraft was placed on the 60ft (18m) launching rail which had been laid downhill into the wind. Orville and Wilbur tossed a coin to find out who would be the first pilot, and it was Wilbur who won. The test, however, was a failure; Flyer I ran down the rail, rose from the carrying truck, climbed steeply, stalled and ploughed into the sand. This caused minor damage to the structure, which was soon repaired. Wilbur admitted

Below:
Orville Wright at the controls of the Flyer I as it leaves the take-off rail on its 120 feet, twelve second flight into history, on 17 December 1903, at Kill Devil Hills, near Kittyhawk, North Carolina.

that the failure was due to their mistake in putting on too much elevator, thus bringing up the nose too high. It should be noted that even if the first trial had been successful, it would not have counted since the take-off was downhill and so was assisted by gravity.

Conditions were suitable again by 17 December, and the take-off rail was laid down on level ground. Local witnesses were summoned yet again, and a camera was set up and trained on the end of the take-off track.

With Orville at the controls, the engine of Flyer I was run up and at 10.35 Eastern Standard Time the holding rope was released. The aircraft lifted from the truck after a take-off run of about 40ft (12m). It made an undulating flight of approximately 12 seconds in which time it covered 120ft (36.5m) — the rise and fall of the aircraft was due to the pilot's inexperience with the elevator, which turned out to be too evenly balanced. Airspeed was approximately 30mph (48km/h).

Although of only a short duration, this was the world's first flight of a powered machine transporting a man, having lifted itself by its own power into the air. It had sailed forward without any reduction of speed and had finally landed at a point as high as that from which it had started. It should be noted at at this stage that the entire flight of Flyer I was only just over half the length of a Boeing 747! Following minor repairs, three more flights were made the same morning the last of which covered just under half a mile (1km). The elevator was damaged in the final landing and the brothers then decided to end all tests for the day. The machine was carried back to the camp where tragically the machine was overturned and wrecked by the wind a few minutes later.

Orville and Wilbur had, in effect, conquered the

air only one and a half years after they had written to the Smithsonian Institute requesting books on flying. Now, in 1903, they had made the first powered, sustained and controlled flights. They also possessed the first potentially practical flying machine. (No aircraft other than the Wrights' could remain in the air for more than 20 seconds until November 1906. Even then it was not until November 1907 that a full minute's duration was achieved by a European machine.)

Back in Dayton, Ohio the brothers began to design their powered Flyer II as well as a new motor. Construction was finished in May, and a new airdrome was established eight miles east of Dayton: the Huffman Prairie was the world's first airdrome for aviation. The new machine was basically similar to Flyer I but had the camber decreased to 1 in 25. A new, much more efficient engine with 15-16 horsepower was used. Many trial flights were made in 1904; although the majority were short, they were nevertheless important.

The first circular flight was made by Wilbur on 20 September, yet it was not until November that a flight of more than five minutes was accomplished. Wilbur undertook almost four cir-

Orville (left) and Wilbur (right) making repairs to their damaged flyer.

cuits of the airfield, covering a distance of 3 miles (nearly 5km). The flights during 1904 were made at very low heights so that during the process of learning both the particular characteristics of the aircraft and the craft of pilotage in general, they had a good chance of survival in a crash. Another reason to fly low was that Flyer II tended to respond poorly to the controls, then stall and go out of control when making a tight turn. This problem was not mastered until September 1905.

The brothers had designed Flyer III by June 1905. The machine proved to be thoroughly successful, and it ranks as the first all-round practical aircraft in history. Flights were becoming longer and longer and increasingly successful. However, despite offers to the American Government for the aircraft, nothing was forthcoming. From the negative reaction they received, the Wrights decided to try overseas, first to Britain and then to France. However, neither Government seemed interested and so finally, after a great deal of trying, Wilbur and Orville gave up on the idea of flight. Little did they realise that less than 70 years later the idea for a flying machine would resolve in an aircraft of the capacity of Concorde!

WRIGHT FLYER

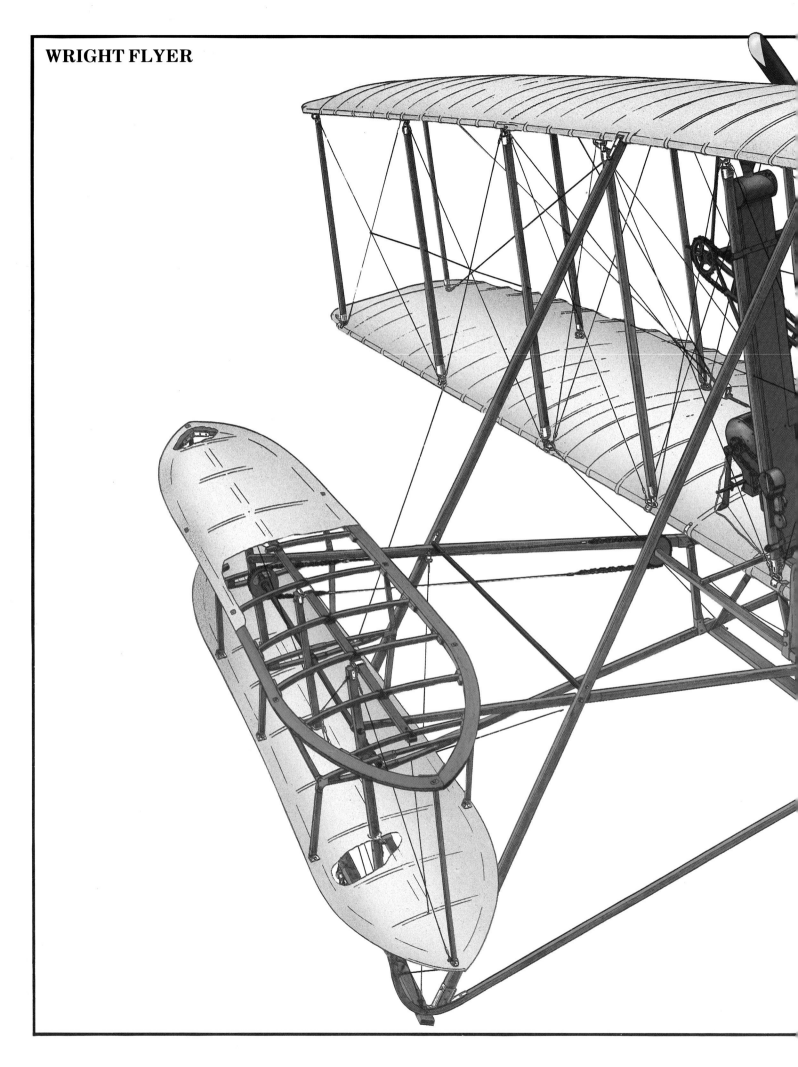

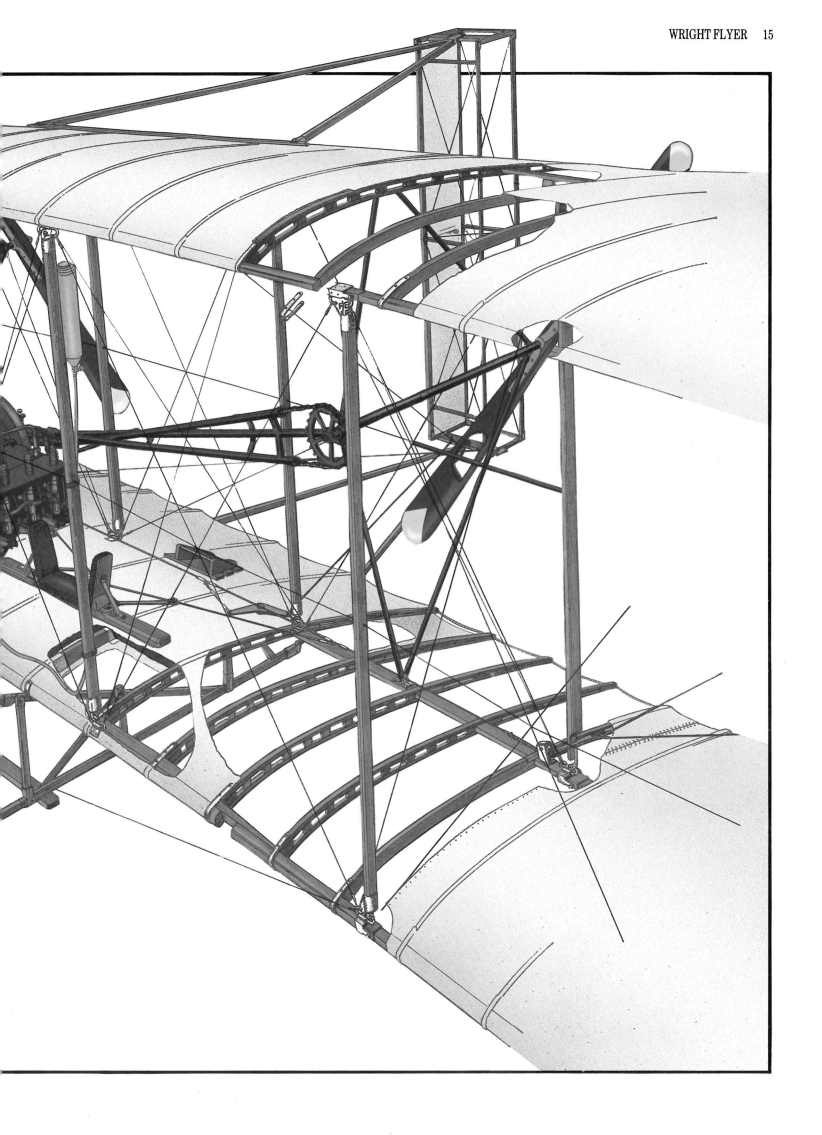

BLERIOT TYPE XI (1909)

In 1909 the British *Daily Mail* newspaper offered a prize of £1,000 for the first aeroplane flight across the English Channel. The best aeroplane of the day was the Antoinette, but the example entered by Hubert Latham twice (and most untypically) suffered engine failure and had to alight in the sea. Louis Blériot had a cruder and most unsuitable aircraft, yet by daring, skill and sheer luck, he succeeded in flying from Calais to Dover on 25 July 1909. Overnight Blériot's name echoed round the world, and within a few months he had taken orders for over 100 aircraft.

Like the Antoinette, but unlike almost all other 'flying machines' of 1909, his aircraft was a monoplane. Blériot made a few short hops with his first monoplane in April 1907. By 1909 he was an experienced designer and pilot, and his Channel conqueror was the Type XI. Some were sold with Gnome rotary engines, in which the crankshaft was fixed to the fuselage and the engine and propeller rotated round it, but he himself used only Anzani engines, usually the three-cylinder of 25hp. This was bolted to a strong metal frame riding on two bicycle wheels

with rubber and coil-spring shock absorbers. The frame was bolted to the front of a simple fuselage with four straight hardwood longerons which were joined together at the tail, where the rudder was pivoted. Only the front of the fuselage was covered with fabric, the rest being open to enable the diagonal bracing wires that gave the fuselage its strength to be checked and, if necessary, tightened with turnbuckles.

By 1909 it was known that wings should have a curved profile, with a subtly arched top of the kind which had been shown to generate the maximum lift for any given airspeed. Blériot's wing was of the kind known as single curvature; in other words it had an upper surface but no underside. Nowhere was it more than 3·5in (89mm) thick, so it would have had very little strength had it not been braced by strong wires above and below to the landing gears and to a triangulated steel frame above the fuselage. The left and right wings were separate and, after releasing the bracing wires, could be removed from their attachments on the sides of the fuselage so that the machine could be sent by rail or towed behind a car. The horizontal tail (in America called the stabilizer) was also removable from its attachment under the rear of the

Left:
Two views of the Salis Collection's, reconstructed Bleriot X I Monoplane, part reconstruction and part original.

fuselage. At the time of the Channel flight the tailplane mid-section was fixed, only the outer portions being pivoted.

The pilot sat in line with the trailing edge of the wings. He held the control column in his left hand, using his right to control the throttle and ignition levers, and also to pump a rubber bulb to pressurize the lubricating oil supply. The control column was carried in a bell-shaped universal joint. Movement fore and aft worked the elevators for diving and climbing. Movement to left or right rolled the aircraft by warping the wings. The rudder was worked by pedals. Most Blériots had a horizontal wheel fixed to the top of the stick, merely to give a better handhold, and often the stick itself carried the engine controls.

Behind the engine were the tanks for petrol (gasoline) and oil, sufficient for about two hours. The engine drove a beautiful Chauvière propeller of carved hardwood, of 82in (2·08m) diameter. This was much more efficient than the crude propellers used by some other constructors, which were often made from bent steel plate, and was perhaps the Blériot's best single feature.

Right:
A Bleriot circles over Hendon airfield in 1912.

Below:
A Bleriot replica on display in Switzerland.

CURTISS JN-4 'JENNY' (1914)

After the Wright brothers, Glenn Curtiss was the greatest pioneer American aviator. Many of his earliest machines were seaplanes, but in 1914 the US Army issued a specification for a trainer, preferring a tractor biplane. Curtiss produced the Model N, while he engaged a British designer, B. Douglas Thomas, to produce the Model J. There were various versions of both, but the most important offshoots were the JN series which combined features of both. Almost all had the water-cooled OX-5 engine, with a flat frontal radiator, while some had equal-span wings with ailerons on all four, and other versions had unequal span, with upper ailerons only.

Early models had the outdated shoulder-yoke lateral control which worked the ailerons by the pilot leaning left or right. This was replaced by a wheel control and finally in the mass-production wartime trainers by plain sticks. The first big order was for 94 wheel-control JN-4s in 1916, an aircraft of the US Army 1st Aero Sqn flying the first US combat mission on 16 March 1916 (against the Mexican bandit Pancho Villa). Nearly all 'Jennies', however, were trainers. Over 10,000 were built, in more than 40 versions, and by many companies in the USA and Canada. By the end of World War I many British pilots, and practically every US and Canadian, had received at least part of his instruction on 'Jennies'. In the 1920s they were used in hundreds for barnstorming, pleasure flying, mail carrying and many other tasks.

In plan view the JN series looked very like the equally numerous British B.E. series and, like them, the 'Jenny' was slow and sedate. This is hardly surprising because it was very big for 90hp, and the long wings were braced by eight interplane struts, over 300ft (91m) of round wire and additional cabane struts and wires to support the overhanging outer sections of the upper wing. To add to the drag, a curved skid protected each lower wing during the inevitable ground loops made by nervous pupils. Like the B.E., the tailplane had a chord (distance from front to rear) almost as great as the span, and all control wires to the hinged elevators and rudder were external.

Its structure was almost entirely wood, and spruce and ash were the most common. Of course, the fuselage was braced by a mass of piano wires, all with turnbuckles to adjust the tension. It was said that rigging a 'Jenny' was something any good piano-tuner could do! The wing aerofoil section was Eiffel 36, not very much deeper in profile than the single-surface wings of the Blèriot, the chord being 59·5in and the gap between the wings 60in (1·52m). The main landing gear had ash struts carrying the cross-axle with rubber bungee springing. Under the tail was a massive skid which swivelled with the rudder to make taxiing easy. There were no brakes, and usually not even an airspeed indicator, so the pilot learned to fly 'by the seat of his pants' and the pitch of the sound from the wires.

Thanks to its low wing loading (weight divided by wing area) all JNs were airborne after a very short run, and general handling was quite good considering their low power and ponderous size. But they were unforgiving, and pupil fatalities were high. The Canadians, who called their versions Canucks, were switching production to the Avro 504K at the time of the Armistice in November 1918.

Below:
The large size, together with the "built-in headwind", of the Jenny's wire bracing contribute to the aircraft's rather sedate performance.

Top and Mid: Barnstorming Jennies. The Curtiss Jenny was a favourite aircraft of the post World War One "Barnstormers", the workhorse of these aerial daredevils.

Below: The external control wires to ailerons, elevators and rudder are clearly visible on this preserved US Army Aviation JN-4D.

FOKKER DR.1

Only 320 Dr.I triplanes were built (the designation coming from *Dreidecker*, three-winger), a trivial number in the context of World War I production. It had several faults, and hardly shone in combat, yet this agile machine is today one of the most famous fighters of all time, largely because a red model was being flown by 'Red Baron' Manfred von Richthofen when he was killed on 21 April 1918.

Fokker saw the British Sopwith Triplanes in action in May 1917. He was very impressed and got his chief designer, Reinhold Platz, to produce a similar machine (though Platz rightly remained unconvinced about a triplane's merits). Later, when a Sopwith was captured, 14 German and Austrian companies produced copies, but Fokker had a head start. The triplane was regarded as a kind of wonder-formula, but this proved without foundation. The reason Sopwith adopted it in the first place was that pilot view was better, the short span improved rate of roll and the narrow chord was thought to improve manoeuvrability generally, but by 1918 no triplanes remained in production.

Platz's D VI prototype was flown by ace Werner Voss in June 1917. This had completely unbraced wings, but the production Dr.I had single interplane struts added, largely to allay pilots' fears. Like most Fokkers of the period, the entire fuselage and tail was made of welded steel tube, accurately assembled in a precise jig. Despite this, there were the usual diagonal bracing wires, tightened by turnbuckles. The wings, however, were almost wholly of wood, and by this time were beginning to assume a deeper

aerofoil section with a fairly flat undersurface. The Sopwith Triplane had had two spars, but Platz used only one. It was in the form of a rectangular plywood box, with four spruce booms (strong strips) at the corners. Ribs were ply, reinforced by spruce vertical strips and peripheral flanges, a large hole being cut in the ply between each pair of uprights to reduce weight. Cross-over diagonal strips and a single square-section spruce boom joined the ribs at the rear of each wing.

Sopwith had used six ailerons, but the Fokker had only two, on the top wing and projecting beyond the tip (almost a Fokker trademark). The Dr.I was one of the last Fokkers to have a rudder but no fin, whereas the horn-balanced elevators were hinged to large tailplanes of the triangular shape which in the 1950s became known as the delta. The rubber-sprung landing gear was again typically Fokker, having a large wing-like fairing enclosing the axle. The tail skid was likewise pivoted and sprung by rubber bungee. Under each wing-tip was a protective skid of ash, attached by steel brackets, though the mind boggles at how the tip could inadvertently have scraped the ground! Similar steel-plate fittings, with single bolts, attached the middle and lower wings to the fuselage.

Most Dr.Is had twin LMG 08/15 (so-called Spandau) guns. The pilot had quite a complicated stick with grips for both hands, the left being pivoted fore/aft as the throttle lever. The right grip had a large trigger for both guns, while between the grips were thumb switches firing left/right guns separately. Between these hinged push-switches was the ignition cut-out button, used for 'blipping' the rotary engine.

Above:
A scarlet Fokker
Triplane replica in
the colours of the
infamous Red Baron.

Right:
German Air Force
Officers inspect a
Dr 1 on an airfield in
France during World
War 1.

Left:
Many Fokker
Triplane replicas
have been built,
some specifically for
film and television
work.

FOKKER Dr.1 (1917)

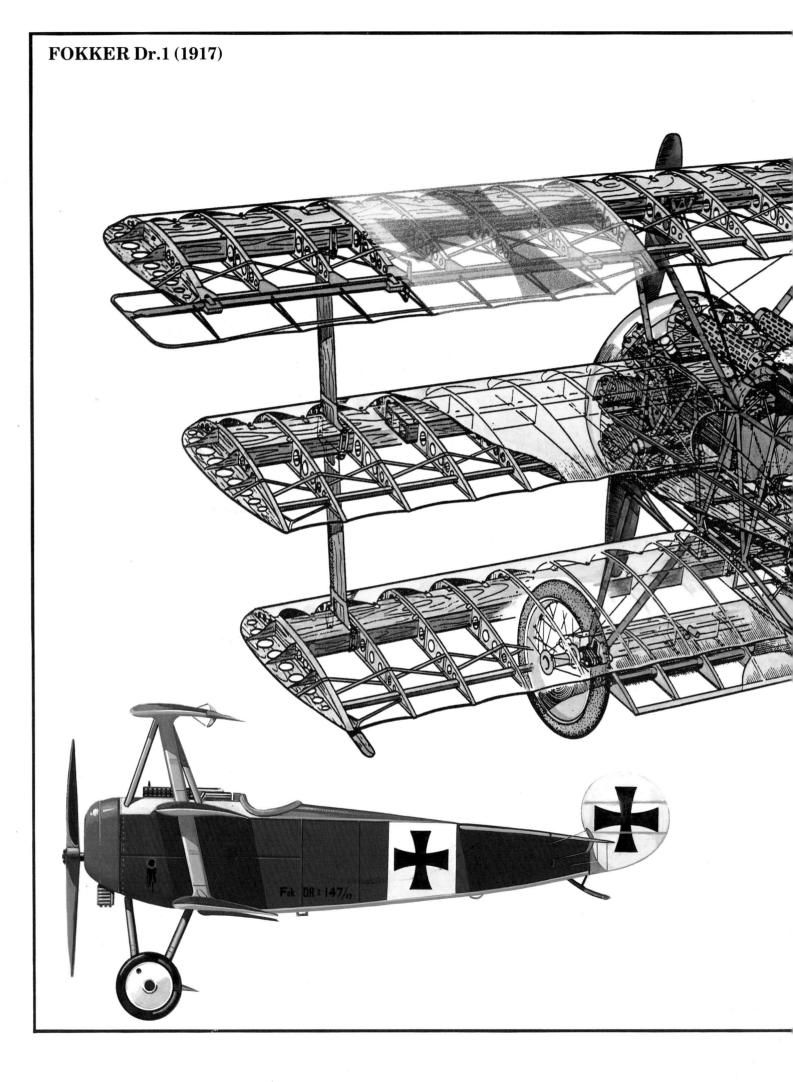

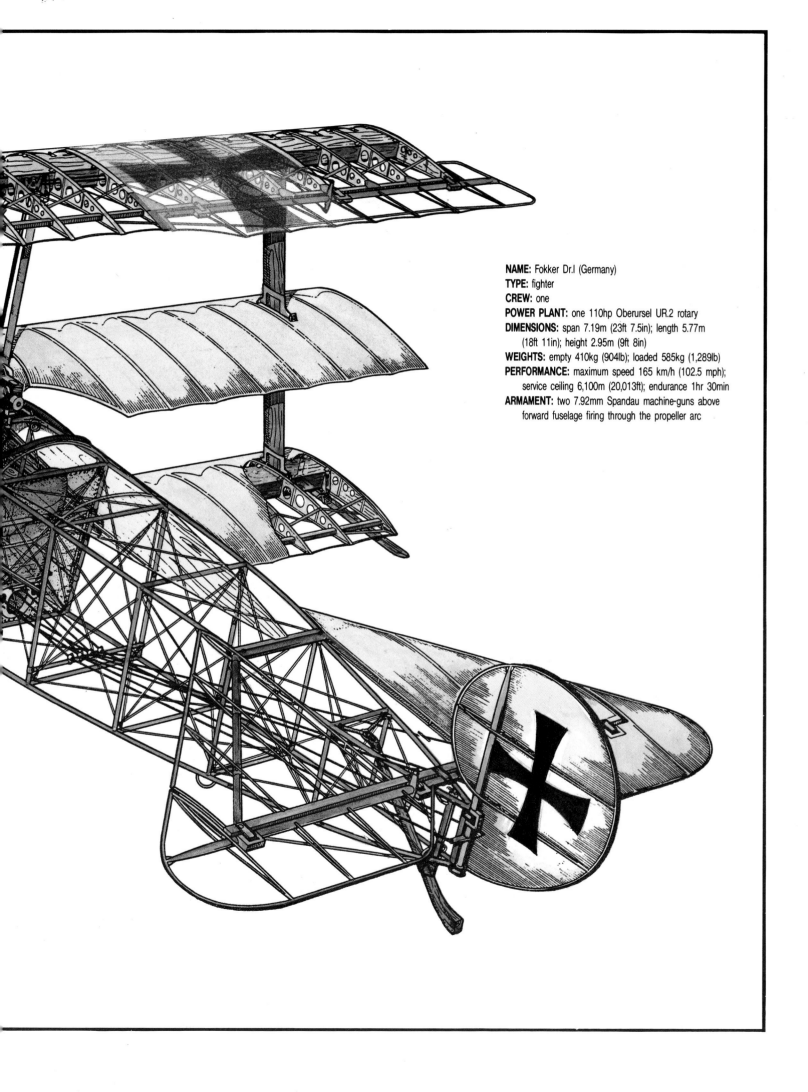

NAME: Fokker Dr.I (Germany)
TYPE: fighter
CREW: one
POWER PLANT: one 110hp Oberursel UR.2 rotary
DIMENSIONS: span 7.19m (23ft 7.5in); length 5.77m
   (18ft 11in); height 2.95m (9ft 8in)
WEIGHTS: empty 410kg (904lb); loaded 585kg (1,289lb)
PERFORMANCE: maximum speed 165 km/h (102.5 mph);
   service ceiling 6,100m (20,013ft); endurance 1hr 30min
ARMAMENT: two 7.92mm Spandau machine-guns above
   forward fuselage firing through the propeller arc

SOPWITH F.1 CAMEL (1916)

Sopwith's design team under R. J. Ashfield and then Herbert Smith probably gained more experience of combat-aircraft design than any rival group during 1914–16. The prototype Camel first flew in December 1916, getting its name from the humpbacked appearance caused by the twin Vickers guns under a bulged fairing. To a degree seen in few other fighters, the big rotary engine, two guns and ammunition (twice the common armament of 1916), fuel, oil and pilot were all grouped in a very short fore/aft distance. This gave the Camel extraordinary manoeuvrability; it also made it a tricky machine to handle. There were many things a pilot could mistakenly do that at low altitude would prove immediately lethal, but in the hands of an expert the Camel was perhaps the supreme dogfighter of the war.

Oddly, the one figure everyone knew between the wars was that the Camel's victory tally of 1,294 exceeded that of all other Allied types. In the 1970s Chaz Bowyer, a British historian, checked original records and soon found that RFC/RAF Camels alone gained over 2,900 confirmed victories!

Aerodynamically the Camel was unusual in having acute dihedral (upward slope) on the lower wing but a horizontal upper wing. There were four ailerons, and what today would be called a conventional tail, the rudder being hinged to a fixed fin and the elevators to a parallel-chord tailplane. Structurally, the Camel was almost all wood, though the firewall behind the rotary engine, and the removable panels over the forward fuselage, were all aluminium, and the guns were bolted to transverse steel-tube mountings. The four main fuselage longerons were ash, but most other members were spruce, and a notable feature was that almost all

Below:
A Sopwith Camel replica, built in 1977 for the Leisure Sports Collection.

large components were spindled: cut away to reduce weight while having little effect upon strength. The usual form of spindling was to cut a large channel along each side to convert the original plain beam into a wooden equivalent of the girder.

The wings each had two spars of solid spruce. The rear spar of the lower wings was not spindled, but the others were deeply cut away except at the attachments of the main compression ribs and interplane struts, of which there was just one pair on each side. The upper wing was made in three parts, the centre section extending beyond the splayed-out struts which supported it above the fuselage. Invariably there was a cut-out in the middle of the centre section to give the pilot a better upward view than was afforded by the circular cut-out in the trailing edge. The right front interplane strut carried a pitot head serving the airspeed indicator. The

main wheels were attached to short stub-axles sprung by multiple rubber bungees and bolted inside a streamlined cross-member instead of having a single continuous axle.

The pilot had an excellent instrument panel, a spade-grip stick with a blip switch and two thumb triggers for the guns, and 'the most exciting view in the world' over the twin Vickers immediately in front. Each gun was fed by a disintegrating-link belt of 250 rounds. There were various armament installations, differing in guns, location, arrangement of link and case chutes, and type of synchronizing gear to prevent the gun(s) damaging the propeller. Night-fighter Camels usually had twin Lewis guns on a Foster mount above the upper wing, the pilot being moved aft by interchanging the positions of the cockpit and the main/secondary fuel tanks.

SOPWITH F.1 CAMEL (1916)

NAME: Sopwith Camel F.1 (Britain)
TYPE: fighter
CREW: one
POWER PLANT: one 130hp Clerget 9B
 rotary
DIMENSIONS: span 8.53m (28ft 0in); length
 5.72m (18ft 9in); height 2.59m (8ft 6in)
WEIGHTS: empty 422kg (930lb);
 loaded 659kg (1,453lb)
PERFORMANCE: maximum speed 181.8
 km/h (113 mph); service ceiling 5,791m
 (19,000ft); endurance 2hr 30min
ARMAMENT: two 0.303in Vickers machine-
 guns mounted in upper fuselage firing
 through the propeller arc

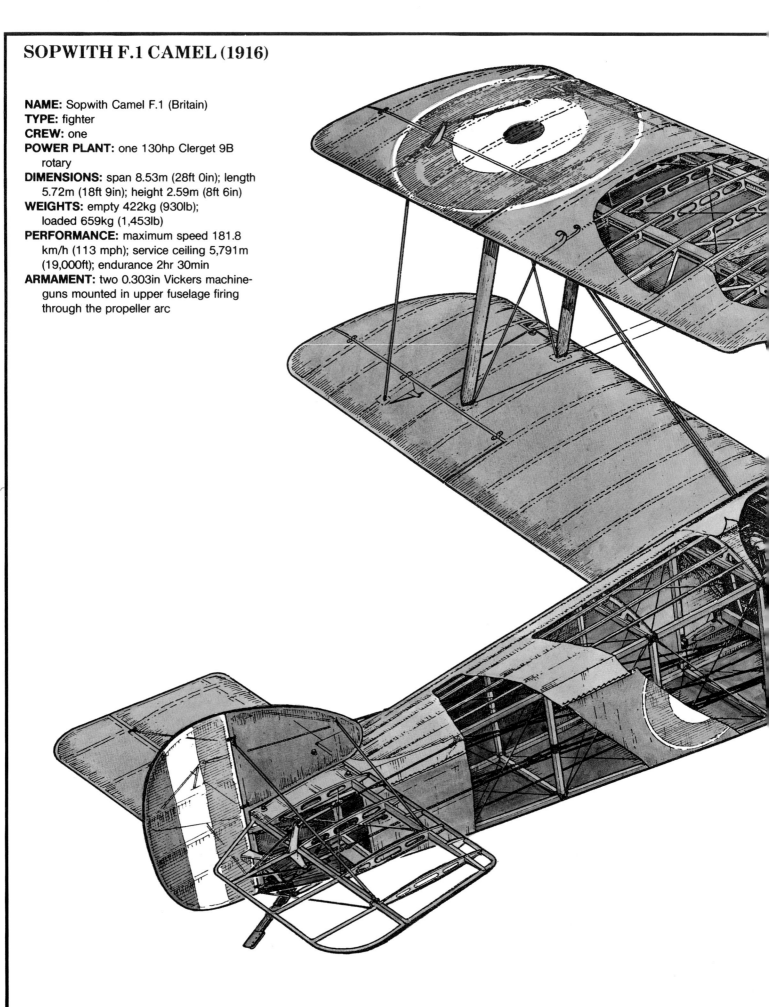

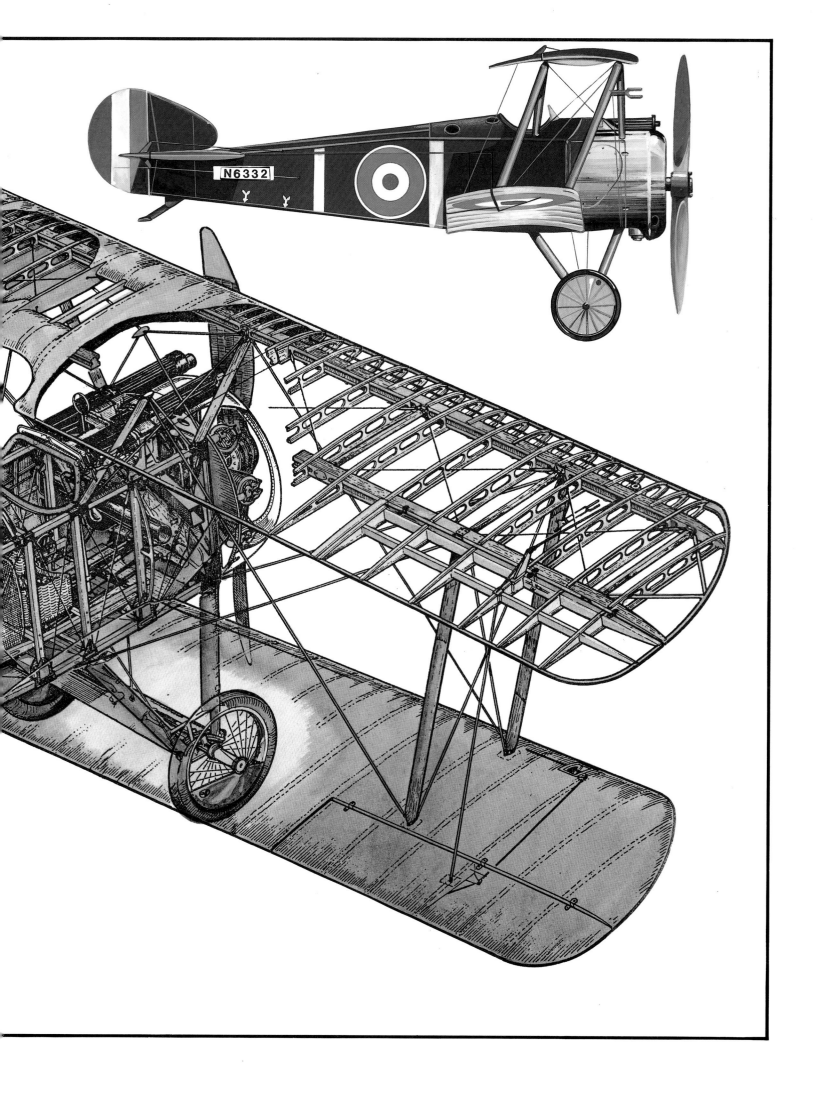

RYAN NYP (1927)

Charles Lindbergh was not the first human to fly the Atlantic but the 92nd; yet his was probably the greatest single-handed achievement in the history of aviation. New York hotelier Raymond Orteig, impressed by Alcock & Brown's Atlantic flight in 1919, offered a prize of $25,000 for the first non-stop flight from New York to Paris. The 1919 technology was inadequate but when Orteig re-offered the prize in 1926 there were reliable and efficient engines.

Young Lindbergh was an extremely experienced barnstormer and mail pilot, who had the advantage of being what he was later called, a 'lone eagle'. He could plan much faster and better than large teams, and asked the Ryan company to build him a special aircraft. The firm was in poor shape, trying to build M-1s on the upper floor of an abandoned fish factory in San Diego. (Ryan was all 'Lindy' could afford; he really wanted a pricey Bellanca.) Designer Donald Hall started with the M-1, already an efficient high-wing monoplane with the excellent Whirlwind engine, and turned out the NYP (New York/Paris) in just 60 days from order to first flight on 28 April 1927. Lindbergh named it *Spirit of St Louis* after the businessmen from that city who put up the money.

Even if designer Hall had started with a clean sheet of paper, the NYP would probably have come out just as it did. Contemporary all-metal stressed-skin construction was too risky and far too expensive. The airframe had to be made by traditional methods, with all the strength in a skeleton of welded steel tubes, strips of spruce and ash and (becoming less important) tight piano wires. The very thick cantilever monoplane wing was widely distrusted and in any case held back speed. The best answer was the wing mounted above the fuselage and braced by strong streamlined struts at about mid-span on each side. These struts, plus others going diagonally up to the wing root, provided attachments for the main landing gear.

On the NYP the landing gear was going to take a terrible beating on takeoff, roaring along a bumpy field for at least a kilometre (3,280ft) with a colossal load of fuel on board. It was essential to have a wide track (distance between the wheels) to give stability on the ground, so on the NYP, as on airliners of the day, each wheel turned on its own short axle fixed to a vertical steel strut supported by multiple strips of rubber inside streamlined fairings. The V-type bracing struts were joined to the bottom longerons of the fuselage by pinned pivots.

Hall had visited the San Diego public library and measured the distance from New York to Paris with a thread stretched round a globe. He then worked out the need for 450 US gallons of fuel (375 Imp gal/1,705 litres). This was awesome. The 2,750lb (1,247kg) weight of fuel meant the wing would have to be enlarged and, despite putting some of the fuel in the wing, there was no way Hall could give Lindbergh forward vision, so he added a periscope. 'Lindy' decided against having radio and relied upon a magnetic compass, an Earth-inductor compass (which senses current in a coil of wire as it cuts through the Earth's magnetic field) and a drift meter which was never used. When Lindbergh landed at Le Bourget airport in darkness on 21 May 1927, after 58 hours without sleep, he had changed the world for ever.

Below:
The Ryan NYP "Spirit of St Louis", which was flown solo across the Atlantic by Charles Lindbergh. The aircraft is on display at the National Air and Space museum, Washington D.C.

SUPERMARINE S.6B (1931)

In 1913 Jacques Schneider offered a trophy to be competed for by racing seaplanes. Today a seaplane would be at a disadvantage compared with landplanes, but before 1930 calm water offered much more room for takeoff and landing than the cramped bumpy fields, so that the Schneider racers of the late 1920s were the fastest aeroplanes in the world. The trophy was contested annually until 1927 and then every two years. It did more than anything else to develop the technology of powerful engines and high-speed aircraft in the pre-1930 era.

One of the early British Schneider designers was Reginald Mitchell, of Supermarine Aviation. One of his lumbering biplane boats won the 1922 race at 145·7mph (234·48km/h), but Mitchell knew such machines would soon be outclassed. For the 1925 race he designed the beautiful S.4, a bold stressed-skin cantilever monoplane with a steel-tube and wood fuselage. It crashed because of wing flutter, a phenomenon then little understood. By 1927 he had more cautiously added bracing wires to the S.5, though these were of thin streamlined section which enabled the main float struts to be thinner, thus reducing drag. Construction was still mixed steel tube, wood and aluminium, the wing being wooden.

To stand a chance in the 1929 race, a new engine was needed. Napier, whose Lion powered the S.4 and S.5, showed little interest, but Rolls-Royce created a new racing engine, the R, which set totally new standards of power (admittedly only for short periods, and while burning special fuel mixtures concocted by F. R. Banks of Associated Ethyl). Mitchell designed the S.6 around the R engine, making it rather bigger and much stronger than the S.5 and with the important difference of an all-metal stressed-skin airframe. Bracing struts were still used, but they were fewer and stronger. Though basically a simple aircraft, the all-metal structure would have posed a terrible challenge to most British constructors; Supermarine were able to tackle it because they had already gone all-metal in their flying boats.

One of the biggest problems was how to dissipate the surplus heat from the fantastically powerful engine, and with minimum drag. Flush surface radiators had already been used in the S.5, but in the S.6 the radiators formed double skins over the wings and also most of the floats. Thanks to the stressed-skin construction, the wing radiators actually carried the flight loads. The oil tank was in the fin, and the oil was cooled by corrugated radiator panels forming the sides of the fuselage.

Fairey provided the steel propeller. Britain was years away from using variable-pitch propellers, and to match the expected flight speeds the pitch of the blades had to be very coarse indeed. At takeoff this was very inefficient; the S.6 needed a long run, and the vicious torque made the left float dig deep into the water. The answer was to carry nearly all the fuel in the right float, instead of in both floats equally.

The two S.6Bs produced for the 1931 race were fitted with R engines further boosted to 2,300hp. The floats were made slightly larger, balances added to the ailerons and rudder, and the rear fuselage stiffened. After a walkover in the 1931 race, one of the S.6Bs was fitted with an engine from which the last safe ounce of power was wrung (2,600hp) and set a world speed record at 406·94mph (654·9km/h).

Below:
This is the Supermarine S.6B that won the Schneider Trophy outright in 1931. On the same day, Flight Lieutenant Boothman of the Royal Air Force (inset) flew the S.6B to a new world speed record.

SUPERMARINE S.6B (1931)

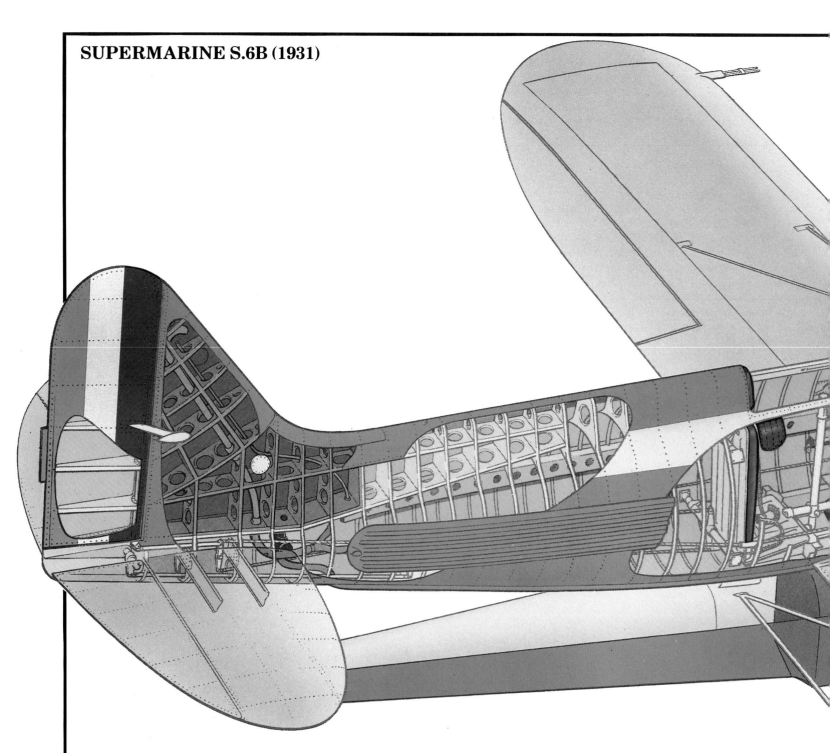

NAME: Supermarine S6.B

TYPE: Schneider Trophy seaplane racer

CREW: one

POWER PLANT: one 2,350hp Rolls-Royce 'R' 12 cylinder
liquid-cooled Vee-type

DIMENSIONS: span 9.14m (30ft 0in); length 8.79
(28ft 10in); wing area 13.47m² (145sq ft)

WEIGHTS: take-off weight 2,761kg (6,086lb)

PERFORMANCE: maximum speed 610.75km/h (379.05mph)

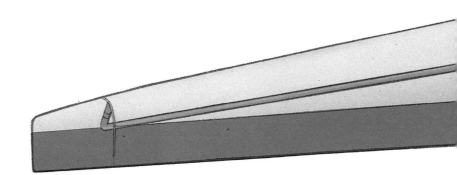

CURTISS BF2C-1 HAWK III (1933)

During the 20 years between the world wars the world's planemakers strove ceaselessly to improve their aircraft, but often the way ahead was far from clear. The engine companies had no such problem: constant effort steadily increased both power and reliability, so that aircraft performance would have kept increasing without much effort by their own builders. But there were many new alternatives, and just when to introduce them was a difficult decision.

In August 1929 a merger between Curtiss and Wright – two of the oldest names in the world of aviation – produced the biggest aircraft company in the United States. Curtiss, often using Wright engines, had established an unbroken line of military aircraft for the Army and Navy, but by 1930 was having twinges of doubt about the future of the biplane. It continued with the traditional formula, one argument being that a biplane fighter tended to have a span close to 30ft (9·14m) whereas an equivalent monoplane spanned 36ft (11m) and so was less manoeuvrable. Another choice concerned the type of engine: water cooled V-12 engines looked more streamlined than air-cooled radials, but when the cooling system and radiator were taken into account they were generally heavier and longer (spoiling manoeuvrability) and had similar drag. The American Pratt & Whitney and Wright radials were so good that no other engines were considered until the late 1930s.

Other choices concerned flaps, controllable-pitch propellers and retractable landing gear. The provision of a glazed canopy over the cockpit generally met with a storm of protest from the pilots, and producing the right aircraft meant

Below:
A prototype XF IIC-3 in United States Navy colours.

balancing innate conservatism and a need to avoid high-risk innovations with the need to stay ahead of the competition – rival companies as well as rival countries which might become enemies.

In October 1932 Curtiss received an order for 28 F11C-2 fighters for the US Navy (later redesignated BFC-2 to emphasize its bomber/ fighter dual role). These were traditional braced biplanes of mixed construction, with welded steel-tube fuselages, aluminium tails and wooden wings, with fabric skinning except for the front and rear upper fuselage which were of aluminium (but not bearing any flight loads). There were few innovations apart from the use of one of the Hamilton company's new variable-pitch propellers. The landing gear comprised neat cantilevered legs with spats to streamline the wheels. The cockpit remained open, but to meet Navy requirements a 41·5 Imp gal (189 litre) jettisonable auxiliary tank could be attached under the fuselage.

In late 1931 a new rival, Grumman, had flown a highly successful two-seat fighter that at 207mph (333km/h) was faster than any Navy single-seater. Its secret was retractable landing gear. Curtiss met the competition by copying it, building the BF2C-1 with the same arrangement in which the wheels were cranked by hand into recesses by a chain drive to a large vertical Acme-thread screw on which ran a nut carrying the upper ends of the legs. This gave trouble in service, and despite its ability to carry five bombs, or four 116lb (52·6kg) bombs and a tank, the BF2C-1 had only a short career in the US Navy. On the other hand, as the Hawk III it was adopted as the main Chinese fighter, and also sold well to Siam and Argentina.

CURTISS BF2C-1 HAWK III (1933)

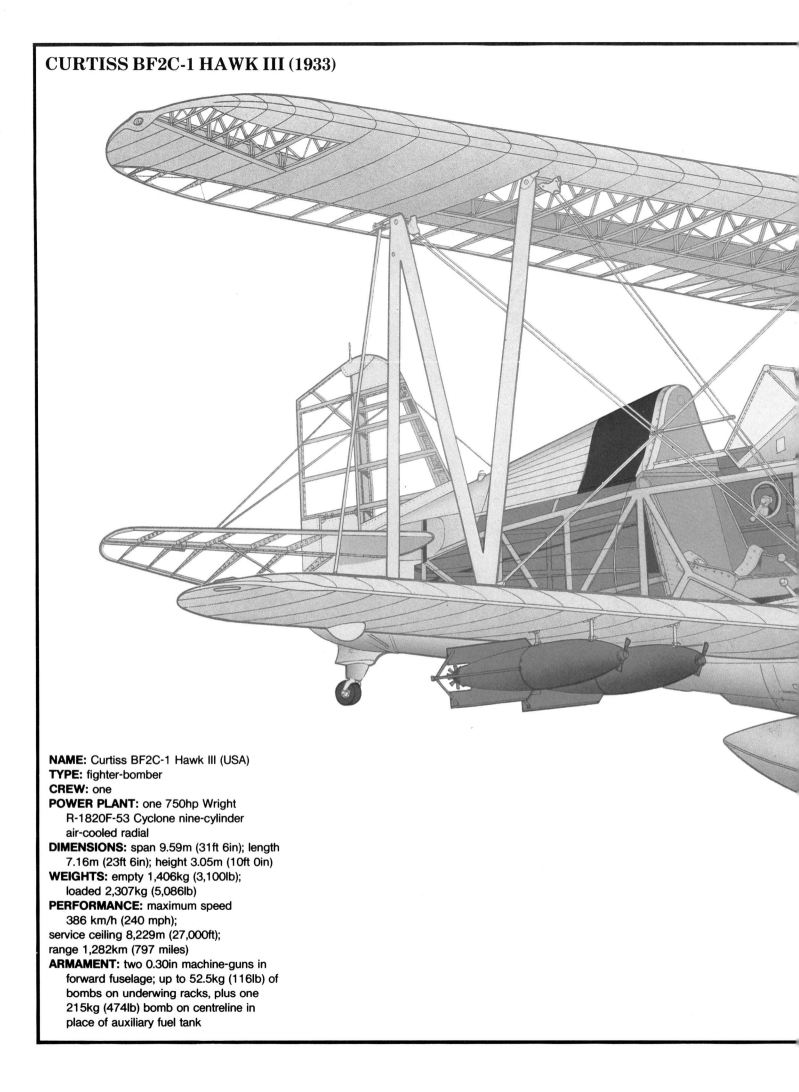

NAME: Curtiss BF2C-1 Hawk III (USA)
TYPE: fighter-bomber
CREW: one
POWER PLANT: one 750hp Wright
    R-1820F-53 Cyclone nine-cylinder
    air-cooled radial
DIMENSIONS: span 9.59m (31ft 6in); length
    7.16m (23ft 6in); height 3.05m (10ft 0in)
WEIGHTS: empty 1,406kg (3,100lb);
    loaded 2,307kg (5,086lb)
PERFORMANCE: maximum speed
    386 km/h (240 mph);
service ceiling 8,229m (27,000ft);
range 1,282km (797 miles)
ARMAMENT: two 0.30in machine-guns in
    forward fuselage; up to 52.5kg (116lb) of
    bombs on underwing racks, plus one
    215kg (474lb) bomb on centreline in
    place of auxiliary fuel tank

CIERVA C.30A (1934)

Modern familiarity with the helicopter obscures the fact that there are also large numbers of light autogyros, many of them built by home constructors. Credit for the invention of the autogyro rests with Juan de la Cierva. A young and handsome Spaniard, he built a huge airliner in 1919, but it was wrecked by a careless test pilot. De la Cierva had a rare combination of money, technical skill and determination, and he asked himself why his aeroplane had crashed. The wings had stalled, in a turn at too low a speed. If the wings were made to rotate they could not stall, thought Cierva, and he began fitting rotors to small aeroplanes.

The key difference between the autogyro (Cierva registered the name as Autogiro) and a helicopter is that the autogyro has a free-spinning rotor. Pulled along by a propeller, the rotor is driven by the air flowing past it. Simple examples thus need a takeoff run, though a very short one. They cannot hover motionless in the air, and their landings are not vertical, though the approach can be steep and the run short.

Cierva took many years to get a worthwhile autogyro, though he succeeded long before anyone succeeded in building a practical helicopter. Moving to Britain in 1925, he had large numbers of Autogiros built by such companies as Avro, Parnall, de Havilland, Airwork, BAMC, and Westland, and also Weymann-Lepère in France. Each successive model introduced some improvement, though nearly all were quite small two-seaters, mostly with open cockpits.

Probably the only serious problem remaining by 1930 was that the aeroplane-type controls were ineffective during very slow landings, so that if (for example) the machine began to roll over sideways, the pilot could not take corrective action. This caused many serious crashes. On the positive side, Cierva had perfected a way of making a cantilever rotor without bracing wires, using steel-tube spars, spruce ribs and covering mainly of fabric. The USA licensee, Pitcairn, devised a reliable gearbox and clutch so that the engine could spin-up the rotor before the start, greatly shortening the run. All that was needed was better low-speed control, and in 1931 Cierva completed the drawings for a 'direct control' Autogiro which he was sure would solve the problem. The rotor hub was pivoted and, by means of a control column hanging down into the cockpit, the pilot could tilt the entire rotor in any direction. At last he had positive control of dive, climb, roll and turn, the machine automatically banking correctly in any commanded turn.

The C.30 prototype flew in April 1933, proving most successful. After redesign of the struts of the pylon and landing gear, it became the C.30A, and Avro at Manchester made 78, 12 of them as the Avro Rota I for the RAF and the rest for civil use or export. It was a very simple machine, with a steel-tube fuselage truss, light wooden fairing stringers and fabric covering. The tail was mainly aluminium, with fabric covering, and the direct-control system enabled the rudder and elevators of previous models to be dispensed with. The tail surfaces were only for stabilization.

In 1933 the original C.30 was fitted with Cierva's new 'Autodynamic' rotor head. This enabled the rotor to be spun up to speed in zero pitch and then suddenly put into positive pitch (a helicopter pilot would call it a collective control) to leap 30ft (10m) into the air, thereafter flying away normally. Sadly, Cierva was killed in 1936 – ironically, in the crash of a fixed-wing aeroplane – and further development petered out.

Opposite top:
Miss Joan Maine stands proudly by her C.30 after becoming the first woman in the world to obtain a pilot's licence for autogiros on 29 October 1934.

Opposite right:
The Kellet KD1, an American derivitive of the Cierva.

Opposite left:
The Cierva C.30's divided control columns hang down from the pivoted rotor head straight into the tandem cockpits.

Below:
Early Cierva Autogiros, this example is on floats, used conventional control surfaces, elevators, rudders and ailerons. However, these proved ineffective at the very low speeds at which the Autogiros can fly.

Below
A Cierva C.30 with "direct control" and unbraced rotors.

CIERVA C.30A (1934)

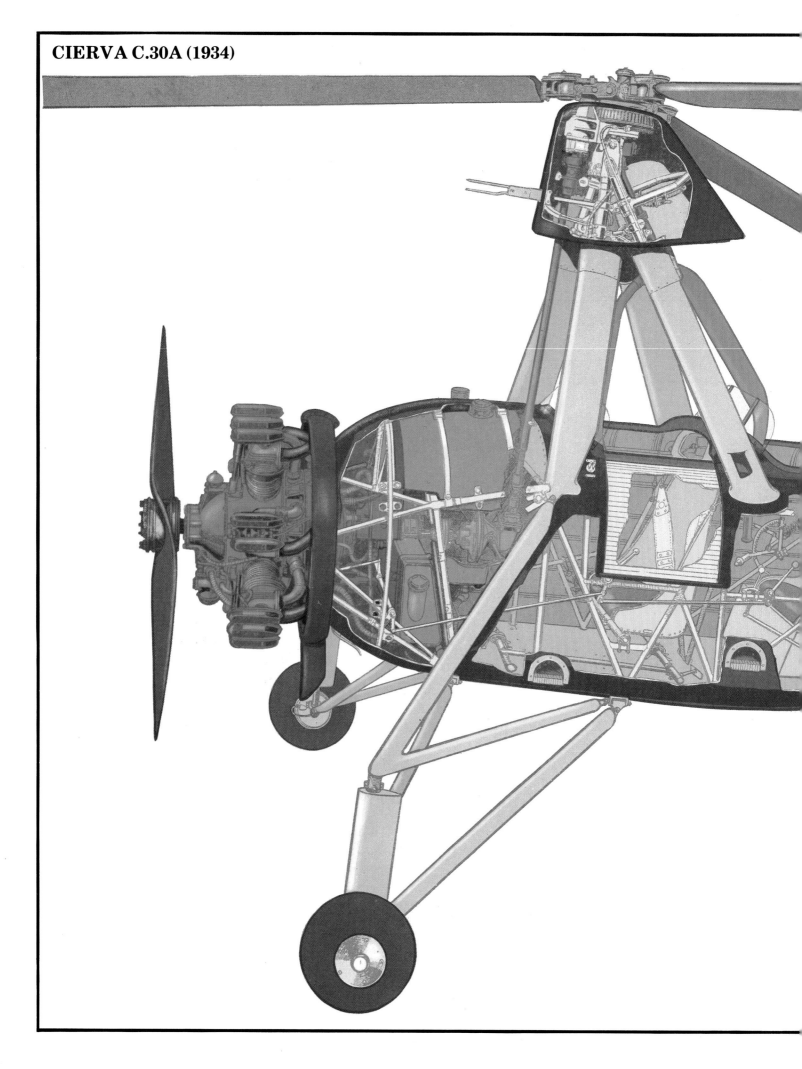

NAME: Cierva C.30A (Avro Rota)
TYPE: civil/military autogyro
CREW: two
POWER PLANT: one 140hp Armstrong Siddeley Genet
     Major seven-cylinder air-cooled radial
DIMENSIONS: rotor diameter 11.28m (37ft 0in); fuselage
     length 6.01m (19ft 8½in); height 3.38m (11ft 1in)
WEIGHTS: maximum take-off weight 862kg (1,900lb)
PERFORMANCE: maximum speed 177km/h (110mph) at
     sea level; service ceiling 2,438m (8,000ft);
     range 402km (250 miles)

DE HAVILLAND D.H.88 COMET (1934)

The Australian state of Victoria celebrated its centenary in 1934, and Sir MacPherson Robertson offered £15,000 in prize money for an air race from London to Melbourne. This distant act did much to jerk Britain's aircraft industry out of the doldrums caused by the failure of the RAF and Imperial Airways to ask for modern aircraft. It was obvious the race would be a walkover for foreign designs, mainly American; so de Havilland Aircraft patriotically said it would build a special 'MacRobertson' racer, even if it mean a large financial loss. In the event, three were ordered, followed by a fourth in 1935, so the Hatfield firm almost broke even.

The performance of foreign stressed-skin monoplanes was far beyond anything attempted in Britain (except for the highly specialized short-range Schneider seaplanes), and it was by no means certain that de Havilland could create a racer with sufficient speed and fuel capacity and still make it safe in operation from existing airfields. At least the company had just produced its Gipsy Six 6-cylinder engine which, with a bit of uprating, offered enough power to a streamlined twin. The choice of a low-mounted cantilever wing was not questioned, but there was so little room in it that all fuel had to be in the fuselage. As the fuel tanks had to be distributed fore and aft of the centre of gravity, the cockpit had to be at the back. There had to be seats for two, so for minimum drag they were placed in tandem covered by a canopy hinged along the right side, were very cramped for long flights.

The firm had no experience of modern all-metal structures, but making the Comet entirely of wood had few drawbacks. Thin veneer or ply skin was used almost throughout, the highly stressed main wing box being covered with two layers each made up of narrow spruce strips arranged diagonally. The only sizeable metal parts were the welded steel-tube nacelle trusses, extended forward to carry the engines in aluminium cowlings. The lowest junctions of these trusses formed the pivots for the landing gear, which was arranged to retract by a manual chain-drive and screwjack arrangement typical of the period, each wheel having its own fairing door.

It was difficult to achieve a landing speed that seemed reasonably low, and so split flaps were fitted over the short span between the nacelles. Britain's accessory industry had no experience of flaps and, like the landing gear, these were manually operated by a large lever like those in old railway signal cabins. Probably the greatest technical problem of all concerned the propellers. Though Britain had experimented with variable-pitch propellers from 1916, the industry had nothing available. De Havilland was itself taking a licence for the American Hamilton, but this excellent bracket type could not be fitted in time. Accordingly the Comets entered the race with curious French Ratier propellers. Before takeoff these were pressurized with a bicycle pump to the fine-pitch position. After takeoff, the increasing air pressure acting on a disc in front of the spinner would suddenly overcome the internal pressure, changing the setting to coarse, each propeller doing this in its own time with no control by the pilot. There was then no way of restoring fine pitch until the bicycle pump was brought out again after landing. Clearly, a missed approach and overshoot in coarse pitch was dangerous. One has to respect the skill of pilots Scott and Black, who took the Comet *Grosvenor House* to Melbourne in the winning time of 70 hours, 54 minutes.

Below: Shuttleworth Trust's DH 88 Comet Racer flying at the 1987 Hatfield Open Day following its restoration by British Aerospace engineers.

CONSOLIDATED PBY CATALINA (1935)

Known as the PBY to the US Navy, the Catalina to the RAF, the Canso to the Canadians and the GST to the Russians (who made it under licence), the Consolidated Model 28 was built in larger numbers than any other seaplane of any kind – well in excess of 4,000. This would have seemed fantastic back in 1935, when large flying boats were usually ordered about eight or 10 at a time. The new boat was so good the US Navy started with an order for 60, easily the biggest since World War I.

Consolidated's chief designer, 'Mac' Laddon, had plenty of experience of earlier flying boats, including large parasol monoplanes. The wing had to be mounted parasol-fashion, high above the hull, to keep the engines and propellers out of waves and heavy spray. These earlier boats were thus a forest of struts and wires, but by 1933 the new stressed-skin aircraft were demonstrating that it was possible to do better. This was the year in which the new boat's prototype was ordered. Laddon achieved several important advances.

For the highest possible efficiency on long-range patrols, the wing was given a high aspect ratio (i.e., the span was very large in relation to the chord, or distance from front to rear). Long slender wings are much lighter if they can be braced, and so this wing was given a pair of bracing struts on each side. Despite these, the wing was almost a true cantilever, and structurally it was made as a large rectangular centre section with slightly tapered outer panels. At the centreline it was joined to the hull by a streamlined pylon which had a step built in to the front and internally served as the cabin for the flight engineer.

The stressed-skin hull was notable for its beam (width), which was considerably greater than the depth from the top to the keel. The upper surface was curved, while the strong planing bottom was typical in having a deep transverse step like a speedboat. On takeoff, the boat would quickly get up 'on the step' and then accelerate to flying speed, the rear planing bottom (tapering to a small rear knife-edge) being completely out of the water. Along each side of the bows was a spray-deflecting strake. For stability on the water some flying boats used sponsons, large boxes projecting on each side of the hull, but the Model 28 adhered to the more common arrangement in having small floats under the outer wings. It broke new ground, however, in arranging for these to retract electrically to form the tips of the wings, reducing drag and adding a little extra range.

There was room for about ten times the normal fuel capacity of 1,457 Imp gal (6,624 litres), and even this modest amount sufficed for an endurance of 30 hours. A key to this great aircraft was the achievement of Pratt & Whitney in raising the power of the Twin Wasp engine from 750hp when it was first produced in 1934 to 1,200hp before World War II. This kept pace with the inevitable growth in weight caused by successive additions in equipment (notably wartime radar) and armament. Some 'Cats' were unarmed, but a typical armament comprised one or two rifle-calibre machine guns in the bow turret, another in a ventral 'tunnel' under the tail and two heavy 0.5in guns (or two pairs of smaller guns) in the giant waist blisters which also offered a marvellous view in searching for U-boats. As early as 1939, Consolidated tested an amphibian version with a retractable tricycle undercarriage.

Below:
A Royal New Zealand Air Force Catalina on maritime patrol duties.

CONSOLIDATED PBY CATALINA (1935)

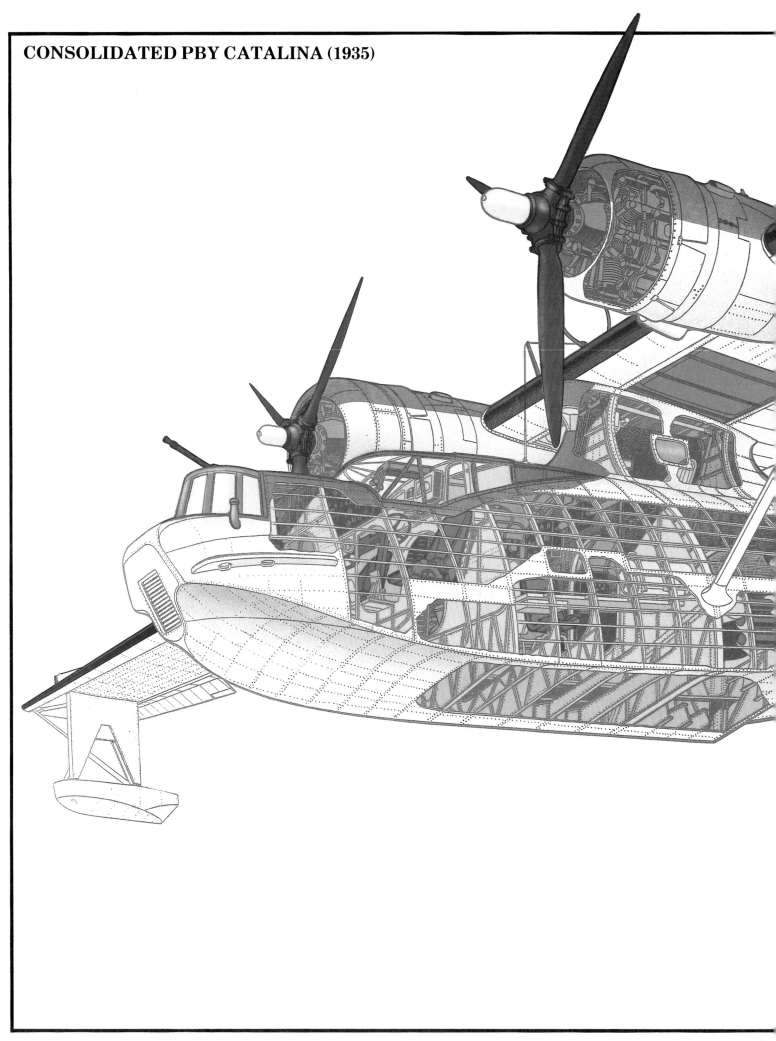

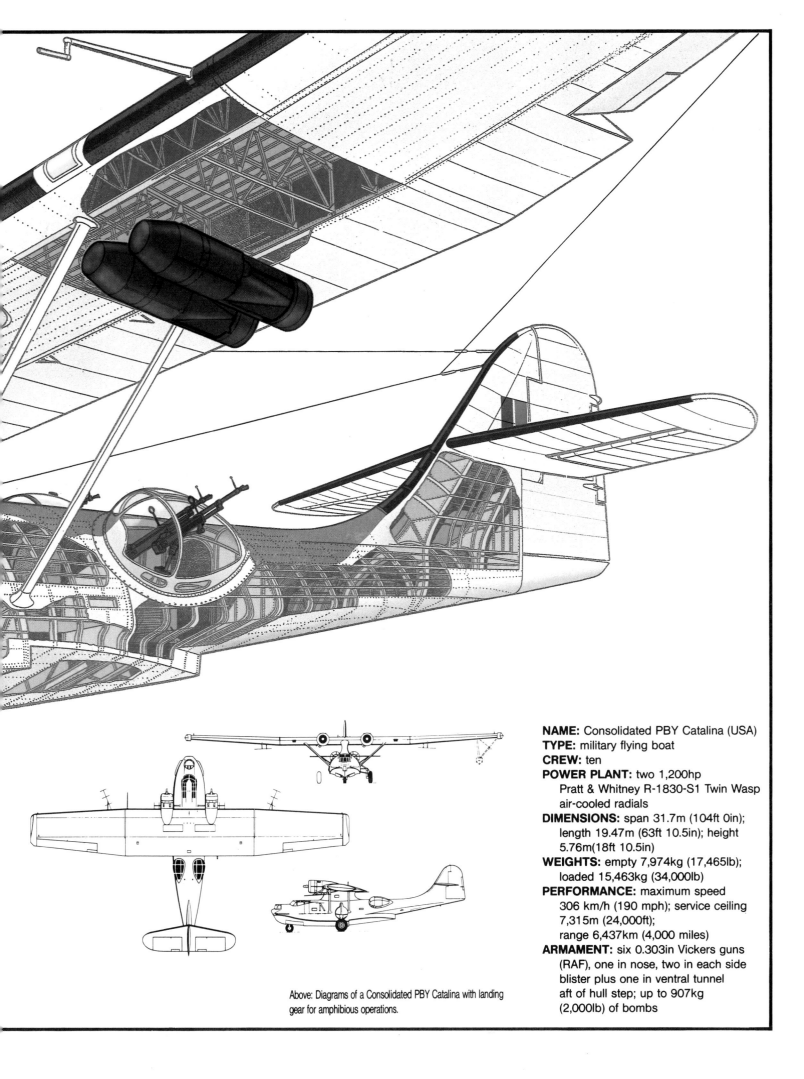

Above: Diagrams of a Consolidated PBY Catalina with landing gear for amphibious operations.

NAME: Consolidated PBY Catalina (USA)
TYPE: military flying boat
CREW: ten
POWER PLANT: two 1,200hp
Pratt & Whitney R-1830-S1 Twin Wasp
air-cooled radials
DIMENSIONS: span 31.7m (104ft 0in);
length 19.47m (63ft 10.5in); height
5.76m(18ft 10.5in)
WEIGHTS: empty 7,974kg (17,465lb);
loaded 15,463kg (34,000lb)
PERFORMANCE: maximum speed
306 km/h (190 mph); service ceiling
7,315m (24,000ft);
range 6,437km (4,000 miles)
ARMAMENT: six 0.303in Vickers guns
(RAF), one in nose, two in each side
blister plus one in ventral tunnel
aft of hull step; up to 907kg
(2,000lb) of bombs

MESSERSCHMITT BF 109 (1935)

When Hitler finally embroiled Europe in war in 1939, his Luftwaffe scythed through all the opposition. To all intents and purposes the Luftwaffe's command of the air was gained by one type: the Bf 109. This was the standard single-seat fighter, and it was made in larger numbers than any other single type of aircraft except the Soviet Il-2 tank-killer. It also shot down more than twice as many enemy aircraft as any other fighter in history.

All the stranger, therefore, to record that in 1933 Willy Messerschmitt was so unpopular with the Nazis he was advised to get a job abroad. With extreme reluctance he was allowed to enter a 1934 contest to build a new fighter, but the resulting Bf 109 was regarded with scorn. With a tiny monoplane wing, rakish lines

and small enclosed cockpit it looked to 1934 eyes (even expert ones) like a racer. Luftwaffe procurement chief Ernst Udet proclaimed, 'That thing will never make a fighter!' That was before he climbed aboard to fly it.

When the first Bf 109Bs went into battle in Spain in the spring of 1937, they demolished all opposition despite having light armament of two small machine-guns (the same as the scouts of World War I). Steadily the 109 was developed, with more powerful engines and increased firepower. By 1939 the standard model was the 109E 'Emil', with a 1,175hp DB 601 engine and two 20-mm cannon as well as the machine-guns. This fought the RAF fighters in the Battle of Britain on very even terms, superior to them in most aspects of performance but unable to match the sustained turn capability of either the Hurricane or Spitfire when flown to the limits.

Left:
A prototype of the first production model Bf 109, the B-1 with a 635hp Junkers Jumo engine.

Below:
The Messerschmitt production line of 109s. Including licence-built examples, nearly 35,000 were built over 21 years.

The Messerschmitt was distinctly smaller than either of its enemies, though its engine was bigger. At low speeds it handled beautifully, and powerful flaps and leading-edge slats countered the drawbacks of a small wing. The cutaway drawing shows the airflow through the under-wing radiators, which had low drag, and whose boundary-layer and main airflows were controlled by flaps. The oil cooler remained under the inverted V-12 engine (which had excellent direct fuel-injection instead of a carburettor) and the supercharger air inlet was on the left side.

The 109 was all-metal stressed-skin structure except for the control surfaces, and it was much simpler and cheaper to make than any of the fighters of the same vintage that it encountered. The left and right wings had a single spar and could be unbolted at the root with the aircraft still on its landing gear. The narrow track of the latter was criticised, but it was deliberate and had several advantages. Perhaps the 109's chief faults were the way its controls (especially the ailerons) became very heavy at high speeds, its uncomfortable posture and narrow cockpit, and pinpricks such as the lack of a rudder trimmer until almost the end of the war.

In 1942 the 109G 'Gustav' replaced earlier types with the DB 605 engine. This was made in colossal numbers and often had very heavy armament, but many aces preferred the 1941 version, the 109F illustrated. This was certainly the best to fly because it had many aerodynamic refinements combined with light weight. Crack shots did not mind the light armament of the F, typically one cannon and two machine guns. By 1943 all versions of the 109 were obsolescent, but the Luftwaffe failed to obtained a good replacement.

Left:
A two seat variant of the Bf 109G

Below:
A close up view of the neat DB 605 installation and "Galland" type cockpit canopy on this late Bf 109G.

MESSERSCHMITT BF 109 (1935)

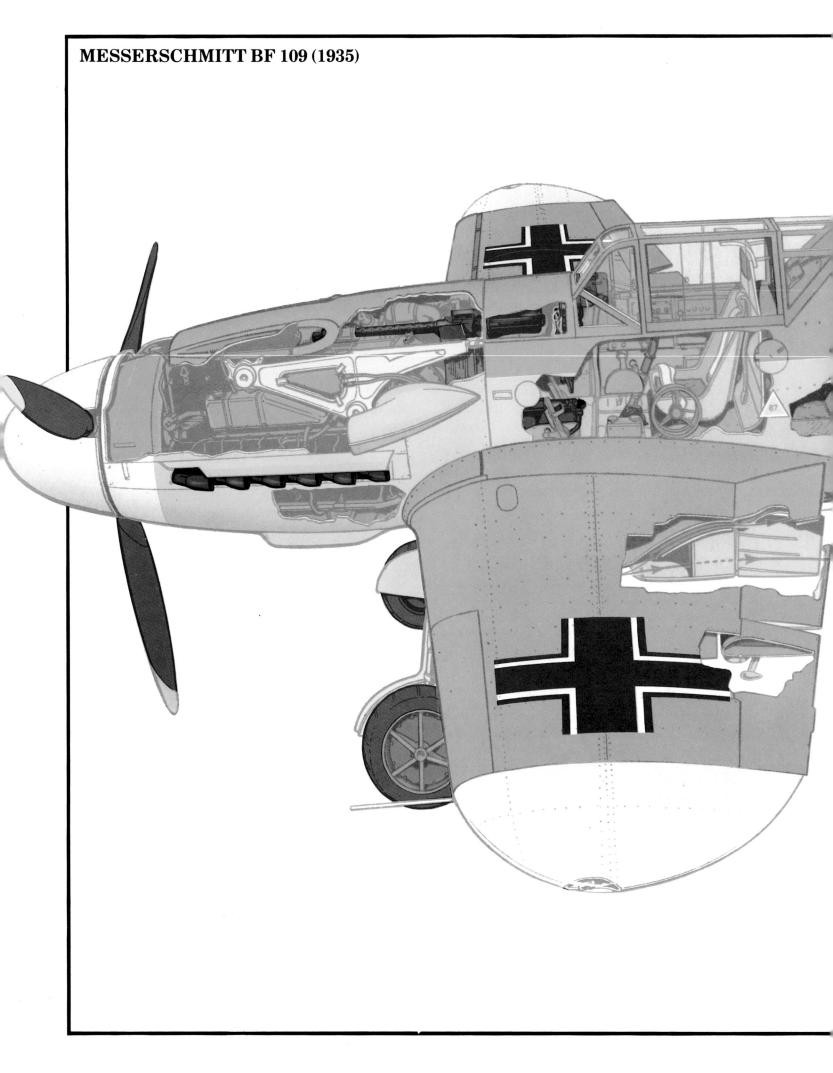

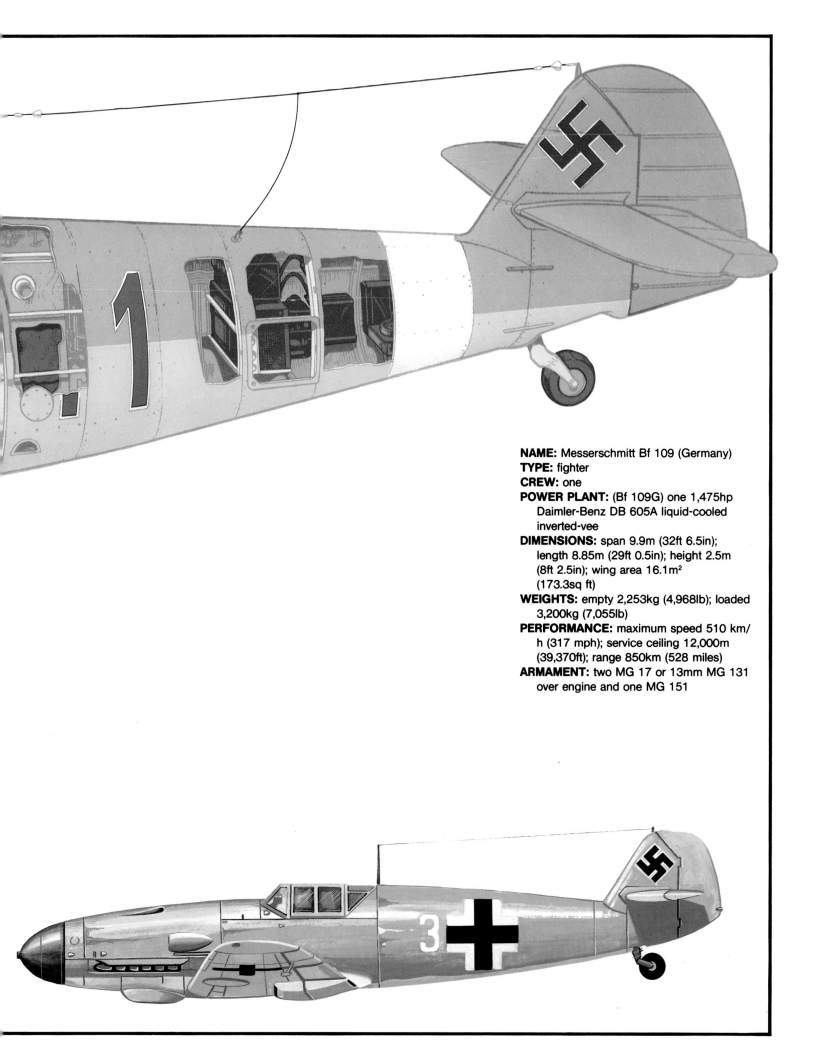

NAME: Messerschmitt Bf 109 (Germany)
TYPE: fighter
CREW: one
POWER PLANT: (Bf 109G) one 1,475hp
Daimler-Benz DB 605A liquid-cooled
inverted-vee
DIMENSIONS: span 9.9m (32ft 6.5in);
length 8.85m (29ft 0.5in); height 2.5m
(8ft 2.5in); wing area 16.1m²
(173.3sq ft)
WEIGHTS: empty 2,253kg (4,968lb); loaded
3,200kg (7,055lb)
PERFORMANCE: maximum speed 510 km/
h (317 mph); service ceiling 12,000m
(39,370ft); range 850km (528 miles)
ARMAMENT: two MG 17 or 13mm MG 131
over engine and one MG 151

HAWKER HURRICANE (1935)

Though it was the name Spitfire that appealed to the media and the public, in fact the chief saviour of Britain (and the Free World) in 1940 was the Hurricane. Far more were in use because it had been started earlier, was easier to make and was wholly traditional. Not least, the directors of Hawker Aircraft had boldly decided to pay for the jigs, tooling and materials for 1,000 Hurricanes in April 1936, long before any official order was placed. Nobody could have foreseen how vital this would be.

Hawker's chief designer was Sydney Camm, one of the giants of the industry. In 1933 he schemed a monoplane version of his biplane Fury, the RAF's newest and fastest fighter. By 1934 the competition abroad had become clearer, Sqn Ldr Ralph Sorley at the Air Ministry had calculated that future fighters would need eight machine-guns instead of the usual two or four, and Rolls-Royce had begun testing the P.V.12, a promising new engine. Camm tore up his Fury Monoplane drawings and began a fresh design. The new engine enabled it to be bigger, to carry the heavy armament, and another change was to retract the landing gear.

In August 1934 Air Ministry specification F.36/34 was written around Camm's new design, and that is all the designation the 'Hawker High-Speed Monoplane' had when it first flew at Brooklands on 6 November 1935. There was still a deep-rooted conviction in the RAF that monoplanes were unsound, but the tough traditional design of the Hawker inspired confidence. There was no way Hawker could mass-produce a stressed-skin machine, so the structure was similar to the preceding biplanes. The main fuselage truss was a Warren (diagonally-braced) girder with steel or aluminium tubes with square-section ends riveted to flat-plate joint fittings. Light aluminium bulkheads and stringers were added to give an oval section, with detachable aluminium panels forward and fabric covering aft. The wing, conveniently made as a horizontal centre section carrying the landing gear and separate outer panels, was again a Warren-braced structure whose spar booms were not machined from solid but built up by riveting rolled strips to form an eight-sided tube. All the great strength was in this framework, because again the covering was fabric.

Where the new fighter differed was in having a sliding cockpit hood, provision for eight Browning guns in the outer wings (where they needed

Below:
A RAF Hurricane Mk II on the ground showing its wide-track, inwardly-retracting undercarriage and sliding cockpit canopy.

no synchronization gear) and a hydraulic system with an engine-driven pump. This system operated the three units of the landing gear, and also the split flaps which occupied the whole trailing edge between the ailerons. The main landing gear, which had wide track and great strength, folded straight in to lie inside the centre section between the spars. This was one of the first neat retractable gears, and also one of the first with air/oil (so-called oleo) shock struts, instead of rubber or springs.

From the start of his design, Camm had studied all-metal stressed-skin wings, which finally came into production in 1939, by which time Hurricanes also had ejector exhausts, anti-spin underfins, rear-view mirrors, bullet-proof windscreens, self-sealing tanks and armour. By 1940 the crude Watts two-blade wooden propeller had at last been replaced by a three-blade Rotol or de Havilland constant-speed type, and the eight machine-guns had become 12 or, more often, been replaced by four 20mm cannon. Total production was 14,231.

Above right:
A flight of six Hurricane Mk Is with fixed-pitch two-bladed wooden propellors and no anti-spin fin.

Right:
The Hurricane Mk IIC, with four 20mm cannon replacing the standard armament of eight 0.303in Browning machine-guns.

HAWKER HURRICANE (1935)

NAME: Hawker Hurricane 1 (Britain)
TYPE: fighter
CREW: one
POWER PLANT: one 1,030hp Rolls-Royce
  Merlin II twelve-cylinder liquid-cooled
  vee-type
DIMENSIONS: span 12.2m (40ft 0in); length
  9.5m (31ft 4in); height 4m (13ft 4.5in);
  wing area 24m² (259sq ft)
WEIGHTS: empty 2,151kg (4,743lb); loaded
  2,820kg (6,218lb)
PERFORMANCE: maximum speed
  496 km/h (308 mph); service ceiling
  10,180m (33,400ft);
  range 845km (525 miles)
ARMAMENT: eight 8mm (0.303in) Browning
  machine-guns in wings; up to 454kg
  (1,000lb) bombs under wings

SUPERMARINE SPITFIRE (1936)

Perhaps the most famous fighter of all time, the Spitfire was designed by the same Reginald Mitchell who had earlier produced the Schneider-winning seaplanes. He had previously built an earlier fighter called Spitfire to the official specification F.7/30. Convinced this was second-rate, he was allowed to go ahead at company expense and design a better and much faster machine, the Supermarine 300; indeed, company director Sir Robert McClean had the courage to tell the Air Ministry, 'In no circumstances will any technical member of the Ministry be allowed to interfere with the designer'. The result was flown on 5 March 1936.

Curiously, some of the Spitfire's features made it difficult to make; one was its elliptical wing, familiar to everyone who ever heard of the aircraft. The structural heart of the wing was a very strong D-section box made up of the heavy leading-edge skin, nose ribs and single spar. Much further aft, a light rear spar carried the split flaps and large ailerons. Construction was all stressed-skin except for the fabric-covered control surfaces and the nose, the latter comprising a steel-tube truss carrying the Merlin engine enclosed in unstressed removable aluminium cowl panels.

The first production Spitfires in 1938–39 had two-blade wooden propellers, but by the Battle of Britain these had been replaced by constant-speed three-bladers which gave better performance. Soon after the battle, the Mk II introduced the Merlin XII using 100-octane fuel, and in 1941 the Mk V received the considerably more powerful Merlin 45. By this time various designs of wing were in production, the A for eight machine-guns, the B for two cannon and four machine-guns, the C for four cannon, and, later, the E for two cannon and two 0·5in (12·7mm),

Below:
The Hurricane and Spitfire of the RAF's Battle of Britain Memorial Flight. The Spitfire is a PR XIX, powered by a Rolls-Royce Griffon engine, and was built as an unarmed photographic reconnaissance aircraft.

and the Universal for any of these, as well as racks for bombs or other stores. Among thousands of modifications, those most noticeable included a tropical filter under the engine, a slipper drop tank fitted snug against the belly, and wingtips which could be clipped (LF, low-altitude fighter) or extended and pointed (HF, high-altitude fighter).

By July 1942 the new Merlin 61, with two-stage superchargers, was being rushed into the Mk V airframe to yield the Mk IX, distinguished by its longer nose, six (instead of three) ejector exhaust stacks each side, four-blade propeller and twin radiators of equal size under the wings. Though an emergency solution to beat the Fw 190, the Mk IX was kept in production at the expense of the properly engineered Mk VIII with neat tropical filter, retractable tailwheel and many other refinements. Many early "Spits" were converted into Seafire naval fighters, after which properly-engineered Seafires were built with folding wings.

From the start of the war the bigger Griffon engine had been considered for the Spitfire, though its cylinder blocks projected into bulges in the cowling. A few Spitfire XIIIs had early Griffons, but late-war Spitfires standardized on the great two-stage Griffon 65 and similar engines, driving five-blade propellers or six-blade contraprops. These aircraft had stronger structures, very broad fins and rudders and, often, a teardrop canopy sliding over a rear fuselage of reduced height giving all-round view. This type of canopy was a feature of the Seafire SVII (post-war called F.17), which is the subject of the drawing. Though there were later and more powerful Griffon-Seafires, the Mk 17 soldiered on with 764 Sqn until November 1954, the last Seafires in service.

A Spitfire Mk XIV with a "teardrop" cockpit canopy, which gave the pilot better all round vision, despite adding slightly to the aircraft's drag.

SEAFIRE Mk.17(1946)

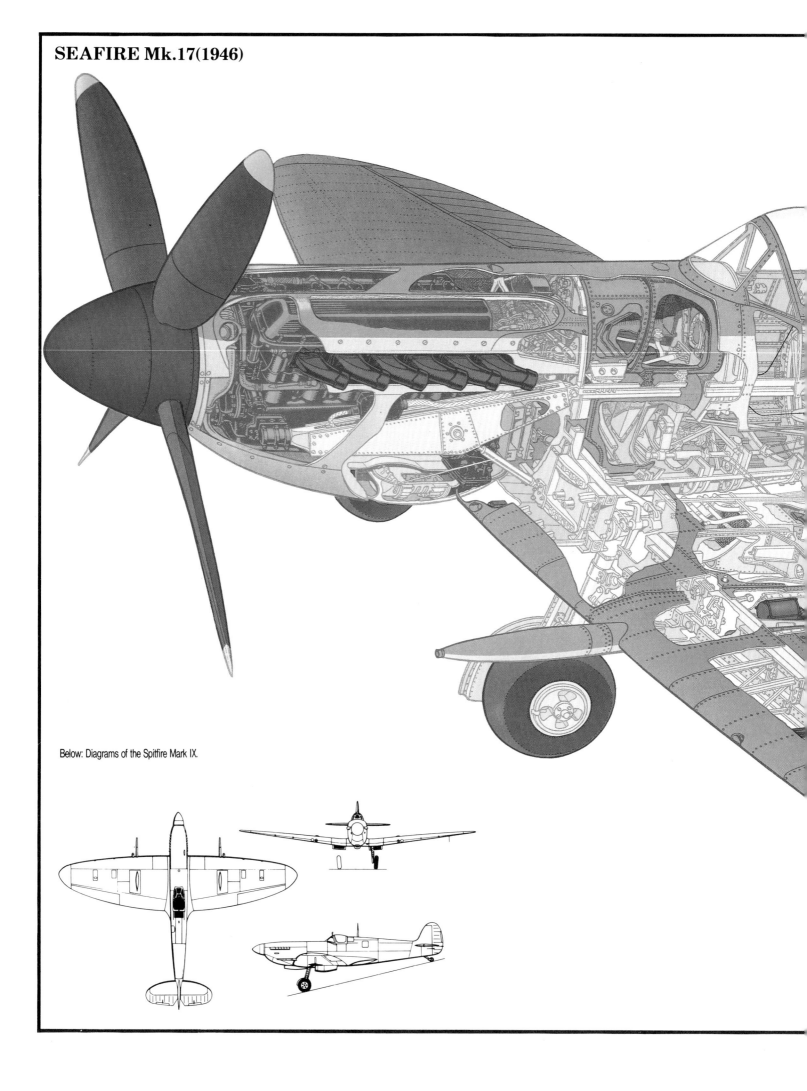

Below: Diagrams of the Spitfire Mark IX.

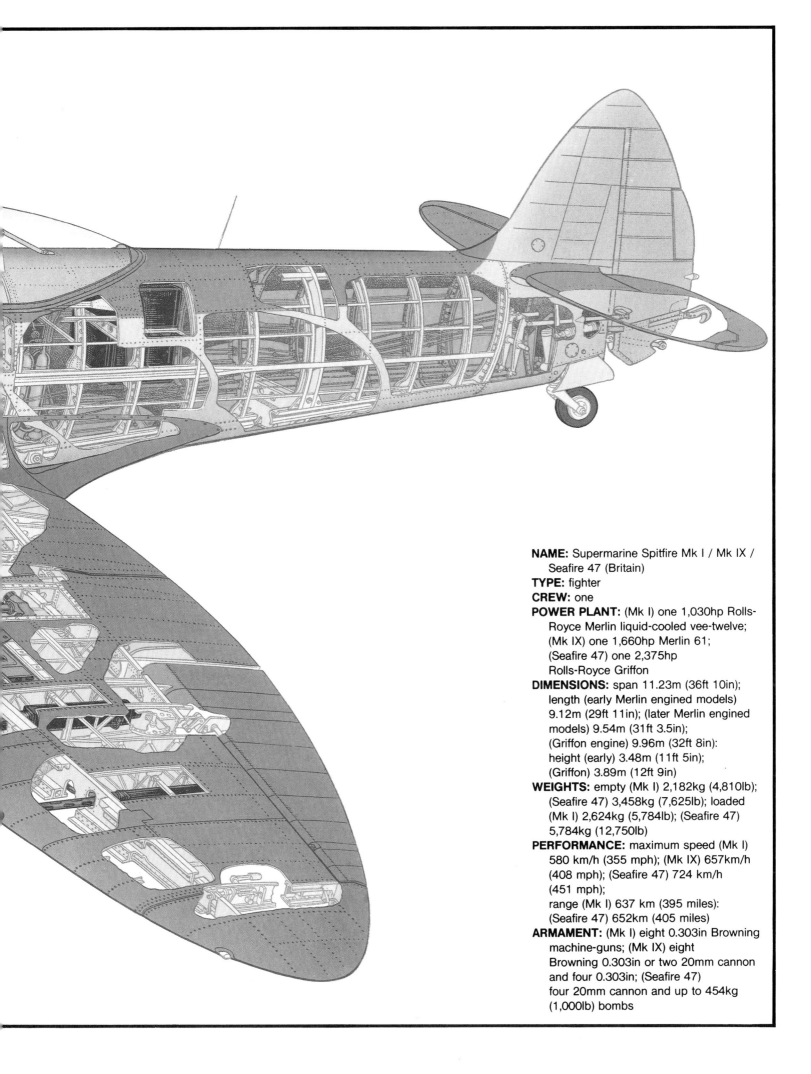

NAME: Supermarine Spitfire Mk I / Mk IX /
Seafire 47 (Britain)
TYPE: fighter
CREW: one
POWER PLANT: (Mk I) one 1,030hp Rolls-
Royce Merlin liquid-cooled vee-twelve;
(Mk IX) one 1,660hp Merlin 61;
(Seafire 47) one 2,375hp
Rolls-Royce Griffon
DIMENSIONS: span 11.23m (36ft 10in);
length (early Merlin engined models)
9.12m (29ft 11in); (later Merlin engined
models) 9.54m (31ft 3.5in);
(Griffon engine) 9.96m (32ft 8in):
height (early) 3.48m (11ft 5in);
(Griffon) 3.89m (12ft 9in)
WEIGHTS: empty (Mk I) 2,182kg (4,810lb);
(Seafire 47) 3,458kg (7,625lb); loaded
(Mk I) 2,624kg (5,784lb); (Seafire 47)
5,784kg (12,750lb)
PERFORMANCE: maximum speed (Mk I)
580 km/h (355 mph); (Mk IX) 657km/h
(408 mph); (Seafire 47) 724 km/h
(451 mph);
range (Mk I) 637 km (395 miles):
(Seafire 47) 652km (405 miles)
ARMAMENT: (Mk I) eight 0.303in Browning
machine-guns; (Mk IX) eight
Browning 0.303in or two 20mm cannon
and four 0.303in; (Seafire 47)
four 20mm cannon and up to 454kg
(1,000lb) bombs

MESSERSCHMITT BF 110 (1936)

In the first half of the 1930s, as the Depression receded, nations began considering twin-engined fighters big enough to escort bombers over the whole distance to the target and back. It was felt such machines might make up in firepower for shortcomings in dogfight manoeuvrability, and be as fast as the single-engined machines. In 1934 German thoughts of a multirole *Kampfzerstörer* began to give way to a pure *Zerstörer*, literally a destroyer but in practice a long-range fighter with no requirement to carry bombs.

Messerschmitt had already prepared a design for the earlier requirement; believing the concept unsound, he and designer Walter Rethel went flat-out for performance and in so doing schemed an aircraft ideal for the *Zerstörer* specification. The Bf 110 first flew on 12 May 1936 and, though having many shortcomings, was probably the best long-range fighter in the world. The idea of great fighters carving swathes through enemy defences appealed to the Nazi leaders, who proclaimed the *Zerstörergruppen* the élite of the Luftwaffe. In Poland all went as

planned, but over southern England the mighty 110s were shot down in droves. Despite this, they saw action all over Europe and North Africa, became leading night fighters, and were built in greater and greater numbers as newer replacements proved a disappointment.

Like its smaller partner the Bf 109, the Bf 110 was an elegant all-metal stressed-skin machine. Like 'destroyers' of the same time in other countries, it had twin fins, tandem seats, a battery of guns in the nose, retractable landing gear and a gun firing aft. Structurally the Bf 110 was unusual in having a single-spar wing. This was built in left and right halves, each joined to the strong spar bridge in the fuselage. The bridge girder was so deep it reached almost to the top of the pilot seat immediately in front of it. To the rear was a seat for a radio operator/navigator and a rear gunner facing aft. A continuous canopy with multiple panes of Plexiglas covered all three cockpits.

Fuel was housed in four tanks ahead of and behind the spar inboard of the engines. The latter were DB 600A inverted V-12s in the prototype, but the lower-powered Jumo 210 had

Right:
The long multi-panel glazed cockpit canopy for the crew of three - a very distinctive feature of the Bf 110.

Below right:
110s over the White Cliffs of Dover in 1940.

Below:
Two Bf 110s in desert camouflage probably over the Mediterranean.

to be accepted for early production Bf 110Bs. Later the standard engines were the DB 601, typically of 1,350hp, and the DB 605 of 1,475hp in the mass-produced Bf 110G family of night fighters. Except for the pre-war versions, which had the coolant radiators under the engines, the radiators were installed in neat ducts immediately outboard of the engines under the wing immediately ahead of the flaps. The latter were of the slotted type and, like the single-leg main landing gears, were operated hydraulically. Like the Bf 109, the 110 had powerful slats along the outer leading edge, and these were particularly welcome on the much heavier G-series, helping these to retain the gentle flying qualities of the light early versions.

Most early Bf 110s had an armament of four MG 17 machine guns round the top of the nose and two MG FF cannon underneath, the latter reloaded with drums of 20mm ammunition by the radio operator. The Bf 110 was used for trials with a vast range of weapons, and later night fighters typically had two 30mm MK 108 and two 20mm 151/20 firing ahead. Large 210mm rocket tubes under the wings were fired against USAAF heavy bombers by day.

MESSERSCHMITT BF 110 (1936)

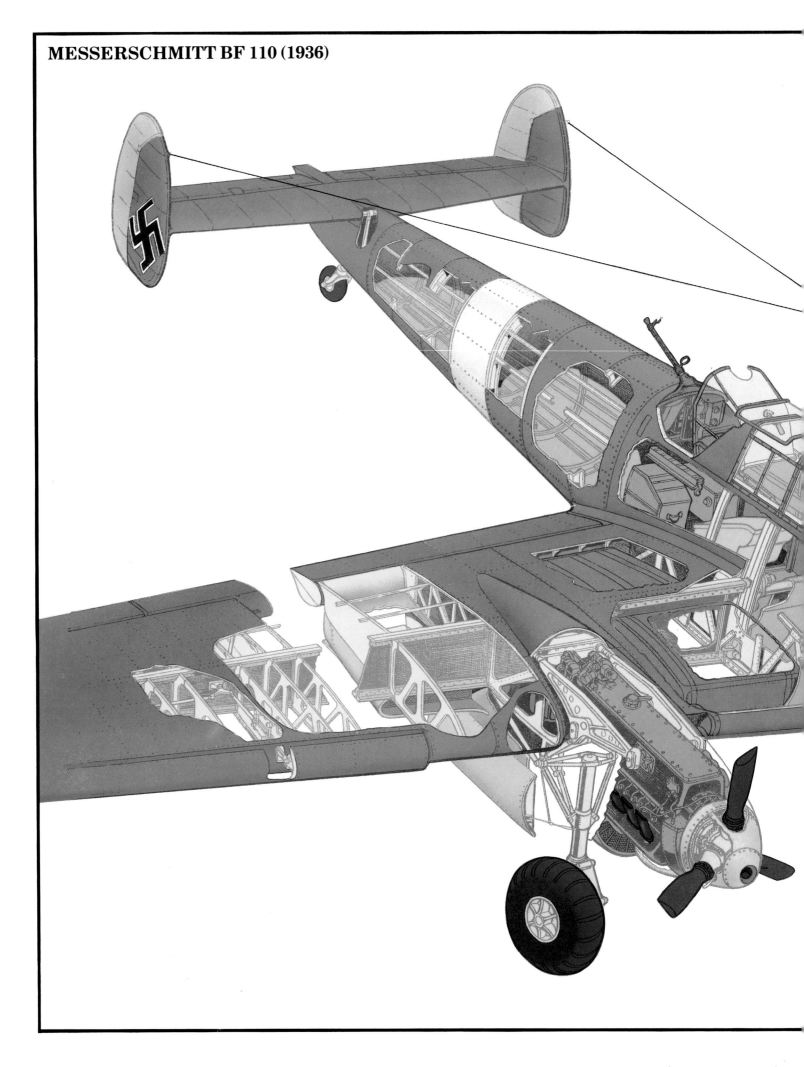

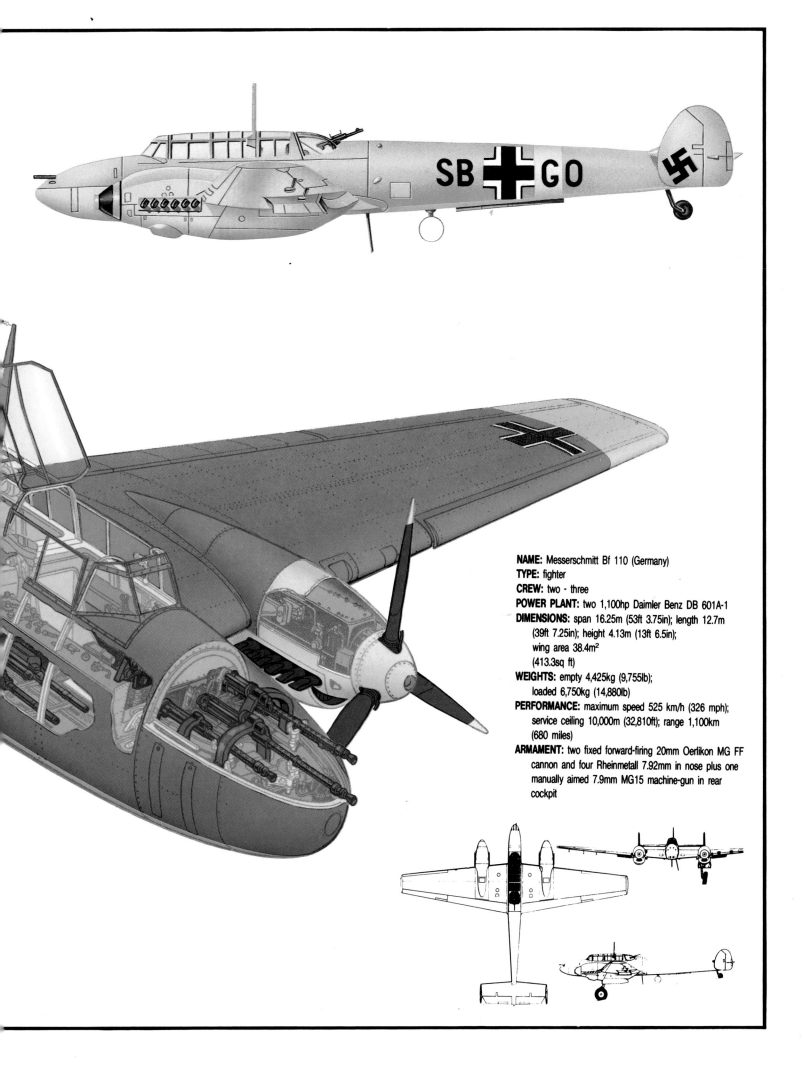

NAME: Messerschmitt Bf 110 (Germany)
TYPE: fighter
CREW: two - three
POWER PLANT: two 1,100hp Daimler Benz DB 601A-1
DIMENSIONS: span 16.25m (53ft 3.75in); length 12.7m
    (39ft 7.25in); height 4.13m (13ft 6.5in);
    wing area 38.4m²
    (413.3sq ft)
WEIGHTS: empty 4,425kg (9,755lb);
    loaded 6,750kg (14,880lb)
PERFORMANCE: maximum speed 525 km/h (326 mph);
    service ceiling 10,000m (32,810ft); range 1,100km
    (680 miles)
ARMAMENT: two fixed forward-firing 20mm Oerlikon MG FF
    cannon and four Rheinmetall 7.92mm in nose plus one
    manually aimed 7.9mm MG15 machine-gun in rear
    cockpit

SHORT C AND G CLASSES (1936)

In 1935 the British Government passed an Act for all mail throughout the worldwide British Empire to be carried by air, and at the existing surface-mail rates. This meant that Imperial Airways had to buy an unprecedented fleet of aircraft. The time had come for Britain to accept modern aerodynamic and structural design, and Short Brothers produced the S.23 'Empire' type, also known as the C-class because each had a name beginning with that letter (the first, *Canopus*, flew on 4 July 1936). Such modern design was hardly compatible with the dangerously small and poorly-surfaced fields that dotted the Empire, so the new transport was a flying boat. Imperial already had many flying-boat bases, and the network was extended from Poole, Hythe (Southampton), and Foynes (Ireland) to the USA, South Africa and New Zealand.

The empire boat transformed not only the Imperial but also the British aircraft industry. It was a streamlined all-metal stressed-skin aircraft of beautifully clean design. The hull was made deep enough for the wing to be mounted directly on it and still be high enough to keep the propellers out of any waves. This depth resulted in a capacious interior with seats at different levels, sleeping berths and promenade deck. In the bows was the enclosed cockpit for captain and first officer at the front of a flight deck with spacious accommodation for a radio officer and navigator and/or engineer, while on the deck below was a cabin for a flight clerk, a large galley (kitchen) and separate male and female toilets. Great stress was laid on mail bags, accommodation for which was under the flight deck, aft of it as far back as the wing, and in the rear of the hull along with a much smaller space for baggage. Crew often outnumbered the passengers.

Though unpressurized, the S.23 had far more extensive 'systems' than previous British aircraft. The efficient aircooled radial engines, which in some versions were of the sleeve-valve variety, drove variable-pitch propellers fitted with de-icing, and behind the engines were electric generators, hydraulic pumps, vacuum pumps and air compressors. By this time engines of any given size were giving far more power, using fuel of progressively higher octane (anti-knock) rating. The first S.23s had engines of 920hp, but with identical 28·7-litre capacity to the Jupiter engines of 400–450hp used in earlier Imperial airliners. Fuel was carried in the wings in unusual cheese-shape tanks.

Structurally, these boats were innovative in many ways. Much of the structure was a new aluminium alloy called Hiduminium, with great strength and corrosion resistance. The booms, the strong spanwise members at top and bottom of the wing spars, were extruded T or L sections, and similar extrusions were found in the hull. The outer skin was flush-riveted to reduce drag, and the electrically-driven flaps had circular upper surfaces so that they could rotate instead of hinge, sliding away from their housings to increase the area of the highly-loaded wings.

Shorts built 42 of various subtypes of C-class, leading to the mass-produced wartime Sunderland ocean patroller.

Below:
The "Golden Hind", taking off for its first flight, on 21 July 1939, along the River Medway, Kent.

JUNKERS Ju 88 (1936)

Designed purely as a *Schnellbomber* (fast bomber), the Ju 88 went on to become perhaps the most versatile combat aircraft in history, with variants for 18 distinct missions. In most respects it was an outstanding machine, and the 14,780 built exceeded the total for all other Luftwaffe bombers and night fighters combined.

All initial versions were powered by two of Junkers' own Jumo 211 engines, large liquid-cooled inverted V-12s of 1,200 or 1,340hp each. In accord with a fortunate requirement, these were mounted as completely equipped power-plants with circular frontal radiators. The cantilever mounting beams forged in Elektron (magnesium alloy) were attached to standardized pick-ups on the fireproof bulkheads so that, in a matter of an hour or two, not only could the engine be changed but also replaced by one of a different type such as the BMW 801D radial which powered many of the later versions.

Structurally the Ju 88 was outstanding, with the most modern all-metal stressed-skin construction. Though the trailing edge of the wing was movable, it was not of the traditional Junkers 'double wing' form; instead it comprised modern slotted flaps and slotted ailerons which, when full flap was selected, drooped as well to increase lift (see cutaway drawing). Early Ju 88s had large slatted dive brakes under the wings and frequently bombed from dives at 60° angle, though most later versions did not dive bomb. Manoeuvrability was excellent, though the rudder and elevators were covered in fabric.

Most versions had a rather cramped four-seat crew compartment (the arrangement was thought to improve morale) with a 'bug eye' nose of multiple Plexiglas acrylic-plastic panes. The pilot sat high on the left with the upper rear gunner behind him (in the October 1940 aircraft illustrated, he has to aim, fire and reload four separate MG 15 machine-guns). The lower rear gun was fired by the radio operator. Exceptionally heavy bomb loads could be carried in the internal bay and on four racks under the inner wings.

The landing gear was an exceptional example of engineering. Each main wheel carried a tyre large enough for use at maximum weight caused by snow, mud or soft sand, conditions accepted as routine by an air force whose front-line units seldom enjoyed the luxury of an airfield. Each wheel was carried on a single massive leg whose shock-absorbing system was a unique stack of *Ringfeder* (ring springs) which, under load, pushed into each other. Their mutual friction when the load slackened prevented the aircraft bouncing. The wheel turned through 90° to lie neatly in a shallow nacelle, the retraction being hydraulic.

For so large an aircraft, some of the later versions had extraordinary performance. The latest night fighters, the Ju 88G series in the sub-types powered by the Jumo 213 engine with GM-1 (nitrous oxide) power-boost, could reach 402mph (647km/h) at high altitude in 'clean' condition, though in combat service they had large flame dampers which reduced performance. Of course the night fighters also carried extensive radar aerial (antenna) arrays which curtailed speed still further, besides being burdened by extremely heavy batteries of cannon, some of them firing obliquely upwards at 70°. This *Schräge Musik* (Jazz) installation destroyed hundreds of RAF bombers.

Below:
A JU88A-4 of
11/LG 1 over the
Mediterranean.

JUNKERS JU 88 (1936)

NAME: Junkers Ju 88 (Germany)
TYPE: night fighter, dive bomber,
   level bomber, torpedo bomber and
   close support
CREW: two - six
POWER PLANT: (G-7) two 1,880hp
   Junkers Jumo 213J liquid-cooled twelve-
   cylinder inverted-vee
DIMENSIONS: span 20.13m (65ft 10.5in);
   length 16.5m (54ft 1.5in); height 4.85m
   (15ft 11in)
WEIGHTS: empty 9,100kg (20,062lb);
   loaded 14,690kg (32,350lb)
PERFORMANCE: maximum speed
   643 km/h (402 mph);
   service ceiling 8,800m (28,870ft);
   range 2,300km (1,430 miles)
ARMAMENT: four MG 151/20 forward-firing
   from ventral fairing, two MG 151/20
   in Schrage Musik installation, plus one
   MG 131 in rear roof

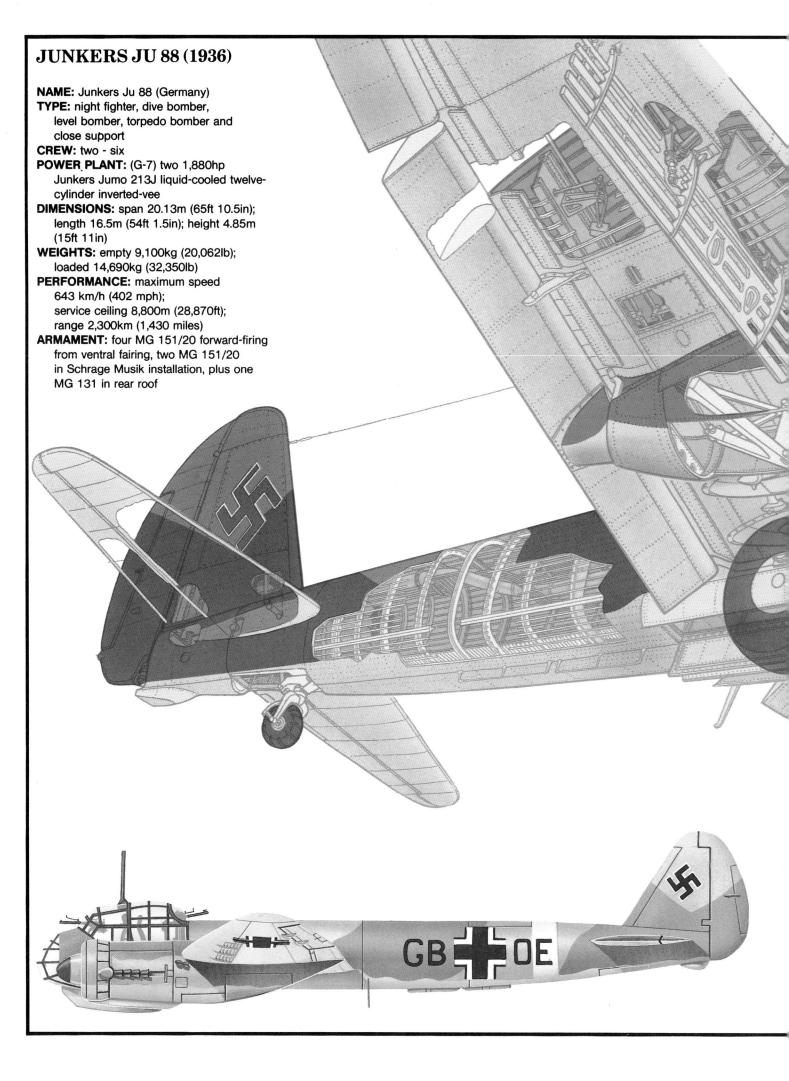

BELL P-39 AIRACOBRA (1939)

The P-39, designed by Bob Woods, became one of the most controversial fighters of World War II. What in theory could be described as the USA's first really 'modern' fighter actually took shape as a close support aircraft for the United States Army Corps. The changes were made in 1937-38 when it seemed certain that the USAAC would not require a purpose-built interceptor. However, in 1941 this forecast was proved well and truly incorrect, and the P-39 was requested to perform in a role that it was not developed to handle. Naturally, the aircraft failed to perform adequately, and so it took a great deal of unjustified and harsh criticism.

The prototype, designated the XP-39, made its inaugural flight on 6 April 1938 at Wright Field, Dayton, Ohio with Jimmy Taylor at the controls. Although lighter than the proposed design weight, because the armament had not been fitted, and with fuel tanks only partly filled, the P-39 achieved a maximum speed of 390mph (628km/h) at 2,000ft (6.096m). Even allowing for a deterioration in performance by having a full load of fuel and armament, the aircraft could still have become a very effective interceptor had the USAAC not demanded so many modifications before they would even consider placing an order. However, once these were done, an order was placed early in 1939 for 12 YP-39s and a YP-39A (the last being a testbed for the 1,150 horsepower Allison V-1710-31 engines for high altitude flying).

The main changes, excluding a reduced wingspan and stretched fuselage, included the

The Allison engines exhaust stubs ejecting to the rear of the cockpit, give away probably the most unique feature of the US Army Air Corps P-39 Airacobra.

repositioning of the air inlets and, most importantly, the choice of the more powerful Allison V-1710-37 engine. This did not have a turbo supercharger, and although it was more reliable and easily serviceable, the Allison only performed well at low and medium altitudes. The authorities were convinced that there was no need for a high altitude aircraft and so all work on the YP-39A was stopped. The modified XP-39 (redesignated the XP-39B) made its inaugural flight in November 1939. Although no armament had been fitted, it was obvious that the aircraft's performance had badly deteriorated.

By this time the French and British Governments had placed orders totalling over 200 units for the P-39 Airacobra. Even after severe criticism of the aircraft, the British not only took over the French order (they had opted out), but went on to place a repeat order for a further 475 which were designated 'the Caribou'. Whatever logic was behind these decisions, by the time the first three P-39Cs had been delivered to the Royal Air Force in 1941, the type was totally rejected. They were condemned as being completely inadequate, and greatly inferior to the Hurricane and Spitfire.

The Airacobras were too slow, handled badly, and were heavy and unmanoeuvrable. In September 1941, No. 601 Squadron (the first and only British Squadron to be equipped with P-39s) had their aircraft withdrawn from service. Such was the ill-feeling of the British that the planes were sold — to the USSR and Australia. Others went to the USAAC which by then had been renamed the United States Air Force.

Despite this blow to the P-39's operational career, American production and use continued uninterrupted, with increasingly heavy weaponry and thicker armour. It was becoming more of a fighter and less of an interceptor, although new, more powerful engines were impractical as there was too little space left in the fuselage.

A total of 9,585 P-39s were built over three years, half of which went to the USSR. The aircraft's wartime career with American forces began with the return of the Airacobras from Britain under the new designation P-400. It was immediately put into service in the Pacific.

The following model numbers show the development of the P-39. The XP-39 (Model 11) was the prototype example. P-39A was the temporary designation that was given to the YP-39. The XP-39B was the name of the first prototype that was modified with the Allison V-1710-37 engine. The YP-39 (Model 12) was a pre-production series variant. The YP-39A (or XP-39A) was the official designation of the last YP-39 which should have tested an Allison V-1710-3 engine suited to high altitude flight, but which was, however, never made. The P-39C (Model 13) was initially designated the P-45: only 20 were built of the 80 ordered.

Airacobra 1 (Model 14) was essentially a variant of the P-39C for export with different armament and an Allison V-1710-35E-A engine. Originally, 200 were ordered by France. On the fall of France, Britain took over the order for the RAF, bringing up the required order to 675 although not all those built were sent to Britain. P-400 (Model 14) are the Airacobra 1s taken and retained by the USA after the Japanese attack on Pearl Harbor.

The P-39D (Model 15) was very similar to the P-39Cs, but had reinforced armaments and pro-

A Portuguese Air Force P-39 Airacobra

vision for bombs and self-sealing fuel tanks. P-39D-1 (Model 15) was the designation given to 705 Airacobras ordered in June 1941. These were identical to the P-39D except for different armament.

The P-39D-2 (Model 14, export variant) was the same as the P-39D except that it had the Allison V-1710-63 engine. It was ordered by the RAF in 1941. XP-39E (Model 23) was similar to the P-39 but was redesignated the P-76 and 4,000 were ordered. The P-39F-1 (Model 15B) was the P-39D with a three-bladed propeller — 229 were produced.

The P-39F-2 was the designation given to 13 P-39Fs that were modified for photoreconnaissance. Another modification of the P-39F was the TT-39F, which was experimentally modified as an advanced trainer with a second cockpit and dual controls. All its armament was completely removed.

The P-39G (Model 20) was the designation for an order of 1,800 aircraft which was placed in August 1941, but after the order the airframes were changed to P-39K, P-39L, P-39M and P-39N types.

The P-39H designation was not assigned.

The P-39J (Model 15B) was identical to the P-39F except for its uprated engines.

The P-39K-1 was originally ordered as the P-39G, and the P-39K-2 was the designation of six P-39Ks modified for photoreconnaissance.

The P-39L-1 was the P-39K but with a Curtiss Electric three-bladed propeller. Its total production was 250. The P-39L-2 described 11 P-39Ls modified for photoreconnaissance.

The P-39M-1 differed from the P-39K only because it had an upgraded engine. The P-39M-2 was the designation of eight P-39Ms which were adapted for photoreconnaissance.

BELL P-39 AIRACOBRA (1939)

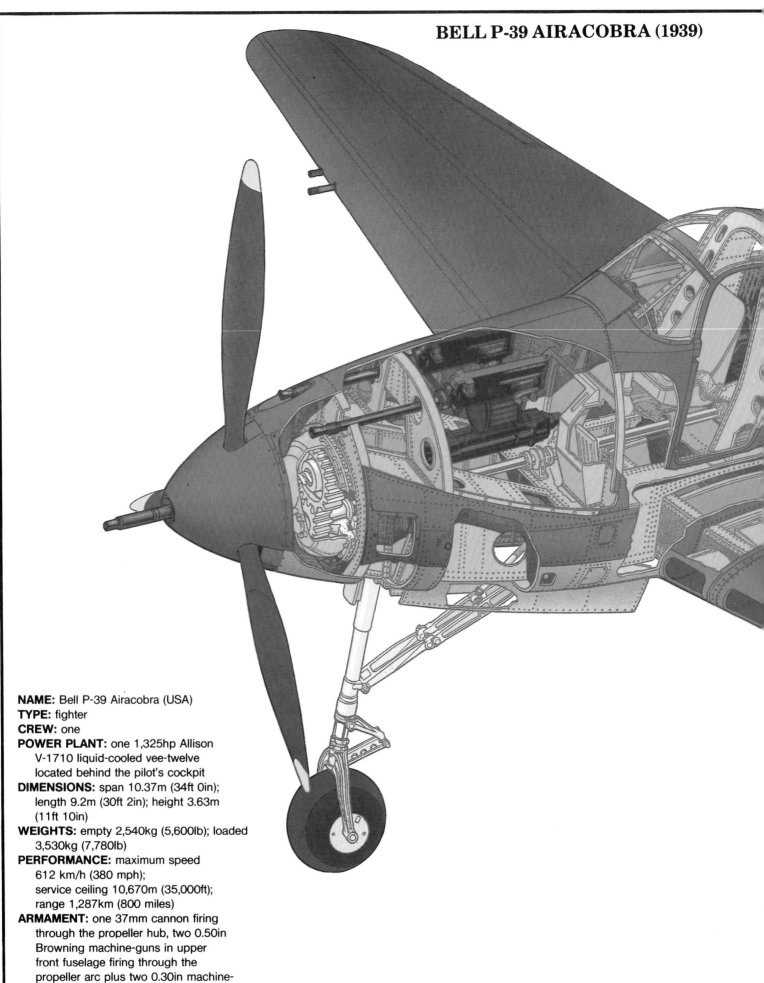

NAME: Bell P-39 Airacobra (USA)
TYPE: fighter
CREW: one
POWER PLANT: one 1,325hp Allison
    V-1710 liquid-cooled vee-twelve
    located behind the pilot's cockpit
DIMENSIONS: span 10.37m (34ft 0in);
    length 9.2m (30ft 2in); height 3.63m
    (11ft 10in)
WEIGHTS: empty 2,540kg (5,600lb); loaded
    3,530kg (7,780lb)
PERFORMANCE: maximum speed
    612 km/h (380 mph);
    service ceiling 10,670m (35,000ft);
    range 1,287km (800 miles)
ARMAMENT: one 37mm cannon firing
    through the propeller hub, two 0.50in
    Browning machine-guns in upper
    front fuselage firing through the
    propeller arc plus two 0.30in machine-
    guns in each wing

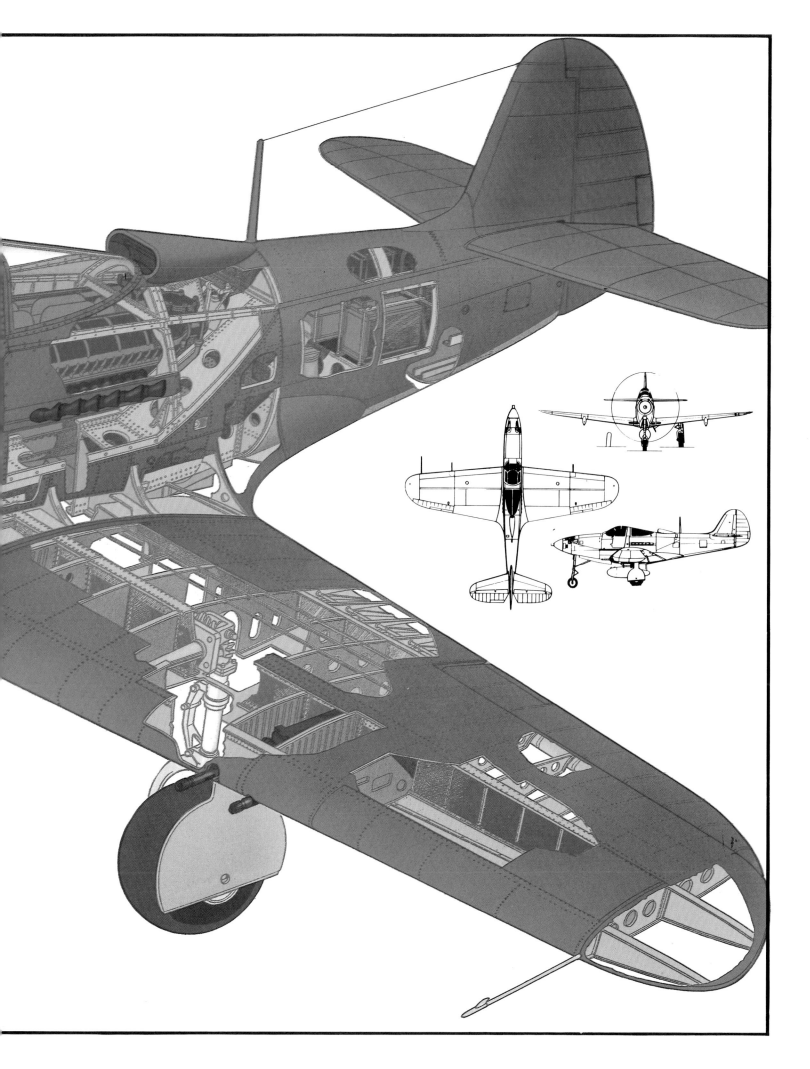

LOCKHEED P-38 LIGHTNING (1939)

One of the greatest fighters of World War II, the Lightning was the sole pursuit aircraft to remain in continuous production throughout the war. An initial service model was delivered to the USAAF in June 1941 (six months before Pear Harbor) with contracts for the final units being cancelled after the war had ended.

Lockheed's proposal for a multi-seat fighter (the XPB-3/XFM-2) had come second to Bell's in the 1936 competition that had resulted in the XFM-1 Airacuda, and consequently Lockheed was invited to take part in the Air Corps' design competition for a twin-engined high-altitude interceptor. Other entries were from Boeing, Consolidated, Curtiss, Douglas, and Vultee, but Lockheed was awarded the contract for one XP-38 prototype in June 1937. Construction began in July and a completed airframe was ready by December after which the aircraft was handed over to the Air Corps for high-speed taxiing trials.

An inaugural flight was completed on 27 January 1939 when Lieutenant Ben Kelsey took the aircraft up for 34 minutes. Unfortunately, the maiden voyage was hampered by very bad vibration of the flaps and the fracture of three flap support rods. A second flight took place on 5 February after repairs had been made. Despite continual problems during the following four test flights, it was decided to attempt a record transcontinental flight. On 11 February 1939, the aircraft left California to New York. After just over seven hours flying time on the last leg, the X-P38 lost power and crashed onto a golf course, some 2,000ft (610m) short of the landing field. The prototype, which by that time had accumulated less than 12 hours flying time, was damaged beyond repair.

In April 1939, Lockheed was awarded the contract for 13 YP-38s and one structural test airframe. These aircraft were powered by V-1710-F2 engines. The first YP-38 flew in September 1940, with subsequent aircraft being used by the USAAC/USAAF for accelerated service tests. Indeed, the type had had an assured future even before its first flight, since an order for 66 aircraft had been issued in September 1939. In August 1940 a follow-up order was given for 410 airframes. The initial order was to be delivered as P-38s, XP-38As and P-38Ds, while the second order consisted of P-38Es, P-38Fs, F-4s, F-4As, F-5s and F-5As. Britain and France showed an interest in the P-38 as early as 1939, and this subsequently led to a joint order for 667 aircraft. The two variants ordered were respectively designated Model 322-B for Britain and 322-F for France. Both were powered by Allison V-1710-C15 engines. Britain took the entire contract for the Model 322 after the fall of France in June 1940. The order was amended to provide for the delivery of 143 Lightning Is and the rest were to be Lightning IIs.

However, the Lightning I was tested by the Royal Air Force at Boscombe Down and considered unsatisfactory, and they refused to take the type, ending up with only three examples. Only one Lightning II airframe was completed and was used by Lockheed for testing smoke-laying canisters on racks between the boom and nacelle as well as for testing the air dropping of two torpedoes from the same racks. Those aircraft built for the Royal Air Force were instead delivered to the United States Air Force.

When the British and French orders are included, Lockheed and Vultee produced over 2,000 Lightnings, which received various designations in the P- (Pursuit) and F- (Photographic Reconnaissance) series.

YP-38 was a service test batch of 13 aircraft that were fitted with Allison V-1710-27/29 engines, turbo-superchargers and counter rotating propellers. P-38-L0 was the first production model, of which 29 were built and were redesignated the RP-38 in 1942. (The 'R' prefix denoted their restricted non-combat role.) The XP-38-L0 was a variant with a pressurized

Left:
This Lightning I was built for the RAF but was soon rejected as its non-turbocharged engines resulted in a poor performance.

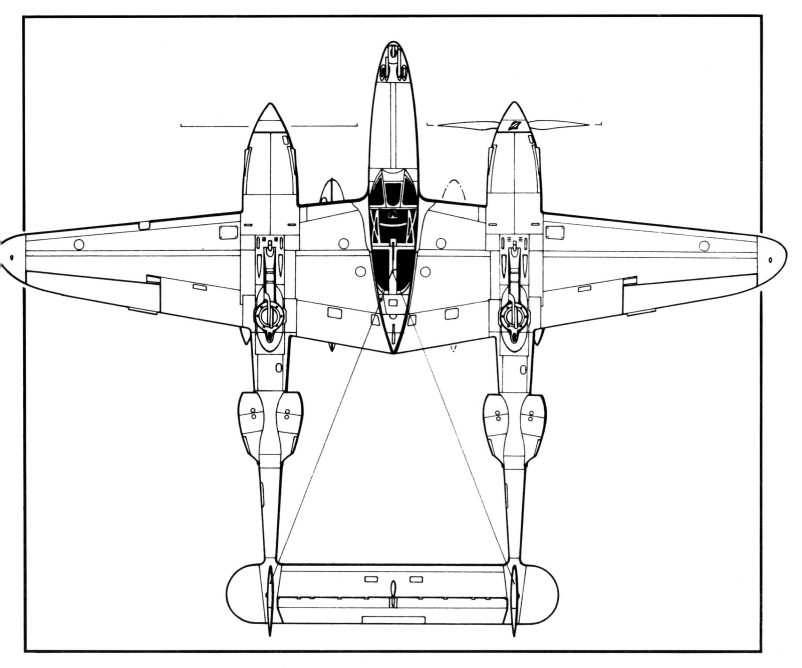

P-38J, machine-guns mounted in the front of the nacelle, superchargers clearly visible just aft of engines and radiators located either side of twin-booms.

cockpit. Trials took place between May and December 1942, and the aircraft was accepted by the USAAF at the end of the year. The engines were the V-1710-37 and 29. The categories P-38B and P-38C were reserved for two variants that were proposed by Lockheed in October and November 1939. but not in fact proceeded with. The P-38D-L0 was built with a low-pressure oxygen system, self- sealing fuel tanks and a retractable landing light.

The P-38E-L0 was the first major production version, and it had improved instrumentation and revised hydraulic and electrical systems. It was still not yet combat-ready, and most examples were redesignated YP-38Es while the rest were used for a variety of tests. In fact, the P-38F-L0 was the first combat-ready variant of the Lightning. All of these were powered by V-1710-49/-53 engines.

The P-38G-L0 had new engines, improved oxygen equipment and a more reliable radio. The P-38H-L0 had V-1710-89/-91 engines and were fitted with automatic oil radiator flaps which were designed to solve a very bad overheating

problem for the engine. The P-38J-L0 was the first variant in which Lockheed fitted a revised powerplant. It included a revised electrical system and modified turbo regulators.

The TP-38J-L0 was the unofficial designation of a number of P-38Js that had been adapted as two-seat trainers with a jump seat aft of the pilot.

The P-38K-L0 was a prototype which combined a P-38G-10-L0 airframe with V-1710-75/77 engines. The final production variant of the Lightning was the P-38L-L0: it was delivered by Lockheed in two blocks and was fitted with V-1710-111/-113 engines. The P-38L-5-VN was a still more improved version that was due to be produced by the Consolidated-Vultee Aircraft Corporation. Unfortunately, due to problems encountered in getting the new assembly line started, only five examples were built and the rest of the order for 2,000 were cancelled. Finally, the P-38M was a single-seat night fighter that had been modified by the US Fifth Air Force by fitting an SCR540 radar with a Yagi Array of antennae in the nose.

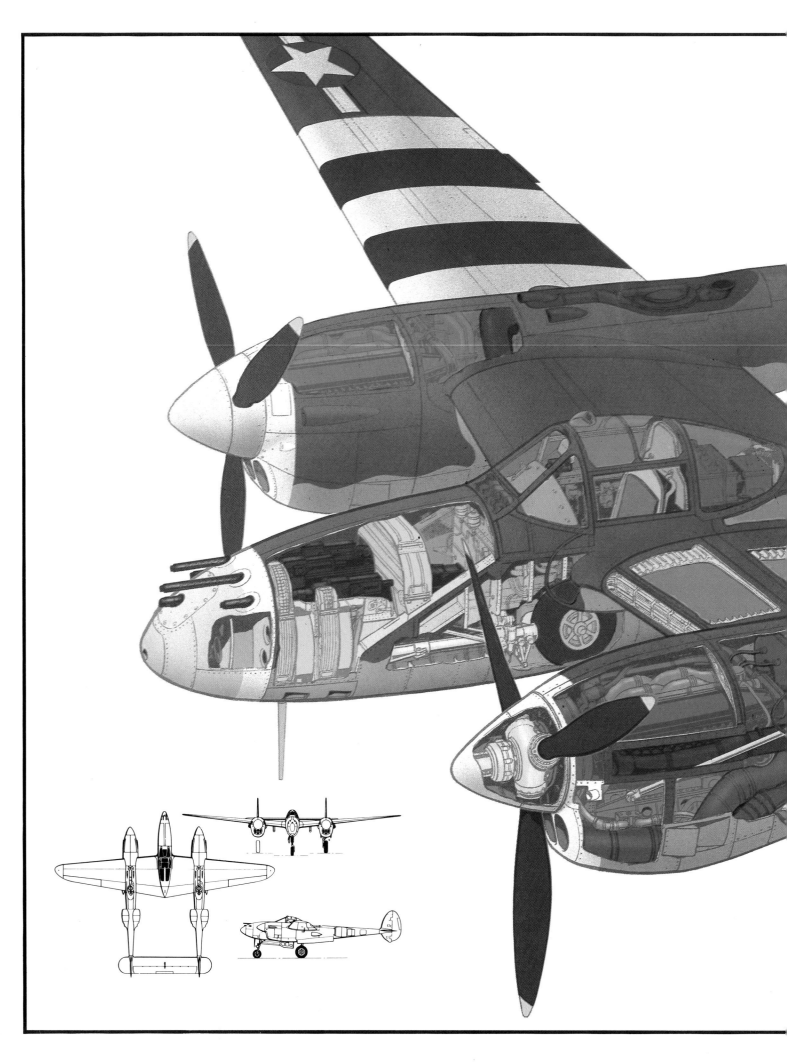

LOCKHEED P-38 LIGHTNING (1939)

NAME: Lockheed P-38 Lightning (USA)
TYPE: long range fighter
CREW: one
POWER PLANT: two 1,425hp Allison V-1710 liquid-cooled vee-type
DIMENSIONS: span 15.86m (52ft 0in); length 11.53m (37ft 10in); height 3.9m (12ft 10in)
WEIGHTS: empty weights varied from 4,990kg (11,000lb) (YP-38) to 6,350kg (14,000lb) in later models, maximum loaded 6,508kg (14,348lb) to 9,788kg (21,600lb)
PERFORMANCE: maximum speed 666 km/h (414 mph); service ceiling 13,410m (44,000ft); range on internal fuel, 891km (1,175 miles); range with maximum fuel 3,650km (2,260 miles)
ARMAMENT: one 20mm Hispano M2 cannon and four 0.50in Colt-Browning machine-guns in the nose; up to 726kg (1,600lb) of bombs under each inboard wing section

CHANCE VOUGHT F4U CORSAIR (1940)

The distinctive bent-wing Corsair was unfortunately delayed by development problems. Developed to meet a February 1938 design contest for a new carrier-based fighter for the US Navy, the XF4U-1 prototype flew in May 1940, but it was late 1943 before any Corsairs went into action. This was a pity, because many think it was the best piston-engined fighter of all time.

To meet Navy requirements the prototype had bomb cells in the wings, armament of two small and two large machine guns, and a bombsight in the floor of the cockpit. The R-2800 engine was the most powerful available, and to absorb its power the propeller had the unprecedented diameter of 13ft 4in (4.07m). To keep this clear of the ground with an efficient right-angle connection of the wing to the fuselage and still have a reasonably short landing gear the wing was bent sharply down in 'inverted-gull' configuration. This was good aerodynamically, and other advantages were improved pilot view and reduced height with the wings folded aboard a carrier. Drag was further reduced by mounting the large air cooler and carburettor air inlets in the centre-section leading edge, where they received maximum ram pressure. The engine itself was cowled very closely.

The main landing gears retracted backwards, the wheels rotating to lie in a shallow compartment completely closed by three doors. Basic structure of the airframe was immensely strong, with thick bulkheads, heavy extruded booms and longerons and thick skin, all of which enabled the underlying 'skeleton' to be simplified. Chance Vought and the Navy developed a new method of attaching the skin using spot-welding, and this was used over almost the whole fuselage and wing, giving a very smooth exterior finish. In contrast all control surfaces were covered with fabric, and this remained the case even though early in its career the Corsair was the fastest aircraft in the world apart from specialized racers. On 1 October 1940 the prototype reached 405mph (625km/h) in level flight. Incidentally, this achievement played a major role in Pratt & Whitney's abandonment of a giant programme of liquid-cooled engines; instead the company concentrated on simpler aircooled radials.

By 1941 the F4U had been redesigned. European fighting showed more firepower was needed. Six 0·5in (12·7mm) guns were accordingly mounted in the wing. This displaced the integral wing tanks, so a huge 237-Imp gal (1,077-litre) tank was put in the fuselage above the wing, which in turn forced the cockpit to be relocated over the trailing edge, where the view on the ground was poor. The flaps were simplified, and then cut down in span to allow the ailerons to be enlarged to improve rate of roll. The bomb cells and sight were removed, though later the F4U received plenty of underwing and fuselage pylons for tanks, bombs and rockets. The engine was made more powerful, the canopy was changed for a bulged frameless pattern giving a much better view.

As a carrier-based fighter the F4U had many shortcomings, notably awkward landing qualities which were almost dangerous. In the air it was superb, and it could outfight almost any other aircraft. It was the only US piston-engined fighter to remain in production into the Korean war, the 12,571st and last coming off the line in December 1952. It was an F4U-7 of the type shown in the cutaway drawing, with four 20mm cannon and a heavy attack load. This version was produced for the French in Indo-China.

Corsairs of the 4th Marine Air Wing in the Marshall Islands, June 1944.

Right:
Pilots of the 1st
Marine Air Wing
warm up their F4Us
engines whilst on-
board a carrier
bound for Korea.

Below:
An F4U, in the
colours of the French
Navy in Indo-China,
at an airshow at
North Weald in 1983.

CHANCE VOUGHT F4U CORSAIR (1940)

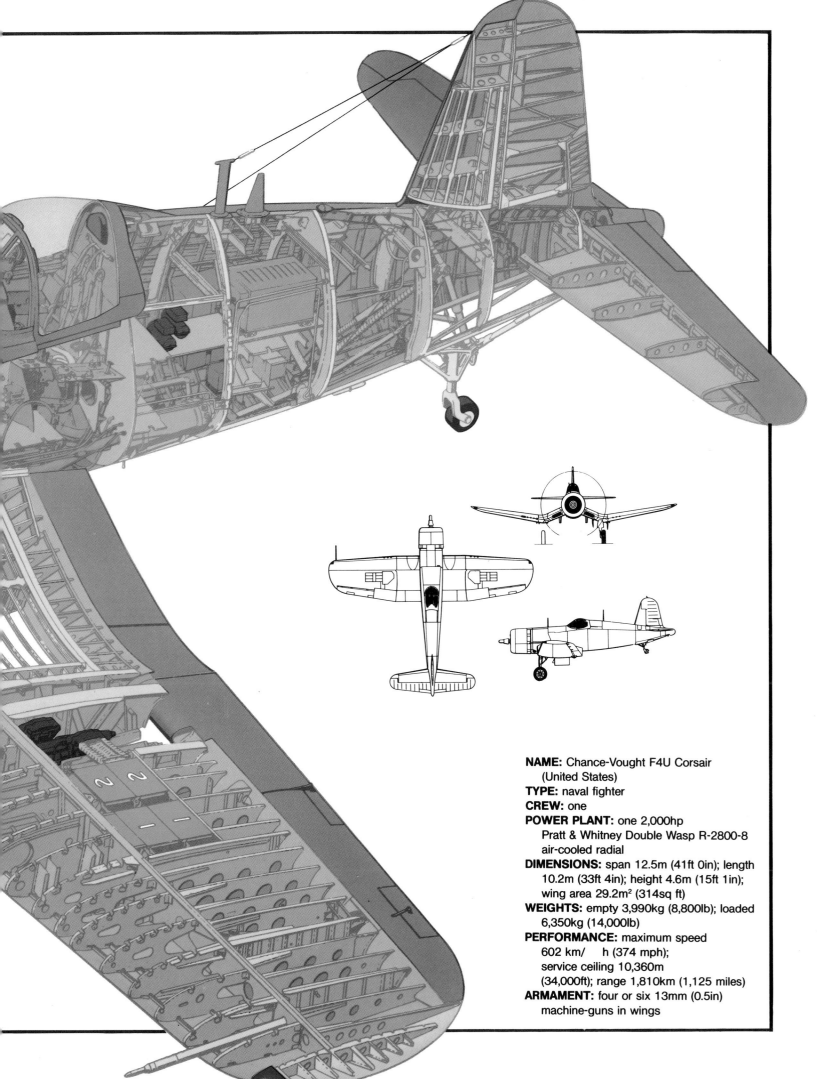

NAME: Chance-Vought F4U Corsair
(United States)
TYPE: naval fighter
CREW: one
POWER PLANT: one 2,000hp
Pratt & Whitney Double Wasp R-2800-8
air-cooled radial
DIMENSIONS: span 12.5m (41ft 0in); length
10.2m (33ft 4in); height 4.6m (15ft 1in);
wing area 29.2m² (314sq ft)
WEIGHTS: empty 3,990kg (8,800lb); loaded
6,350kg (14,000lb)
PERFORMANCE: maximum speed
602 km/ h (374 mph);
service ceiling 10,360m
(34,000ft); range 1,810km (1,125 miles)
ARMAMENT: four or six 13mm (0.5in)
machine-guns in wings

NORTH AMERICAN B-25 MITCHELL (1940)

One of the most important classes of aircraft in World War II was the twin-engined light or medium bomber. The United States mass-produced such important machines as the Douglas A-20 Boston/Havoc and A-26 Invader, the Martin 167 Maryland, 179 (B-26) Marauder and 187 Baltimore and Lockheed Hudson and Ventura, but in terms of numbers built the most important of all was the North American B-25 Mitchell. North American Aviation at Inglewood (Los Angeles) and Kansas City built 9,889 during the war, and they served on all fronts with virtually all the Allied forces.

The original NA-40 prototype flown in 1939 had 1,100hp engines, three seats and dihedral (upslope of the wings) from the roots. It featured the new nosewheel-type or 'tricycle' landing gear which offered many advantages but was very slow to be adopted by traditionalist Britain. Further development resulted in a new design with a wider fuselage, doubled bombload of 3,600lb (1,635kg), five seats and a pilot cockpit lowered flush with the top of the fuselage but wide enough for side-by-side seats. This was the basis of the B-25, but after building nine aircraft the outer wing panels were tilted down to the zero-dihedral (horizontal) position, giving a distinctive 'gull-wing' appearance. All production aircraft had the Cyclone 14 engine of 1,700hp.

Structurally the B-25 was typical of the period, with all-metal stressed-skin construction throughout except for fabric covering on the ailerons, elevators and twin rudders. The wing had a single massive spar with extruded booms at top and bottom and plate webs. The ribs were light-alloy sheet, with numerous flanged lightening holes, and light spanwise stringers were added before attaching the skin panels with flush rivets. The fuselage was capacious, but movement from one part to another was restricted by the mid-mounted wing, with bomb bay beneath, though a cramped crawlway low on the left side linked the bombardier's glazed nose compartment with the rest of the fuselage. Fuel was housed in wing tanks which from the B-25A onwards were self-sealing, armour also being added for the crew.

The twin-row radial engines were neatly cowled in long nacelles projecting behind the wing, providing room for the large main gears. The latter had single oleo legs and retracted backwards hydraulically. So did the nose gear, which had a shimmy damper (to prevent 'supermarket trolly' behaviour) and centring device used on takeoff and landing, but steering on the ground was accomplished by differential use of the toe-operated brakes, the nosewheel castoring right or left as needed. The engine oil coolers were inside the outer wings, with ram-air inlets in the leading edge and twin outlets in the upper surface just ahead of the flaps. The latter, of the slotted type, were operated hydraulically. A peculiarity of the B-25 was that lowering a little flap enabled the aircraft to fly further. It had the effect of tilting the aircraft level, from the normal nose-high cruise attitude, allowing the last 40 gallons of 100/130-octane fuel in the front of each tank to be used.

There were many major revisions of armament. In the Pacific most attacks were from low level, and the bombardier was often replaced by a 'solid' nose mounting a giant 75mm gun, reloaded shell by shell by the navigator. About four rounds could be fired on each attack (see cutaway drawing).

Left:
An American
Mitchell bomber
waits on an airfield
in wartime England.

Above:
A Royal Air Force
B-25 Mitchell
bomber flies over
Southern England
during World War
Two.

Right:
A B-25 Mitchell
bomber on an
English airfield in
1943. This was one
of the most
important Allied
bombers and flew in
every war zone.

NORTH AMERICAN B-25 MITCHELL (1940)

NAME: North American B-25 Mitchell (USA)
TYPE: medium bomber/attack
CREW: four - six
POWER PLANT: (B-25B) two 1,700hp
   Wright R-2600 Double Cyclone
   14-cylinder two-row air-cooled radial
DIMENSIONS: span 20.6m (67ft 7in);
   length 16.1m (52ft 11in);
   height 4.8m (15ft 9in)
WEIGHTS: empty 9,580kg (21,100lb);
   loaded 13,018kg (28,640lb)

PERFORMANCE: maximum speed
   482 km/h (300 mph);
   service ceiling 7,315m (24,000ft);
   range 2,414km (1,500 miles)
ARMAMENT: twin 0.5in machine-guns in
   electrically powered dorsal turret and
   retractable ventral turret;
   up to 1,363kg (3,000lb) bombs

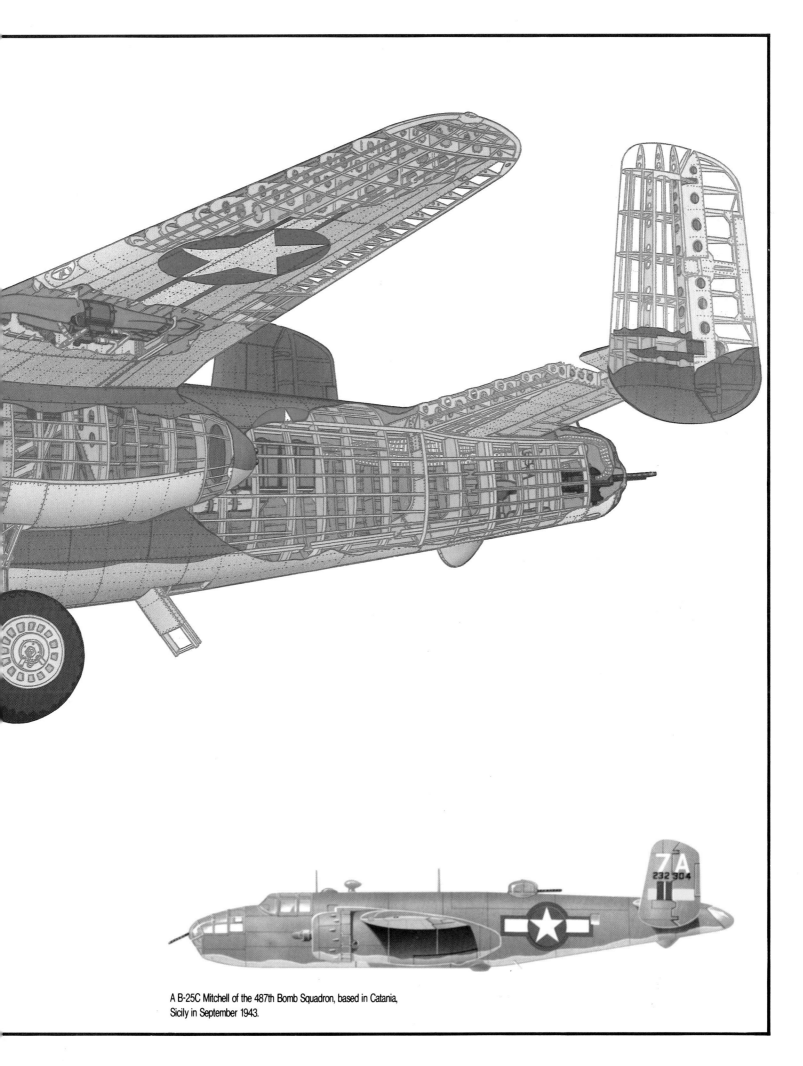

A B-25C Mitchell of the 487th Bomb Squadron, based in Catania,
Sicily in September 1943.

NORTH AMERICAN P-51 MUSTANG (1940)

Perhaps the most glamorous fighter of World War II, the Mustang was also one of the most modern, having been designed after that conflict began. In late 1939 the British Direct Purchasing Commission asked North American Aviation (NAA) to build the RAF Curtiss P-40s under licence. NAA, very unimpressed, suggested instead that they should design a much better fighter. The company were at last given the go-ahead on 10 April 1940, and the prototype N.A. 73X flew on 26 October 1940.

Named Mustang by the British, the new fighter was a winner from the start. It owed nothing to any previous design. The fact NAA had never built a fighter had troubled the customer, but it almost certainly was a prime reason for the Mustang's excellence. It abounded in cautious innovation. The wing had the new so-called 'laminar' section, with convex camber below as well as above and with maximum thickness much further aft than in traditional wings. The engine, an American Allison V-1710, was cooled by a glycol radiator in a duct under the rear fuselage giving minimum drag. Heavy armament comprised eight machine-guns, four of 0·3in (7·6mm) and the others heavy 0·5in(12·7mm) weapons.

The all-metal structure was extremely efficient yet designed for easy mass-production. Stressed-skin was used throughout, even for the control surfaces, and handling was quickly brought up to a superb level, with no shortcomings. Very large slotted flaps kept down the landing speed despite the new high-speed wing profile, these and the three units of the neat wide-track landing gear being operated hydraulically. The well-arranged and comfortable cockpit had armour and a side-hinged canopy, the left window panels dropping down to the left and the rest folding over to the right.

The most outstanding feature of the Mustang was its aerodynamic efficiency and performance. Powered by an engine of lower power than that of a Spitfire, the new US fighter was appreciably faster than the British machine at all heights up to 13,000ft (3,962m). Nevertheless, its fuel capacity was much more than twice as great, and its combat radius roughly three times that of the British fighter.

In retrospect it seems unbelievable that so superlative a fighter should have been consigned to army co-operation, reconnaissance and attack-bombing, all because its engine power dropped off too rapidly at high altitude. Indeed, one wonders why the US-built Merlin engine was not specified from the start. As it was, it was left to various individuals, notably Rolls-Royce pilot Ronnie Harker, to suggest re-engining the Mustang with the Merlin. The result was a great success, to such a degree that, even though the P-51B, C, D and K really only got into the war in 1944, they eclipsed the Allison-engined models that fought the rest of the war.

The Allison-Mustang had been bought in large numbers by the USAAF as the P-51 and the A-36 dive bomber, the former having four 20mm cannon. Curiously, the Merlin-engined P-51B had armament reduced to four 0·5in (12·7mm) all in the wings. Many P-51Bs and similar Dallas-built P-51Cs were refitted in Britain with a Malcolm canopy, a bulged sliding type giving a better view. The mass-produced P-51D and K had six 0·5in (12·7mm) wing guns and a beautiful sliding 'teardrop' canopy similar to today's fighters. With an additional tank of 71 Imp gal (323 litres) behind the cockpit, and two 90-gal (409-litre) 'paper' drop tanks, they could defeat the Luftwaffe over Berlin and fly home to Britain with fuel to spare.

Left:
A Royal South African Air Force P-51 preparing for a sortie in Korea.

Left:
Two Cavalier
Mustangs which are
post war derivatives
of the P-51H.

NORTH AMERICAN P-51 MUSTANG (1940)

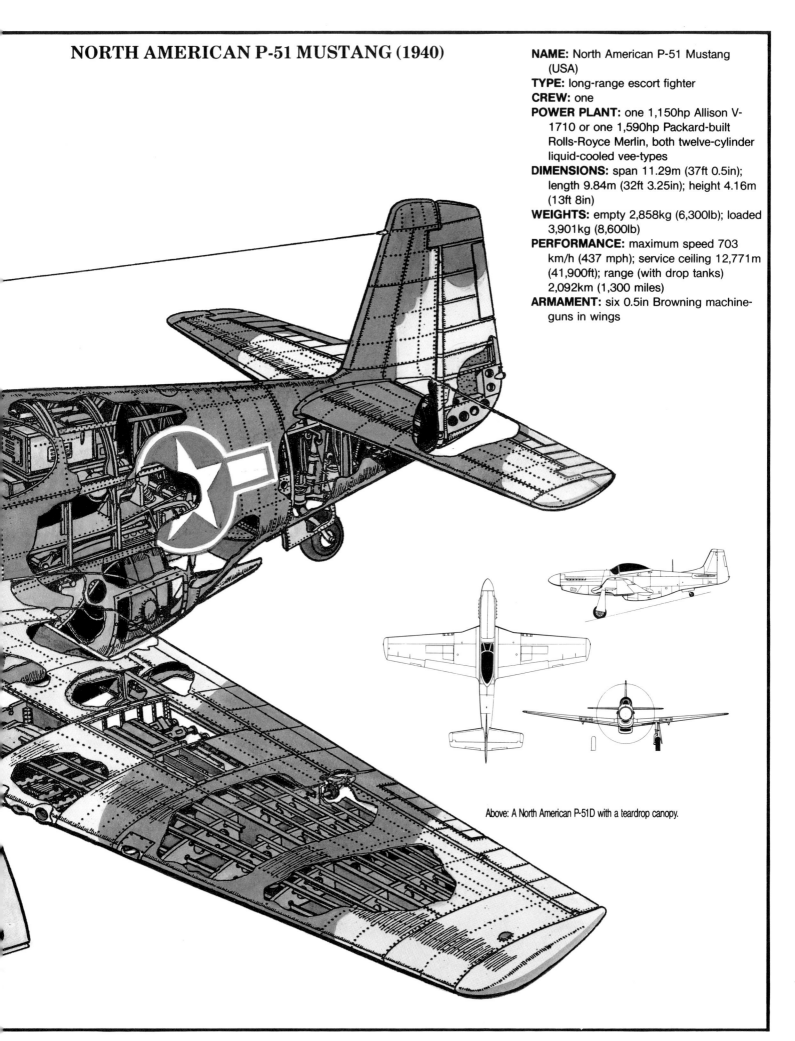

NAME: North American P-51 Mustang (USA)

TYPE: long-range escort fighter

CREW: one

POWER PLANT: one 1,150hp Allison V-1710 or one 1,590hp Packard-built Rolls-Royce Merlin, both twelve-cylinder liquid-cooled vee-types

DIMENSIONS: span 11.29m (37ft 0.5in); length 9.84m (32ft 3.25in); height 4.16m (13ft 8in)

WEIGHTS: empty 2,858kg (6,300lb); loaded 3,901kg (8,600lb)

PERFORMANCE: maximum speed 703 km/h (437 mph); service ceiling 12,771m (41,900ft); range (with drop tanks) 2,092km (1,300 miles)

ARMAMENT: six 0.5in Browning machine-guns in wings

Above: A North American P-51D with a teardrop canopy.

AVRO LANCASTER (1941)

The Avro Lancaster was formed by mating the airframe of a Manchester (an earlier unsuccessful bomber) with a new centre-section, and the prototype (BT308) made its inaugural flight on 9 January 1941. There followed very successful trials at the Aeroplane and Armament Experimental Establishment, Boscombe Down, and the British Air Ministry found with a great deal surprise that they had an excellent machine on their hands. They demanded that Avro and Metropolitan Vickers cease production of the Manchester in favour of the Lancaster as soon as possible.

The first Avro-built machine flew on 31 October 1941 and the first one from Metropolitan Vickers flew in early 1942. In complete contrast to the Manchesters, Lancasters started to reach the first operational squadrons within a very short period of time after the first production aircraft flew. In December 1942, No. 44 Squadron at Waddington began to receive their first aircraft. As more and more aircraft arrived, the squadron began to work up to operational status.

At first the Lancaster's crew complement consisted of two pilots, a navigator, two wireless operator/air gunners, and two air gunners. However, the second pilot was soon replaced by a flight engineer. No. 97 Squadron began to re-equip in January 1942 and were followed by 207 Squadron in March. Each Lancaster could carry four 1,000lb (454kg) general purpose bombs that had an 11-second delay so that they could be dropped from a low altitude without endangering the crew. As bomb development was carried out, individual bombs grew in size. Al-

Lancaster PA474 of the Battle of Britain memorial flight over the Royal Air Force College at Cranwell.

though the possibility of transporting an 8,000lb (3,629kg) bomb had been discussed at the time of the Manchester, none had existed then. The first of these were dropped on Essen in April 1942, and the even larger 12,000lb (5,443kg) bomb was first carried in September 1943.

There are few aircraft that have maintained their original form throughout their production and service life. The Lancaster did exactly that except for a few changes for specific purposes. An example of this was when the Lancasters of 617 Squadron were adapted to carry the famous Wallis 'bouncing bomb' on their dam busting raids. Another example was when turrets were taken out to permit the transportation of 2,200lb (9,980kg) bombs at the end of the war.

Although Avro was the main producer of Lancasters, there were several other production factories elsewhere. The main Avro works was at Chadderton, Manchester, but final assembly took place at Woodford which also received those Lancasters made by Metropolitan Vickers at Trafford Park. From there they were transported in sections to the Avro airfield. There was also a production line at Yeadon which had its own airfield. Armstrong Whitworth had built a factory at Bitteswell to supplement its existing facility at Baington where Whitley bombers had been built.

There was also a production line in Canada for the Lancaster Bomber, and a regular ferry route sent them to Canadian bomber squadrons in No. 6 (RCAF) Group in Britain. The production run was huge and the requirement for engines was, to say the least, crucial. Shortages were effectively avoided with the establishment of a Merlin engine production line at Packard Motors in the

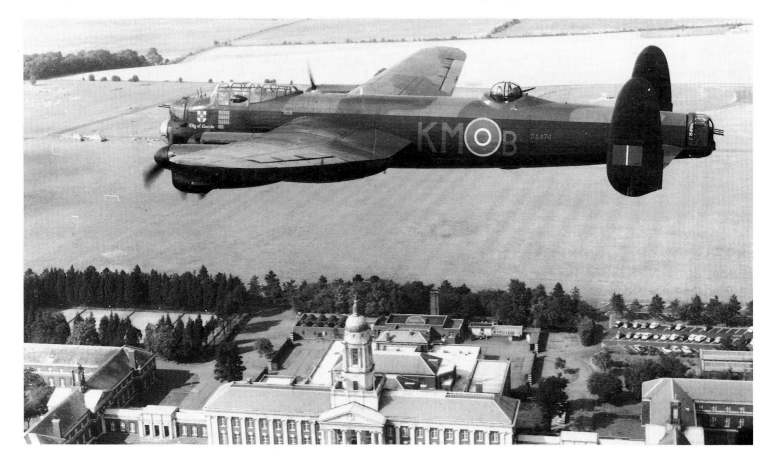

This aircraft was built in 1945 as a basic reconnaissance/ bomber for use in the Far East, but was remodified for photoreconnaissance. It is painted in the standard Lancaster camouflage.

USA. These engines were called Merlin 28s and the Lancasters that they powered became Mark (Mk) IIIs. Merlin 85 or 87s were fitted to the latter mark to become a Mk IV. Other mark numbers given to the aircraft included the Mk VII, which had dorsal and tail turrets for two 0.5in (1.27cm) guns. Many of these were adapted for use in the tropics as the B.VII(FE), and as the Mk X which designated the Canadian-built aircraft.

Mks IV and V later became the Lincoln bomber which first appeared in 1945. A modification that was frequently made to the basic Lancaster airframe was the addition of H2S scanners in a radome under the rear fuselage. Variants produced after the war included the GR 3 for maritime patrol, and the ASR 3 for air-sea rescue; the latter was able to carry an airborne lifeboat on a hook that protruded from the bomb-bay doors. These aircraft were used by Coastal Command squadrons and in the Middle East. They were also the last of the maritime Lancasters left in service on 15 October 1956.

Some unarmed Lancasters were fitted with cameras and were used by No. 82 Squadron in air surveys including in West and East Africa mapping territory which had remained uncharted in detail until then.

The Canadian Lancasters that had been sent home at the end of the war were modified for maritime reconnaissance, arctic survey, photographic, search and rescue and drone-carrying duties.

The Canadians also led the way in converting Lancasters for civilian service by adapting a number of Lancasters to fly passengers over the trans-Atlantic run from 1945 onward. This variant was renamed the Lancastrian. All of the military equipment had been removed and fairings were fitted to the nose and tail. The rear fuselage was fitted with nine seats which converted for night flights into six bunks. Windows were fitted into the starboard side of the fuselage and seats were arranged along the port facing sideways. Ninety per cent of the baggage was carried in the nose. There was a crew of six which included a steward. The Lancastrian had the advantages of long range and speed but had no hope at all of being an economical transport for airline use.

Some Mk II military Lancasters were produced, but most stayed at maintenance units for their entire RAF service. The Mk III was a civilian variant that had seats for 13 passengers, and the Mk IV was a similar model for the RAF.

AVRO LANCASTER (1941)

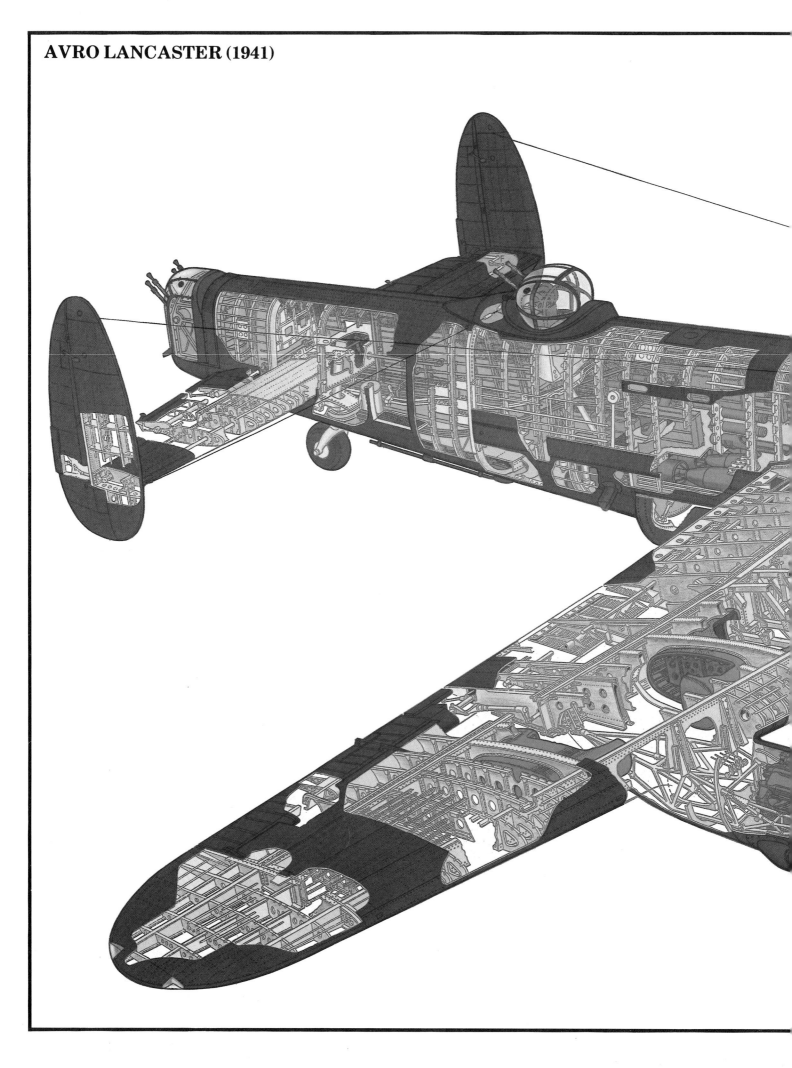

NAME: Avro Lancaster (Britain)

TYPE: heavy bomber

CREW: seven

POWER PLANT: four 1,460hp Rolls-Royce (or Packard-built) Merlin twelve-cylinder liquid-cooled vee-type

DIMENSIONS: span 31.1m (102ft 0in); length 21.1m (69ft 4in); height 5.97m (19ft 7in)

WEIGHTS: empty 16,705kg (36,900lb); loaded 30,800kg (68,000lb)

PERFORMANCE: maximum speed 462 km/h (287 mph); service ceiling 7,467m (24,500ft); range 2,675km (1,660 miles)

ARMAMENT: two 0.303in Browning machine-guns in the nose and dorsal turrets plus four in the rear turret; normal bomb load of 6,350kg (14,000lb) or 9,979kg (22,000lb) "Grand Slam" bomb with modification

DE HAVILLAND DH 98 MOSQUITO

The DH 98 can trace its roots back as far as 1938 when the original concept for this wooden bomber arose. It was envisaged as a small two-engined bomber to be powered by two Rolls-Royce Merlin engines and with a range sufficient to get a worthwhile load of bombs to Berlin. However, in 1938 the project was cancelled by the British Air Ministry which could not see any virtue in unarmed wooden aircraft. It was not until the end of December 1939, with the enthusiasm and foresight of Sir Wilfred Freeman, Air Council member for Research, Development and Production, that a detailed design emerged for a light bomber with a range of 1,500 miles (2,400km) and a capacity to carry a bomb load of 1,000lb (454kg). It was also intended to be equally capable in unarmed reconnaissance and as a long-range fighter.

Finally on 1 March 1940, after much official reluctance, an order for 50 aircraft was placed. The aircraft was designated the DH 98 Mosquito and was an all-wooden cantilever monoplane with a tapering fuselage built of cedar wood and balsa wood. The aircraft was powered by two 1,250 horsepower Merlin engines which were housed in a retractable undercarriage.

The prototype Mosquito (the E0234) was built under intensive secrecy in a small hangar at Salisbury Hall, and made its maiden flight on 25 November 1940 piloted by Geoffrey de Havilland Jnr. The aircraft's performance amazed everybody, none more so than the manufacturers. It was the Mosquito's fighter-like manoeuvrability and upward rolls from ground level, on one engine, that at last attracted official interest. The prototype was renamed the W4050 in February 1941 and underwent further flight tests. It established itself as the world's fastest operational aircraft — a distinction which it enjoyed for the next two and a half years: some later models could reach a maximum speed of 425mph (680km/h).

On 15 May 1941 the Mosquito night fighter prototype made its inaugural flight. It was equipped with strengthened wing spars to allow for excess movement in combat and had four 20mm Hispano cannons under the floor, four machine guns in the nose, a bullet-proof windscreen and the AI Mk IV radar. This aircraft (the W4052) was used for the development of night fighter tactics. It involved the fitting of a pneumatically operated segmented air-brake around the mid-fuselage.

The last of the three prototypes (the W4051)

A de Havilland Mosquito B.IV. The bomber versions differed from the fighter variants mainly in having a glazed nose to give the bomb aimer a good view downward.

made an inaugural flight on 10 June 1941, and was handed over for evaluation to the Photographic Reconnaissance Unit at Benson the following month.

By May 1942 Mosquito bombers and fighters were operational in all three variants. From then onwards, de Havilland progressively developed the aircraft, making them faster, heavier and increasingly difficult to intercept.

The first production bomber was the B Mk IV Series 1, which had increased tankage. It had been discovered that if the bomb vanes were cropped, it was possible to carry four 500lb (227kg) bombs thus doubling the Mosquito's capacity before it went into service. Initial deliveries included an order for 263 B Mk IV Series 2 aircraft, which were distinguishable by their longer nacelles which projected aft of the wing and divided into wing flaps.

It was this model which bombed to destruction the Gestapo Headquarters in Oslo, Norway in September 1942 after which modifications were made to 26 aircraft so that each could transport a 4,000lb (1,815kg) bomb plus 50 gallon (227 litre) drop tanks under the outer wing panels. This enabled Mosquitoes for the first time to reach and bomb Berlin at the end on January 1943. Towards the end of the war, a large number of B Mk IVs were modified to carry an even greater load, and so becoming torpedo bombers. Bomber development carried on via the B Mk V which had a strengthened wing. This was able to carry either two 6500lb (227kg) bombs or 100 gallon (455 litre) drop tanks.

In 1942 De Havilland Aircraft of Canada began building the Mosquito under licence, their

A Mosquito T.III dual control trainer. This variant was first flown in January 1942, but was mainly used after World War Two.

variant being called the Packard-Merlin, and more than a thousand were produced by the time production ended. Some of these types were responsible for air records in flying the Atlantic, and the best time was five and a half hours.

The final bomber variant was the B Mk 35 whose prototype flew on 12 March 1945 and the 122nd, and last, being rolled out in August 1946. Although it was too late for the war, it entered post-war service with Nos. 109 and 139 Squadrons.

Photographic reconnaissance Mosquitoes kept the whole of Europe under daily reconnaissance and flew 3,000 photographic and meteorological sorties during 1943. At the end of the year, the type saw service in the Far East, and in 1944 made aerial surveys of Burma and photographed enemy seaports in Malaya and the Dutch East Indies.

The T Mk III, a dual control trainer version, first flew on 30 January 1942 and was built in small batches in 1943. About 14 airframes were shipped to Australia to be built there by de Havilland Aircraft. Destined for the Royal Australian Air Force, the first aircraft (the A52-1) made its inaugural flight in Sydney on 23 July 1943.

Although ageing, the Mosquito still had quite a considerable military potential in the early post-war years, and a large number of surplus airframes were cheaply acquired by many nations. Some had already been in service in Russia, while others went into service in Belgium, Burma, Canada, China, Czechoslovakia, Dominica, Israel, Norway, Sweden, Turkey and Yugoslavia.

NAME: de Havilland Mosquito (Britain)

TYPE: high-speed day bomber, night fighter, pathfinder

CREW: two

POWER PLANT: two 1,640hp Rolls-Royce Merlin twelve-cylinder liquid-cooled vee-type

DIMENSIONS: span 16.5m (54ft 2in);
length 12.34m (40ft 6in); height 4.66m (15ft 3.5in)

WEIGHTS: empty 6,410kg (14,100lb);
loaded 7,955kg (17,500lb)

PERFORMANCE: maximum speed 660 km/h (410 mph);
service ceiling 10,520m (34,500ft); range 2,990km
(1,860 miles)

ARMAMENT: dependent on mark and use, four 20mm
Hispano cannon and four 0.303in Browning
machine-guns in the nose in the night fighter
variants, or up to 4,000lb of bombs in
internal bomb bay

DE HAVILLAND MOSQUITO(1941)

GLOSTER METEOR (1943)

It is commonly 'known' that the Me 262 was 'the first jet fighter in service'. In fact, though it was half-heartedly made in trivial numbers and had almost no influence on the war, the British Gloster Meteor actually reached a regular combat unit (616 South Yorkshire Sqn) on 12 July 1944, well before any Me 262s were delivered to a regular combat unit of the Luftwaffe. What is much more significant is that the Meteor might have been in service six months earlier had it not been for the outrageous situation that was allowed to develop between Whittle's Power Jets company (which was developing the engines) and the Rover Car Co (which was supposed to produce them).

Be that as it may the Gloster twin-jet was the sole exception to the rule that, until well into World War II, the British authorities were so incapable of assessing whether Frank Whittle's invention of the turbojet had any value that they omitted to order any jet aircraft. Designer George Carter at Gloster Aircraft had already produced the small E.28/39 experimental machine to fly the Whittle engine, first flown on

15 May 1941, and began work on the concept of a jet fighter in January 1940. Later the company type number G.41 was allocated, and the official name Thunderbolt was bestowed, to be changed to Meteor when the US Thunderbolt fighter appeared. The fighter was designed to specification F.9/40, and in August 1941 the first order was received, for a batch of 20.

Carter naturally used stressed-skin construction throughout, and tried to avoid risk by making the Meteor as traditional as possible, but found himself in a series of cleft sticks. Though turbojets were rapidly growing in power and reliability, it seemed essential to use two engines. The Whittle-type engine needed to draw in air all around it, whereas the Metrovick axial and Halford (DH) centrifugal could have direct inlet ducts from the front. In the absence of any other jet aircraft, Carter had to make the Meteor able to take any of the many types of engine, so he mounted them well outboard on the wings. After much agonizing he arranged for the centrifugal engines to be fitted between the widely spaced spars, with circular 'banjo' hoops linking the spars of the centre section to those in the outer wing. The wide gap between the front

Far right:
Side views of the Meteor NF 12 night fighter (top) with extended nose housing radar and tandem seat cockpit and (bottom) the single seat Mk8.

Below right:
The front wing spars are clearly visible just inside the engine intakes of this Mark 4 aircraft.

Below:
Two Mk 8 Meteors, the nearest with two 1,000lb bombs and auxiliary fuel tank under fuselage.

and rear spars made the wing very broad, which in fact helped to reduce the thickness/chord ratio for high-speed flight.

The centrifugal engines thus had a fat cowling centred on the wing, with a plain hole at the front. The Metrovick F.2 engine was underslung below the wing (this remained a prototype). Levered-suspension tricycle landing gear was used, taking full advantage of the absence of propellers to reduce aircraft height above the ground. The large size of the aircraft was inevitable, but the enormous fuel tank for the new kerosene fuel fitted neatly behind the cockpit in the nose with an outstanding view (and, later, an ejection seat). The tail, however, had to be unusual to avoid problems caused by the high-speed jet wakes. Flight controls were manual, the ailerons (which gave a lot of trouble) being driven by chain/sprocket rotary shafts from ahead of the front spar.

The drawing shows the much more powerful MK 4 aircraft, with enlarged nacelles (though the engines were no bigger), which set world speed records in 1945 and 1946. Incidentally, Carter made provision for six cannon, but only four were ever fitted.

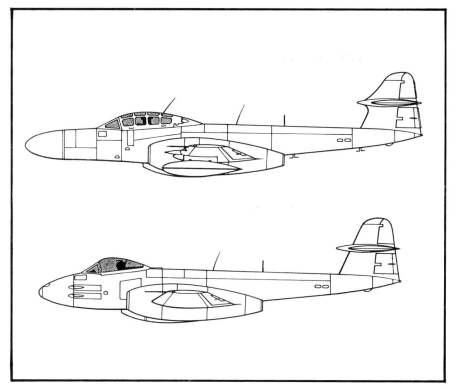

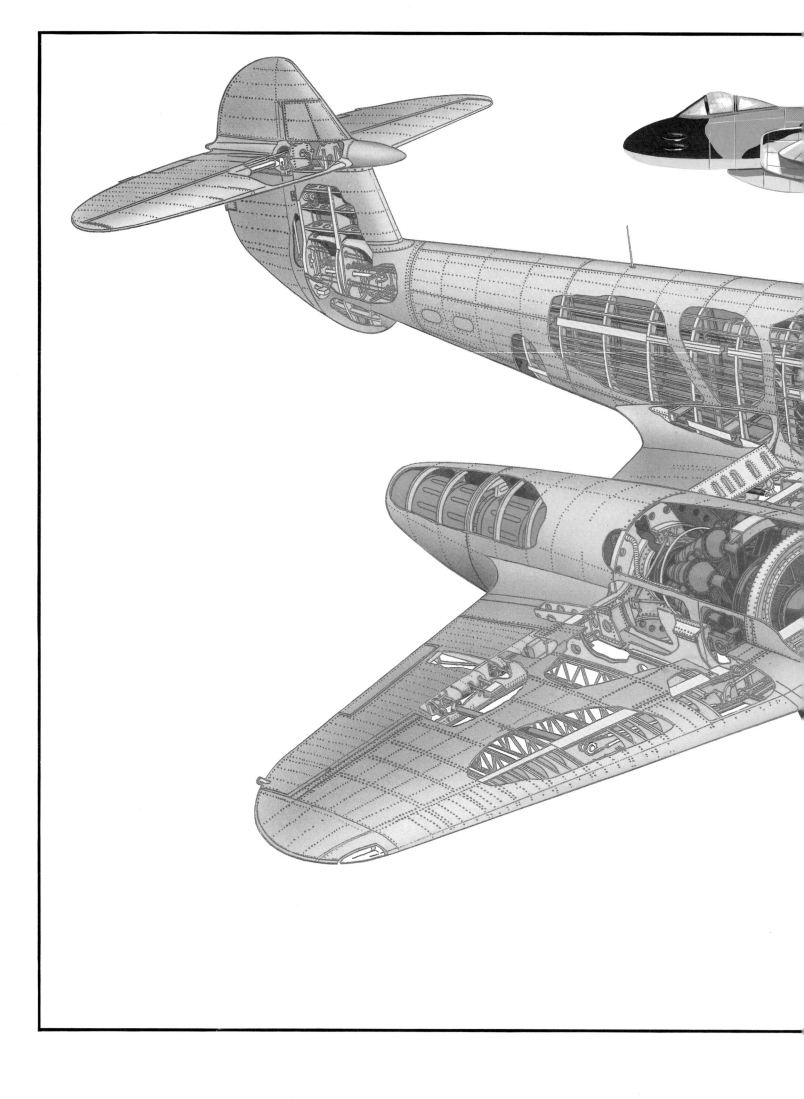

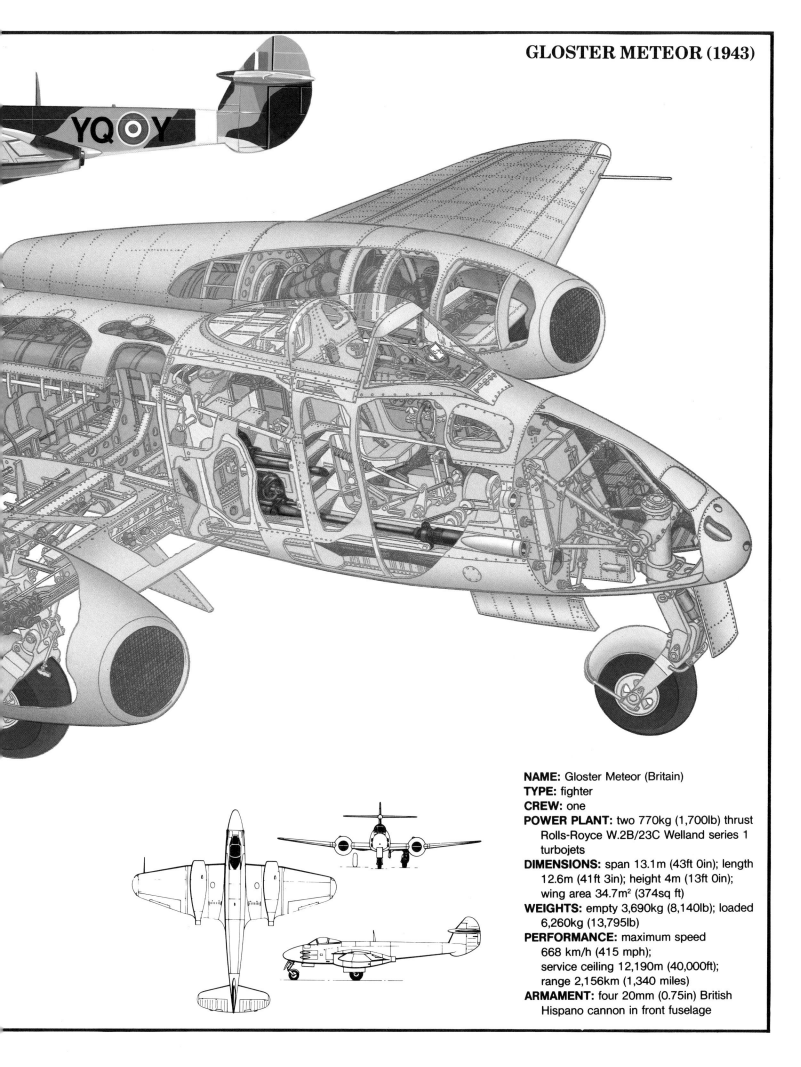

GLOSTER METEOR (1943)

NAME: Gloster Meteor (Britain)
TYPE: fighter
CREW: one
POWER PLANT: two 770kg (1,700lb) thrust
Rolls-Royce W.2B/23C Welland series 1
turbojets
DIMENSIONS: span 13.1m (43ft 0in); length
12.6m (41ft 3in); height 4m (13ft 0in);
wing area 34.7m² (374sq ft)
WEIGHTS: empty 3,690kg (8,140lb); loaded
6,260kg (13,795lb)
PERFORMANCE: maximum speed
668 km/h (415 mph);
service ceiling 12,190m (40,000ft);
range 2,156km (1,340 miles)
ARMAMENT: four 20mm (0.75in) British
Hispano cannon in front fuselage

DORNIER DO 335 (1943)

One of the strangest and fastest piston-engined aircraft ever built, the Do 335 never quite entered service. Today it is remembered (and only by a few) as just another of the wealth of piston and jet types on which Hitler's industry was frantically working in the final year of the war to try to make up for the almost complete lack of proper planning in earlier years. Mainly because of the advent of jet propulsion, the push/pull propeller fighter died with the 335, but the fact that this machine was still an expanding programme at the time of the final collapse shows what an impressive aircraft it was.

In the pre-jet era the main barrier to faster fighters, apart from the aerodynamic limitations of propellers, was getting enough power into the propeller. Giant piston engines were unattractive, but one solution was to use two engines in tandem. Schneider racing seaplanes had been built with two engines at the extremities of a central nacelle, with push/pull propellers (the tail being carried on twin booms) and with tandem engines driving counter-rotating propellers at the front, one propeller's drive shaft being a tube surrounding the other. In the Do 335 Dornier found a third solution, with the pusher propeller behind the tail of an ordinary fuselage.

This scheme has much to commend it. It is generally preferable to twin booms, as there is no asymmetric problem if an engine fails and the frontal area is no greater than for a single-engined machine. On the other hand the rear propeller operates in the slipstream of that in front, it must be prevented from hitting the ground, and it invariably needs a long

Below:
A frontal view of the Dornier DO 335.

driveshaft. Nevertheless, from the first flight on 26 October 1943 the first Do 335 – popularly called *Pfeil*, arrow – handled excellently. Despite its two massive engines so widely distributed fore and aft it showed outstanding manoeuvrability, and at an early stage demonstrated 560km/h (348mph) in level flight with the front propeller feathered! Gradually new versions appeared, including day fighters, night fighters, fighter/bombers, reconnaissance aircraft and trainers, and late in the war Heinkel was given the task of improving the Do 335's high-altitude performance and designed wings of extended span. Most of the planned versions never flew.

An exception was the Do 335 V10 (10th prototype), which was to lead to the Do 335A-6 night fighter that first flew in 1944. This was fitted with a second cockpit behind the first, raised on a higher level to leave room for a large fuel tank underneath which occupied the space used for an internal bomb bay in the fighter-bomber version. The rear cockpit housed an instructor in the trainer version, but in the night fighter the occupant managed the FuG 217J-2 *Neptun* air-interception radar, whose arrays of dipole aerials (antennae) were carried ahead of the outer wings. Only three cannon were fitted in this version, all in or above the front engine.

There were many interesting features in all 335s. The massive nose gear retracted backwards, the wheel turning through 45° to lie obliquely under the pilot's seat. Leading edges were de-iced, those of the fins being wood and incorporating radio aerials. Not least, to enable the crew to escape in emergency, they had ejection seats, and by firing explosive bolts the rear propeller could be severed in flight!

DE HAVILLAND VAMPIRE (1943)

The prototype single-seat, Vampire interceptor jet fighter first flew on 23 September 1943 only 16 months after detailed designs were begun. It was originally conceived as an all-metal aircraft except for the Mosquito-style plywood and balsa cockpit section. The powerplant was a Goblin 1 turbojet which had 2,700lb (1,227kg) of thrust. The engine was fitted behind the pilot in a short nacelle, and had been designed by Major F.B Halford. The tail unit was mounted on twin booms, and the tailplane was set high on tall square fins. The aircraft was able to sit low to the ground on a short, retractable nosewheel undercarriage now that there was no longer any need to allow for airscrew clearance.

Two further prototypes were produced after which a contract was signed on 13 May 1944 to build a total of 120 units — the order was subsequently increased to 300.

The Vampire was the world's first fighter to have a top speed of 500mph (805km/h), and was readily identifiable by its square-cut, vertical tail surfaces. The 41st and subsequent aircraft (the Vampire F Mk I) were powered by the more powerful Goblin 2 engine, and were fitted with one-piece canopies.

Although Vampires were too late for World War II, the 2nd Tactical Air Force flew them between 1946 and 1951. Their public debut was made with a fly-past over London by No. 247 during the victory celebrations of 8 June 1946. The Vampire also became the first jet to fly for the Royal Auxiliary Air Force.

Below:
A Vampire in
level flight.

Three early production models (the TG276, TG280 and TX807) were used as testbeds for the Rolls-Royce Nene I engine. They were distinguishable by the intakes on top of the nacelle which fed air to the double-sided impellers, and because of this were nicknamed 'elephant ears'. These test machines were used for performance trials under the designation Vampire II. The TX807 was later modified by dispensing with the dorsal intakes and was subsequently shipped to Australia. As the A78-2, it served as a development machine for the Nene powered F Mk 30 engine.

On 8 May 1947, the TG278 flew as a testbed for the de Havilland Ghost turbojet. The aircraft was fitted with a 4ft (1.22m) extension to each wing tip and a special hood. In the course of trials, it established a new world altitude record of 59,446ft (18,199m). The TG278 was later fitted with a Mk 3 tailplane during the development of a Ghost-engined version which was initially known as the Vampire Mk 8. However, the model was eventually built as the DH 112 Venom.

The airframes of the TG283 and the TG306 were transferred to the DH 108 programme. The Royal Canadian Air Force was supplied with one Vampire F Mk I, while another type (the TG372) went to Canada for winter trials. Switzerland became interested in the aircraft, and their requirements were met when they fitted the TG433 with a 3,300lb (1497kg) Goblin 3 engine. This prototype became the Vampire FB Mk 6, and 75 of them were ordered by the Swiss Government. The Swedish Government also

DE HAVILLAND VAMPIRE (1943)

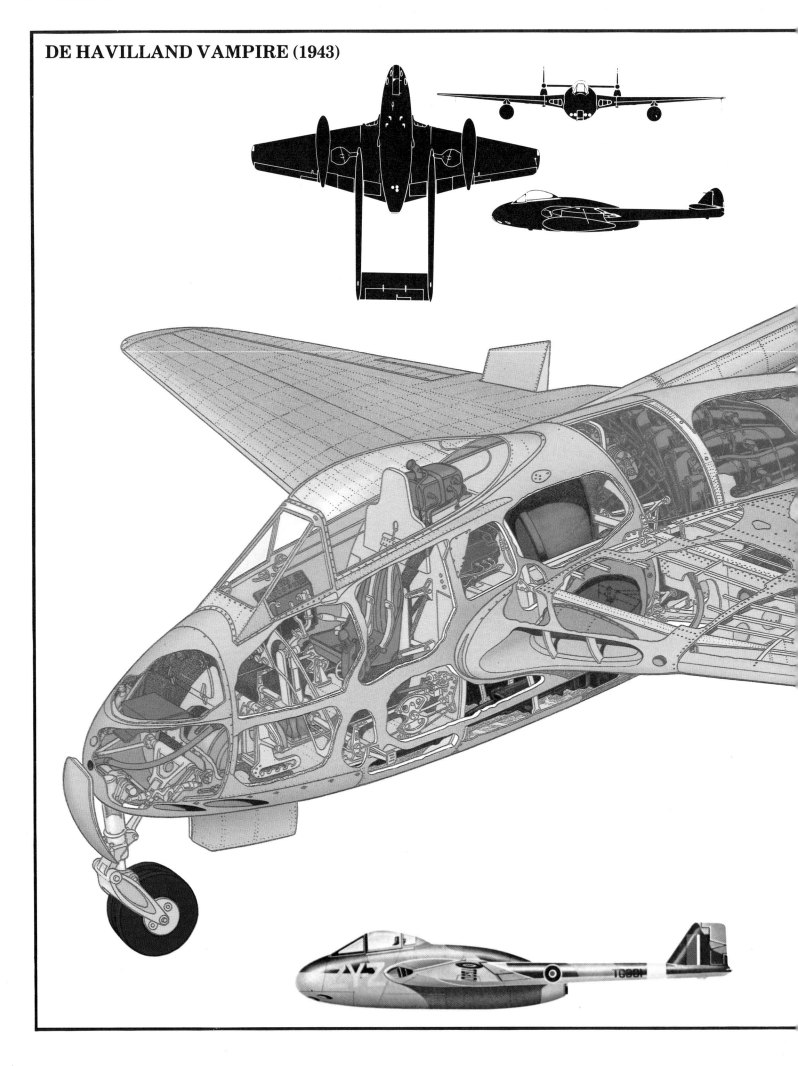

NAME: de Havilland Vampire (Britain)
TYPE: fighter, fighter-bomber
CREW: one
POWER PLANT: one 1,420kg (3,100lb) de Havilland Goblin centrifugal turbojet
DIMENSIONS: span 12.19m (40ft 0in); length 9.37m (30ft 9in); height 2.7m (8ft 10in)
WEIGHTS: empty 2,890kg (6,372lb); loaded 3,890kg (8,578lb)
PERFORMANCE: maximum speed 869 km/h (540 mph); service ceiling 12,500m (41,000ft); range 1,175km (730 miles)
ARMAMENT: four 20mm Hispano cannon with provision for two 1,000lb bombs under the wings

took this plane and the first of 70 Vampire F Mk Is arrived in 1946 — some of these were fitted with Swedish-built Goblin engines. When these aircraft were superseded, many were sold to the Dominican Republic as fighter bombers while others were sold to Austria for civil use.

Later types were routinely fitted with 100 gallon (455 litre) tanks, although this had an adverse effect on the aircraft's stability. The problem was overcome by an increase of the tailplane chord, reduction of the elevator, and the fitting of acorns to the fin and tail junctions. Manufacturing was also simplified by lowering the tailplane by 13in (33cm), and the vertical tail surfaces were changed to the standard de Havilland shape. Long-range wings also increased the total fuel capacity to 326 gallons (1,428 litres). Provision was also made for drop tanks that could hold 100 gallons (455 litres) or 200 gallons (910 litres). In this guise, the aircraft became the prototype Vampire F Mk III and was first flown in November 1946. It subsequently replaced the Vampire F Mk I in Germany and Britain.

Vampires in service with No. 54 Squadron, Odiham became the first jet fighters to fly the Atlantic under their own power. With two Mosquitoes they reached Goose Bay, Canada via Iceland and Greenland in July 1948, and took part in displays in Canada and the USA.

Vampire IV was the official designation given to the Vampire III airframe fitted with a Rolls-Royce Nene engine. None were built in the UK, and the model was developed in Australia as the F Mk 30. De Havilland manufactured 80 of them and they were powered by Australian built Rolls-Royce Nene 2 VH engines. The prototype was flown on 29 June 1948.

The Vampire F Mk I (TG444) began trials with a clipped wingspan of 38ft (11.58 metres). This aircraft preceded the introduction of the Vampire FB Mk 5 which was a ground-attack variant with a strengthened wing for the carriage of bombs or rockets.

A considerable amount of overseas interest in Vampires was aroused by an excellent demonstration at the Farnborough Air Show in 1948. France bought 30 of the FB Mk 51. Other countries that bought the Vampire in its various forms included Egypt, Finland, Iraq, Italy, Lebanon, Norway and Venezuela. The Indian and South African Air Forces also both bought a number of FB Mk 5s.

Following experience with the latter model, de Havilland built the FB Mk 9 which was a tropical variant. It had cockpit air conditioning as well as Godfrey refrigerating equipment in the main plane.

The last Vampire entered service with the RAF in December 1953. A total of nearly 1,600 had been built, including exports, except for those built by Hindustan Aircraft Ltd for the Indian Air Force.

The twin boom layout was adopted by De Havilland for most of its post-war jets, so as to place the tailplane (also known as the horizontal stabilizer) above the hot jet efflux. Large drop tanks on this Vampire helped nearly to double its range to 2,253km (1,400 miles).

KYUSHU J7W1 SHINDEN (1945)

Developed in the last year of World War II, the J7W flew only just before the Japanese surrender, on 3 August 1945. Thus, though one of the two prototypes still exists, very little was generally known about the type until enthusiasts carried out research 40 years later. It is not too much to claim that this strange machine was the pinnacle of piston-engined fighter design, if only because it was one of the last to be started.

For obvious reasons a fighter would rather have its propeller at the back than at the front. This was the usual arrangement of the very earliest armed aircraft in 1913–15. Those early pushers carried their tail on a network of booms and struts, but Capt Masaoki Tsuruno of the Imperial Japanese Navy had by 1943 come to the conclusion that there was much to be said for the canard (tail first) arrangement. In fact, with hindsight it is amazing that this excellent configuration (now likely to become almost standard for fighters) was ignored by all the great fighter designers. Apart from the Italian S.S.4 and American Curtiss XP-55 the J7W was the only canard fighter to fly in World War II. Admittedly they achieved little, but in the case of the Japanese Navy fighter this was because there was no time. It might have proved the most formidable piston-engined fighter of all.

Tsuruno first had the basic stability and control of the concept proved with low-speed gliders in 1943, and it was June 1944 before engineering design of the Shinden (Magnificent Lightning) went ahead. In some respects it resembled the Northrop XP-56, though that American fighter was not a canard but truly 'tailless'. Both were extremely short close--coupled machines which in effect were the smallest airframes that could be wrapped round the most powerful engine available. In each case the engine was an 18-cylinder aircooled radial, and the MK9D engine of the J7W drove a unique six-blade propeller, the only single-unit six-blader to fly and a harbinger of today's multi-blade propfans.

One reason behind Tsuruno's configuration was its suitability for later conversion to jet propulsion. The J7W itself appeared to have jet inlets, though these deep but narrow ducts admitted the cooling air, with separate auxiliary ducts further outboard which curved sharply in to feed air to the supercharger and thence the cylinders. Crude panic solutions were conspicuously absent. The engine installation was a masterpiece of advanced yet compact engineering. A separate slit on the inner wall of the main inlet diverted sluggish boundary-layer air, and though the engine tended to overheat on the ground, cooling in the air was excellent. The only engine problem met in the three test flights, on 3, 6 and 9 August was vibration of the long drive shaft.

Control surfaces, all stressed-skin, comprised tabbed ailerons, forward tabbed elevators and twin rudders, the latter being in the hard-left position during takeoff to counter the massive torque pull to the right, the right main gear being pressed hard into the runway. The small tailwheels were retractable. Other movable surfaces comprised canard slats and area-increasing flaps on the main wing. Landing behaviour was excellent, though the touchdown at 117mph (188km/h) was considered fast. With four devastating 30mm armament, this potentially formidable fighter was intended for operation from land bases.

This strange aircraft was one of the few canard fighters of World War Two.

KYUSHU J7W1 SHINDEN (1945)

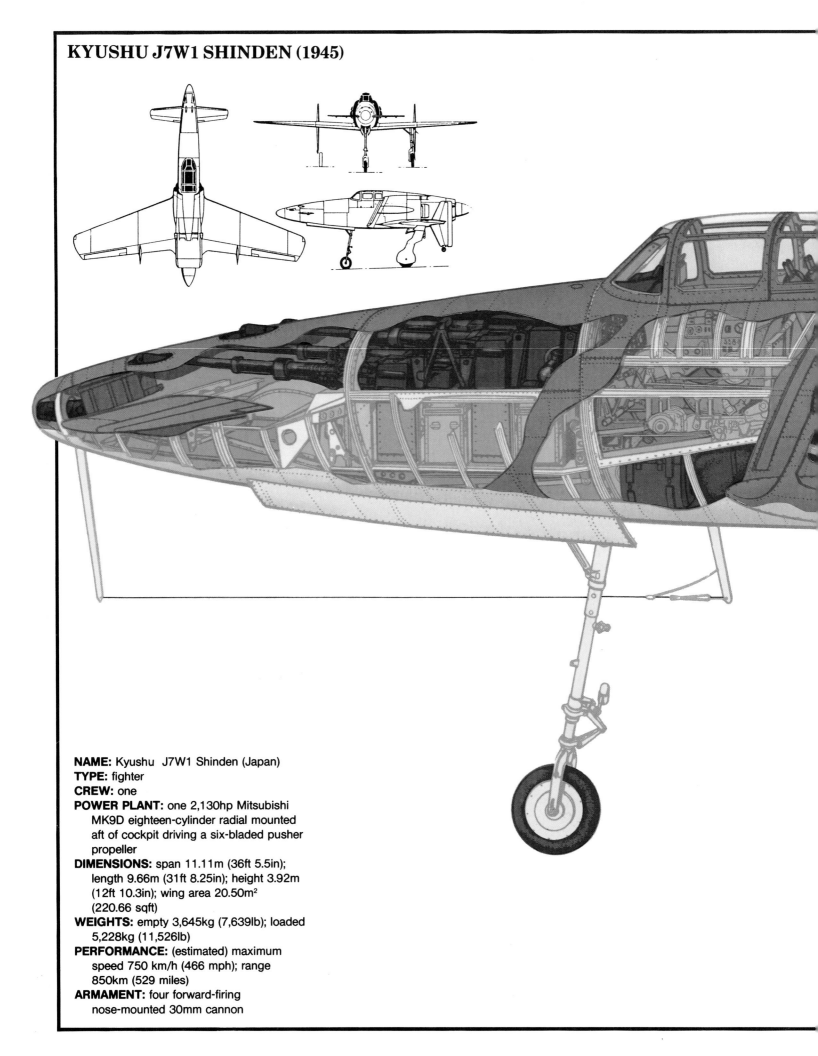

NAME: Kyushu J7W1 Shinden (Japan)
TYPE: fighter
CREW: one
POWER PLANT: one 2,130hp Mitsubishi
  MK9D eighteen-cylinder radial mounted
  aft of cockpit driving a six-bladed pusher
  propeller
DIMENSIONS: span 11.11m (36ft 5.5in);
  length 9.66m (31ft 8.25in); height 3.92m
  (12ft 10.3in); wing area 20.50m²
  (220.66 sqft)
WEIGHTS: empty 3,645kg (7,639lb); loaded
  5,228kg (11,526lb)
PERFORMANCE: (estimated) maximum
  speed 750 km/h (466 mph); range
  850km (529 miles)
ARMAMENT: four forward-firing
  nose-mounted 30mm cannon

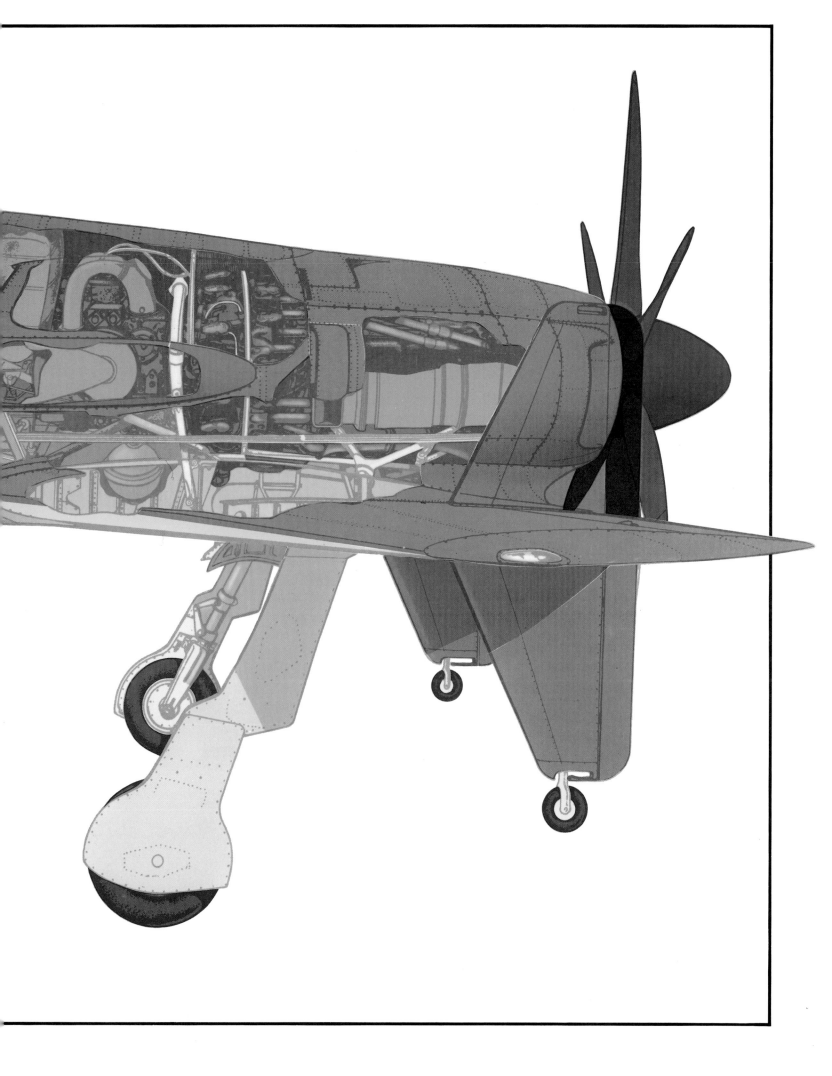

WESTLAND WYVERN (1946)

In 1926 Dr A. A. Griffith at Farnborough published a new theory of turbine design. In 1929 he schemed an axial-compressor turboprop, but the compressor was not built until 1936. Towards the end of the war this led to the Armstrong Siddeley ASP engine, later named Python, which finally went into just one type of aircraft, the Wyvern. This had a brief career in the Fleet Air Arm (1953-57). It was a typically British story in which true pioneering led to no significant result.

The Wyvern was originally designed as a long-range naval fighter to Specification N.11/44, using the Rolls-Royce Eagle 3,500hp piston engine. It was too be capable of carrying a torpedo, bombs or rockets, and was much larger than most single-seaters, the empty weight being roughly the same as that of a DC-3. However, during development it encountered many problems, some due to the eight-blade contra-rotating propellers, and these did not stop when the Eagle was replaced by the massive Python turboprop. Though an impressive machine with many fine qualities the Wyvern managed to kill four experienced test pilots, and had its fair share of trouble in service.

Technically the Wyvern was excellent, with a smooth skin both flush-riveted and spot-welded covering a mass of advanced technology. The wide centre section was built integral with the giant humpbacked fuselage, and it carried very powerful Youngman area-increasing flaps and perforated airbrakes. The hydraulically folding outer wings also had airbrakes, pivoted near their mid-point at the trailing edge, with small fences between them and the spring-tab ailerons. Despite the width of the centre section, the massive landing gear had to be so long that the parallel-linkage legs were arranged to shorten

during retraction, giving clearance for the propeller. The tailwheel also retracted, into a bay with twin doors.

After a vast amount of development Armstrong Siddeley made the Python run at constant speed, so that rapid thrust control could be achieved by varying the propeller pitch only. It was a revere-flow engine, the air entering near the back, travelling forwards through the 14-stage compressor and back through the 11 combustion chambers. Amazingly, the Python had the same two-stage turbine as its predecesor ASX turobjet! Downstream the jetpipe bifurcated to pass under the cockpit to jet nozzles on each side above the wing root. One of the last modifications before the Wyvern S.4 went into production in 1951 was to cut back the front of the annular air inlet surrounding the engine, which had been close behind the propeller. This was done to facilitate reloading engine-starter cartridges. Last of the visible modifications was to add auxiliary fins on the dihedral tailplane.

The pilot was perched 12ft (3·7m) up on a Martin-Baker seat where he had an excellent view. The high cockpit left room for the vast amount of fuel, but most of the space was taken up by the jetpipes. Westland still managed to squeeze in 51 Imp gallons (2,323 litres), but the Python used it up so fast at low level that even with two drop tanks endurance was only 3 hours. Extra wingtip tanks were provided for in a field modification, but not used. With four cannon and 16 rockets or three 1,000-lb (454kg) bombs the Wyvern was a useful attack aircraft, and it saw action with 830 Sqn during the ill-starred Suez campaign in 1956. Perhaps surprisingly, it was well-liked by its pilots in the Royal Navy squadrons.

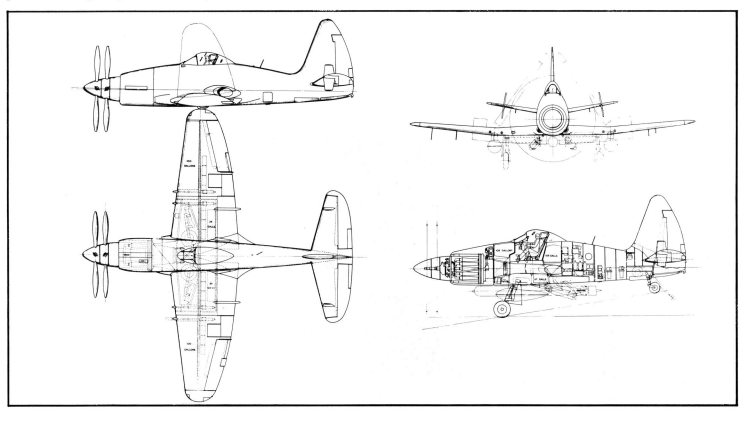

Above:
A Royal Navy Fleet
Air Arm Westland
Wyvern.

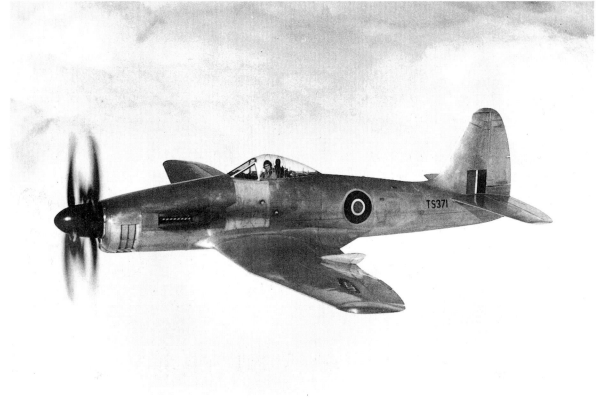

Right:
This Wyvern is one
of the early models
to enter service and
is fitted with the
piston engine that
was later replaced.

WESTLAND WYVERN (1946)

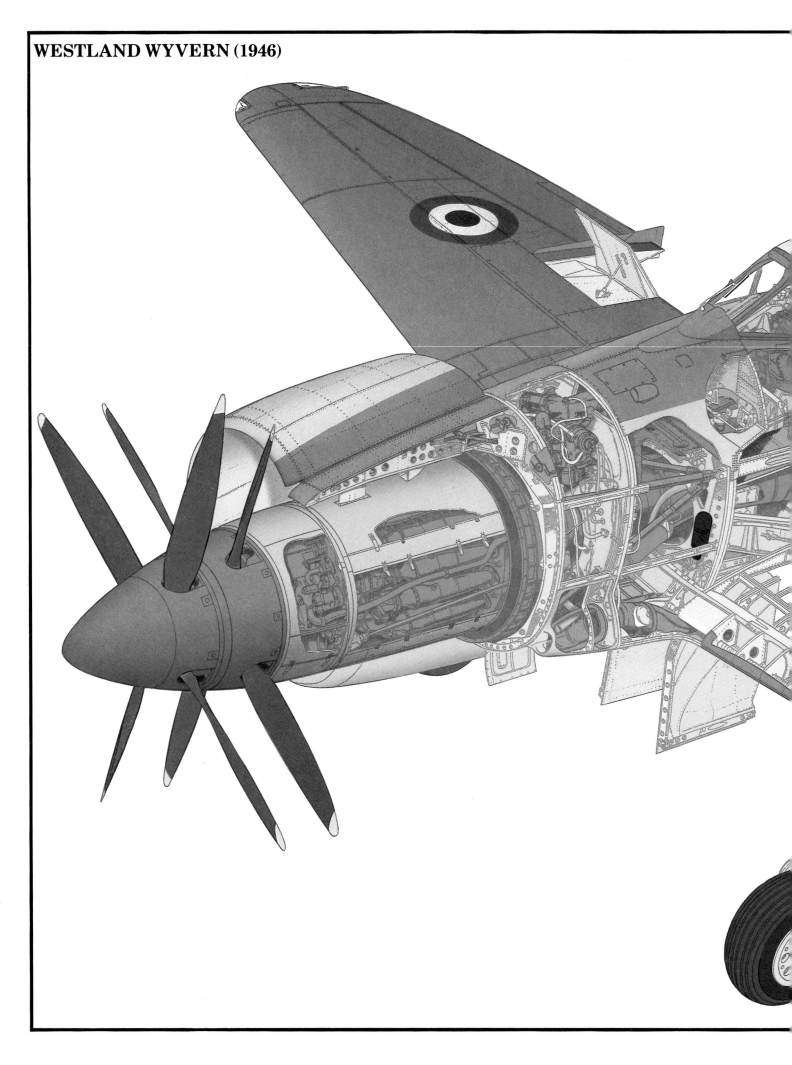

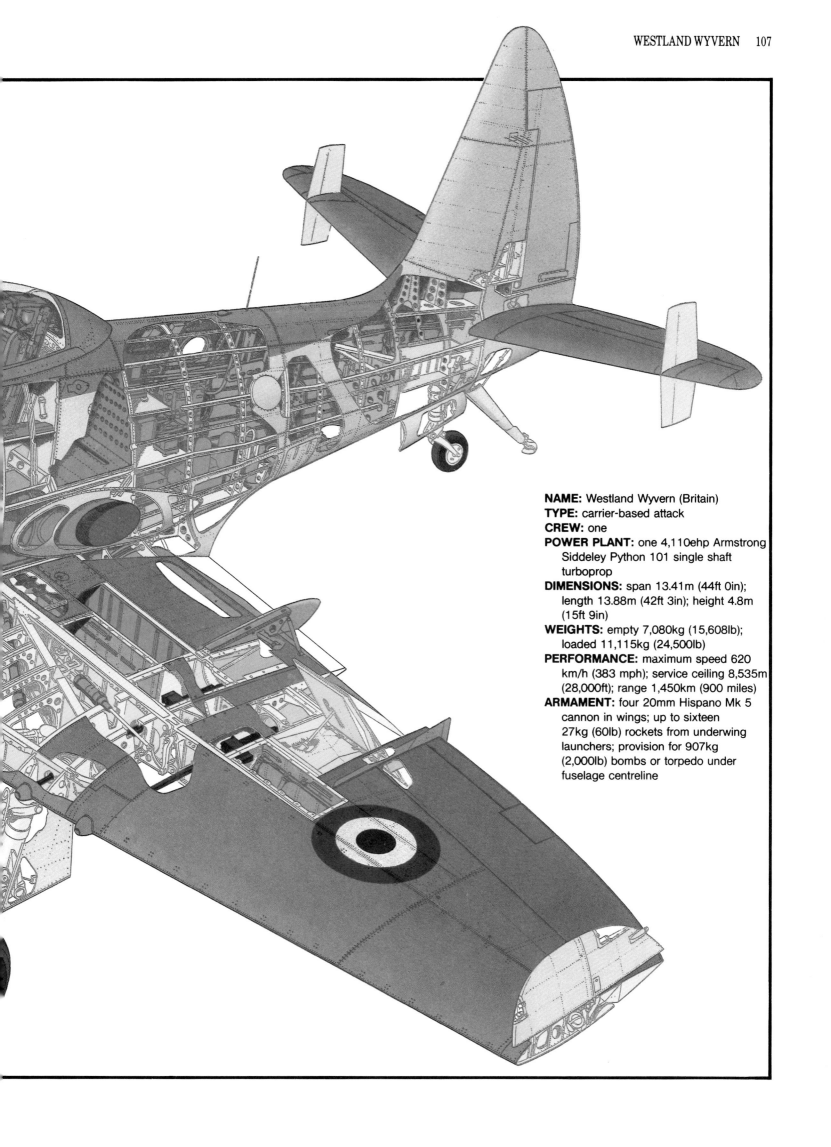

NAME: Westland Wyvern (Britain)
TYPE: carrier-based attack
CREW: one
POWER PLANT: one 4,110ehp Armstrong
Siddeley Python 101 single shaft
turboprop
DIMENSIONS: span 13.41m (44ft 0in);
length 13.88m (42ft 3in); height 4.8m
(15ft 9in)
WEIGHTS: empty 7,080kg (15,608lb);
loaded 11,115kg (24,500lb)
PERFORMANCE: maximum speed 620
km/h (383 mph); service ceiling 8,535m
(28,000ft); range 1,450km (900 miles)
ARMAMENT: four 20mm Hispano Mk 5
cannon in wings; up to sixteen
27kg (60lb) rockets from underwing
launchers; provision for 907kg
(2,000lb) bombs or torpedo under
fuselage centreline

MIG-15 MIDGET (1947)

The MiG-15 must be one of the most famous aircraft of all time. Its production marked the first occasion when a Soviet aircraft bettered any of its Western counterparts in speed of design and development. It also made a big impact when it was encountered in combat in Korea in November 1950.

The initial brief was for a high-altitude day interceptor capable of operating from rough airstrips. The plane was to be able to fly at Mach 0.9, have good manoeuvrability at high altitude, and have a flight endurance of over one hour. It was designed with a mid-mounted swept wing on the shortest circular section fuselage and with a large T-tail. The choice of engine lay between two competing designs of 4,400lb (2,014kg) thrust.

Design was well underway by September 1946 when, under the terms of a trade agreement, the UK agreed to export the Rolls-Royce Nene engine to the USSR. Ten engines were shipped immediately with a further 15 following shortly afterwards. The prototype MiG-15, designated the I-310, was rumoured to have flown on 2 July 1947 and crashed on its inaugural

A Czechoslovakian built MiG-15. Many of these aircraft were later converted to the MiG-15UTI standard as two-seat trainers.

flight. A second prototype was flown on 30 December 1947. It differed from the original version by having a shorter rear fuselage and a greater fin sweep.

The prototype was successful and the first pre-production model was delivered for testing in May 1948. It was fitted with an RD-45 engine, which was a modified version of the Nene engine, and full armament as well as a Soviet ejector seat, RSI-6M radio and a British-derived gyro gunsight.

Although the test pilots gave a good overall report on the MiG 15, there were many shortcomings including a tendency to spin and stall in a tight turn, and poor behaviour at any high angle of attack (even at low speed!). Handling also became increasingly difficult as the speed increased above Mach 0.88. However, in October 1948 clearance was given to manufacture MiG-15s. These models were powered by an improved RD-45F powerplant.

A two-seat trainer (the MiG-15UTI) was designed from August 1948 with a reduced fuel capacity, rear over-wing cockpit with a sliding canopy, and front student cockpit with a right hinged canopy. It was available from March 1949, and was still in service long after the

The MiG-15LL ('Letayuschye Laboratorii' — the flying lab) came next. It had a reduced sweep upper fin and an added side fin, which gave a much greater side area. It also had a fully powered rudder, an increased-chord horizontal tail and many other flight control alterations.

There followed the MiG-15SD which had an improved VK-1 engine. It flew for the first time in September 1949; the airframe was carefully looked at, and the structural weight reduced to 199lb (90kg).

The MiG 15PB ('Podvesnyi Bakami' — underwing tanks) variant was built with the addition of slipper tanks which had a capacity of 132 gallons (600 litres) in each. This was the version that was fitted with the pre-production Izumrud radar.

In 1949 and 1950 the MiG-15 and its more powerful variant, the MiG-15bis, were fitted with a great deal of additional equipment. This included new avionics, beacon receivers and radio altimeters.

The MiG-15SP-1 prototype was a single-seat all-weather interceptor with a large nose radar. It was armed with two cannon. A small number of less well known SP-5 (dual) and MiG-15bisP

(single seat) Izumrud-equipped interceptors were built. They too were armed with cannons. The MiG-15bisS was an escort variant which had 132 gallon (500 litre) slipper fuel tanks.

Photoreconnaissance was the task of the MiG-15bisR which had one or usually two vertical cameras located under the cockpit floor.

The MiG-15bisSB ('Istrebitel Shturmovik', also known as ISh) was a dedicated ground attacker and was equipped with inner axial beams which carried tandem bombs or rocket pods.

A single MiG-15U, also known as the SU, was built. it had lateral engine inlets and a pair of cannon mounted on transverse pivots in a new nose-firing round vertical arc for ground attack.

Production of the MiG-15 and its variants was maintained from at least two factories, and over half the total of airframes were manufactured in Kuibyshyev. Overseas licences to build the aircraft were awarded to Czechoslovakia (the S102 and S103bis), Poland (the LIM-1 and LIM-2) and Hungary (as the Jaguar). At least 5,000 airframes were eventually manufactured as well as several thousand MiG-15UTI trainers built under licence as CS-102 and LIM-3.

Two illustrations of the MiG-15. Below: a single-seat fighter of the Bulgarian Air Force. Bottom: a two-seat advanced trainer of the Indonesian Air Force. Many of these dual-seaters are still in service all over the world.

MiG 15 (1947)

NAME: Mikoyan MiG-15 Midget
(Soviet Union)
TYPE: fighter
CREW: one
POWER PLANT: one 2,270kg (5,505lb)
thrust RD-45 single-shaft centrifugal
turbojet
DIMENSIONS: span 10.08m (33ft 0.75in);
length 11.05m (36ft 3.25in); height 3.4m
(11ft 1.75in)
WEIGHTS: empty 4,000kg (8,820lb); loaded
5,700kg (12,566lb)
PERFORMANCE: maximum speed 1,075
km/h (668 mph); service ceiling 15,545m
(51,000ft); range 1,424km (885 miles)
ARMAMENT: one 37mm N cannon under
right side of nose and one 23mm
NS cannon under left side plus two
underwing hardpoints for up to 500kg
(1,102lb) of ordnance or drop tanks

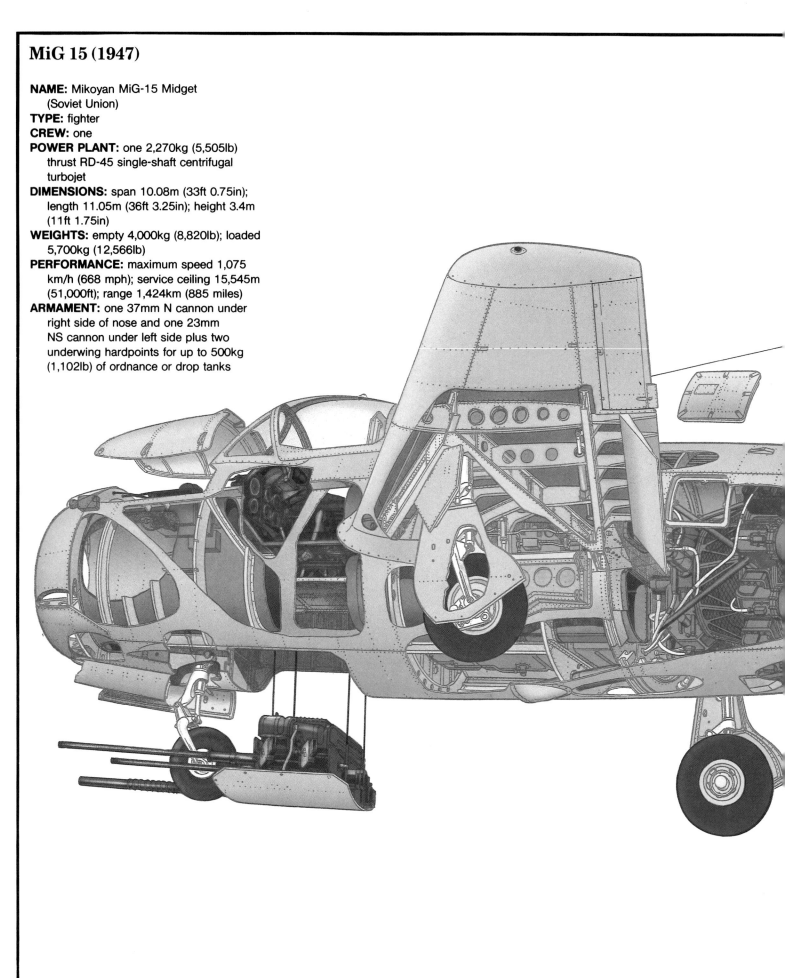

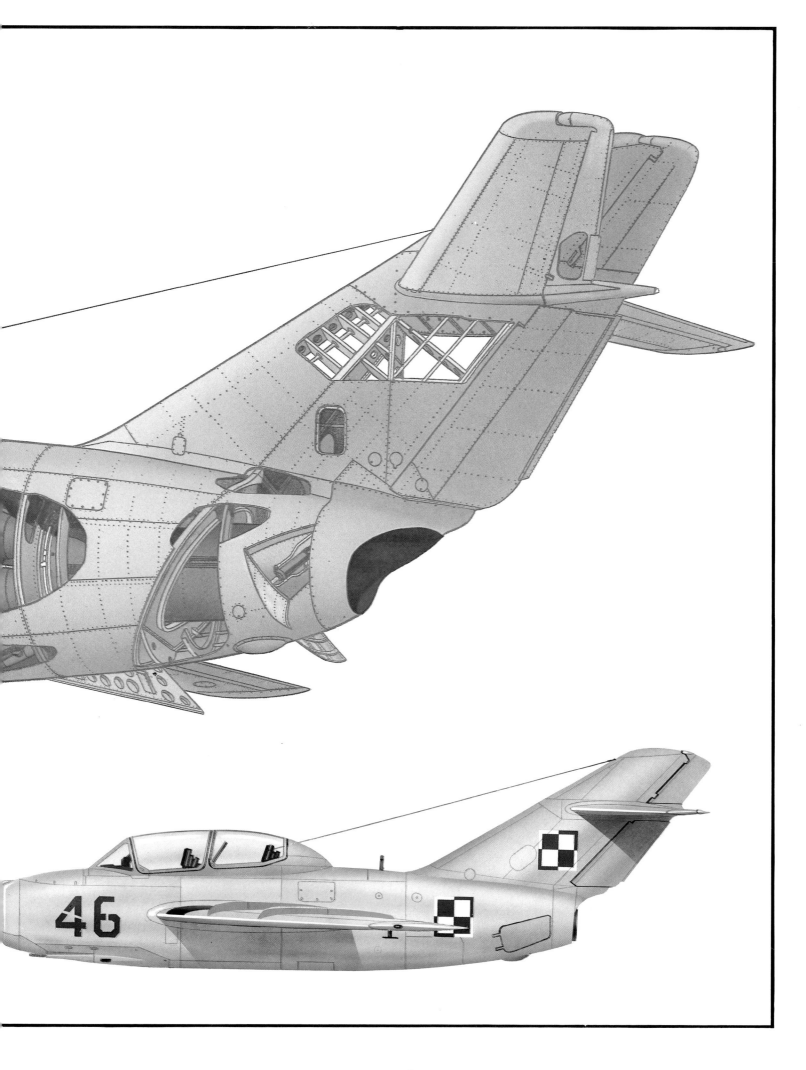

NORTH AMERICAN F-86 SABRE (1947)

In an exact parallel to the B-47 bomber (next entry) this fighter was already in advanced design at the end of World War II when captured German research showed the importance of sweepback in postponing the severe rise in drag caused by air compressibility as the speed of sound is neared. Like Boeing, North American Aviation risked losing everything by delaying the project for a year while it was redesigned with wings and tail swept at 35°. From the first takeoff, on 1 October 1947 (with a very new axial J35 of only 3,750lb/1,701kg thrust), it was clear the Sabre was an absolute winner. It was a joy to fly, and not least of its attributes was that though the cockpit had perhaps twice as many switches as pilots had ever seen before, every switch worked.

It is not too much to claim that the Sabre saved at least the 'face' of the Allies in the Korean war, if not the war itself. Without it there would have been no fighter able to take on the MiG-15, supplied in large numbers to North Korea. As it was, the Sabre established clear ascendancy over its foe, though this was almost entirely because of pilot superiority. Subsequent Sabres, built in much larger numbers than any other non-Soviet jet aircraft (including carrier-based Fury versions, 9,796), served all over the world in many variants, the most numerous (2,504) being the extremely complex F-86D all-weather interceptor with an afterburning engine, nose radar and rockets instead of guns.

All versions broke completely new ground in having wings not only swept but of 'laminar' section, with maximum thickness halfway back from the leading edge, and with thickness of 1·1 per cent at the root, thinning to 10 at the tip. The

skins were machined plate, in double layers forming upper and lower sandwich panels which, when joined to the spars, formed very large but shallow integral tanks. Speed brakes could not be added to the wings, so they were put on the rear fuselage (by chance, the MiG-15 adopted the same answer), and the ailerons and elevators were hydraulically boosted to make quite sure no compressibility problem or combat situation would find the pilot lacking in muscle power. By 1950 the F-86E introduced the 'all-flying tail' in which for the first time the tailplane (horizontal stabilizer) became a primary control surface, the hinged elevators being geared to increase camber and tailplane power.

The slim axial engine was fed by a nose inlet leading to a duct that passed under the cockpit and then rose sharply to meet the engine. As in many early American jets the entire tail could be unhitched and pulled away on a dolly for all-round access to the engine, or to change engines. Sabres were flown with dry and afterburning J47s, with the same maker's J73, the Rolls-Royce Avon, Canadian Orenda and Wright J65 (Sapphire). Many experienced fighter 'jocks' consider the Orenda-engined Canadair Sabre 6 the greatest dogfight jet of all time – certainly in the pre-F-16 era.

A weak point in the otherwise futuristic F-86 was the armament of six 'fifty calibre' guns of basically 1917 design, though a new and valued feature was a radar-ranging gunsight. Other versions had four 20mm or two 30mm cannon, and the F-86D had a rapid-fire tray of 24 computer-aimed air-to-air rockets. All versions had a pressurized cockpit with ejection seat, steerable nosewheel, and neat, unbreakable main gears whose wheels retracted.

Below:
An illustration of the F-86 Sabre in the markings of the Greek Air Force.

Above:
F-86 Sabres, North American redesigned the Sabre to incorporate a 35 degree swept wing and tail, after German research data was captured at the end of the war.

NAME: North American F-86 Sabre (USA)
TYPE: fighter
CREW: one
POWER PLANT: one 2,200kg (4,850lb) thrust General Electric J47-1 single-shaft axial turbojet
DIMENSIONS: span 11.31m (37ft 1.5in); length 11.43m (37ft 6in); height 4.47m (14ft 8.75in)
WEIGHTS: empty 4,820kg (10,606lb); loaded 7,374kg (16,223lb)
PERFORMANCE: maximum speed 1,085 km/h (675 mph); service ceiling 15,240m (50,000ft); range 1,368km (850 miles)
ARMAMENT: six 0.5in Colt-Browning M-3 Machine-guns plus underwing hardpoints for 454kg (1,000lb) of ordnance

BOEING B-47 STRATOJET (1947)

No aircraft in history has ever looked so truly futuristic as the prototype XB-47 (Boeing Model 450) did on its first flight on 17 December 1947 coinciding with the 40th anniversary of the Wrights' first flight. Nothing remotely like it had been seen before, and like NAA with the F-86 (preceding entry in this book) Boeing willingly delayed the project about a year and took a colossal technical risk in order to be technically more advanced. As a result, while the competition faded, the B-47 was built in quantities which, for a gigantic 100-ton bomber developed after World War II, might seem astronomic. The total was 2,289.

Ironically, Britain, which had better jet engines, omitted to order any jet bombers until four years after the USAAF's start in 1943. By 1945 the idea of a 'jet B-29' had given way to the Model 432 with a battery of turbojets in the top of the fuselage behind the cockpit. Then suddenly Boeing engineers in Germany learned about swept wings. There were no half-measures: the Model 450 was planned with 35° swept wings and tail, the wing being amazingly thin and, despite having skins four times thicker than anything previously built, extremely flexible. Not least of the innovations was to hang the six axial-compressor engines in 'pods', two twins and two singles. These helped spread weight along the wing and, by adding mass well outboard, damped possible flutter.

Almost perfectly streamlined, the huge fuselage housed the crew, bombs and more fuel than had ever been put in any aircraft before. By April 1946 it had been decided the landing gear had to be a tandem twin-wheel 'bicycle' arrangement, with small outrigger wheels under the

Opposite:
One of Strategic
Air Command's
B-47 Stratojets
banks steeply.

Below;
Ground shot of a B-47 showing main
gear and outriggers.

inner pods. Structurally and aerodynamically the B-47 was the greatest challenge ever faced. One of the few factors making it easier was that the crew comprised only three, in a pressurized nose section. All were in ejection seats, the navigator in the nose ejecting downwards and the pilot and copilot under a giant fighter-type canopy in tandem seats fired upwards. Navigation/bombing radar was in a blister under the nose.

Production B-47s dispensed with nose glazing and relied entirely on electronics for navigation and bomb-aiming, and also for remote aiming of the tail defence guns, which at first were 0·5in (12·7mm) but were later twin 20mm. Not only did the B-47 demonstrate much less than the predicted drag but it had amazing capacity for growth. Designed for a gross weight of 125,000lb (56,700kg) the B-47A went to 160,000lb (72,570kg), the B-47B to 200,000lb (90,720kg) – with two monster drop tanks under the wings – and the major production model, the B-47E, to 230,000lb (104,328kg)! Even with powerful Fowler flaps the takeoff and landing needed an unprecedented length of good runway. A mighty drag chute was another feature not seen before. A battery of rockets could be added behind the rear landing gear to boost takeoff, the main engines also being boosted by water injection.

Despite the wing's tremendous strength it was anhedral when at rest but curved upwards in flight, the wings and pods thereafter flexing awesomely in any kind of rough air. At high altitudes and at full load it was possible to get into what the media – and the pilots – called 'coffin corner' where the aircraft had to fly straight and level with neither increase nor decrease in speed until a few dozen tons of fuel had been burned off.

NAME: Boeing B-47 Stratojet (USA)

TYPE: medium bomber

CREW: three

POWER PLANT: six 2,707kg (5,970lb) thrust 3,266kg (7,200lb) thrust with water injection for take-off) General Electric J47-25A single-shaft turbojets

DIMENSIONS: span 35.36m (116ft 0in); length 33.5m (109ft 10in); height 8.52m (27ft 11in)

WEIGHTS: empty 36,281kg (78,200lb); loaded 99,790kg (220,000lb)

PERFORMANCE: maximum speed 980 km/h (606 mph); service ceiling 9,754m (32,000ft); range 5,794km (3,600 miles)

ARMAMENT: two 20mm cannon mounted in remotely-controlled tail turret; up to 9,979kg (22,000lb) bombs internally

SIKORSKY WESTLAND S-55 WHIRLWIND

In May 1949 the technical department of Sikorsky was given the testing task of creating a new helicopter in a maximum of seven months. It was necessary for the machine to be able to carry 10 passengers as well as a crew of two.

The first of five YH-19 prototypes, ordered by the American Air Force, made its debut flight on 7 November. The novelty of the design lay in the location of the power unit in the nose of the fuselage. It was so mounted that the drive shaft sloped up to the base of the rotor pylon, clear of the main cabin situated below the main lifting rotor. At first, another characteristic of the helicopter was the horizontal stabilizer attached to the starboard side of the tail. This, however, was subsequently replaced in production by two anhedral tail surfaces.

In November 1950, Westland announced that it had obtained the manufacturing rights for the S-55, and production soon began at the company's base at Yeovil, Somerset. The helicopter was capable of transporting up to 10 fully-equipped troops (equal to a standard platoon), up to eight stretcher cases or a load of special military equipment, and the S-55 figured prominently in Western re-armament. Lack of a British power source at first compelled Westland to fit the 600 horsepower Pratt and Whitney Wasp engine. It was in November 1952 that the first British-built Whirlwind was delivered to No. 705 Squadron at Gosport.

A Westland-built example of the Sikorsky S-55, which was named the Whirlwind by this Yeovil-based company; this particular helicopter is a company demonstrator.

Meanwhile in the United States, the production line continued with the H-19B. This had an upgraded 700 horsepower Wright R-1300-3 engine and a larger-diameter main rotor. A total of 270 were constructed for the United States Air Force when the SH-19B variant is included in the figures. (This variant was a transport aircraft.) In 1952, the United States Army ordered 72 H-19Cs, which were soon nicknamed 'Chicka-saws' and redesignated the UH-19C and UH-19D in 1962.

Variants of the S-55 were acquired by the United States Navy, and a total of 119 were delivered from late 1950 to 1958. This figure includes 10 H04S-1s (the H-19A equivalent) and 61 H04S-2s. Approximately 31 of these were built for the Coast Guard. The United States Marines also purchased 99 of the HRS-2 variant and 84 of the HRS-3 which were used as troop transports.

Whirlwinds saw service with American forces quite late in the Korean War, but the Marines were able to utilize their HRS-1s for tests on rapid assault operations, which were anticipations of full-scale landing operations. The various techniques and roles pioneered with the S-55 in Korea were later to form the basis of new military doctrine. These roles included landing operations behind enemy lines, troop support, recovery of damaged vehicles and their capacity for counter-attack and engagement. There was another task of the helicopter, and that was casualty evacuation or the rescue of pilots who had come down behind enemy lines.

A Royal Navy
Westland Whirlwind
from HMS *Protector*,
the Navy's Ice-Patrol
ship, hovers over
Elephant Island in
the South Shetlands
in the Antarctic
Ocean. The Seal and
Chinstrap Penguin
appear completely
indifferent to this
example of modern
technology.

In the UK, the RAF ordered the S-55 for transport and rescue missions. The Whirlwind HAR Mk 2 joined Transport and Coastal Command in 1955. The Mk 3 was powered by Wright R-1300 engines, and entered production with the Royal Navy in 1953. It operated from both ship and shore bases for many years.

The RAF HAR Mk 4 variant was adapted for the tropics and powered by a new version of the Pratt and Whitney R-1340. It was used in the insurgency in Malaysia. A Leonidas Major engine had been fitted to the Whirlwinds by 1955. It was de-rated to 750 horsepower although it had been delivered with 882 horsepower.

In March 1952, the S-55 obtained its American approval for civil use. The model with R-1340 engines became the S-55A while the variant with the Wright powerplant became the S-55B. It was also in 1952 that the Whirlwind became the first rotary wing transport to be used in commercial links in Europe. Sabena, the Belgian national airline, flew them from the

principal towns in Belgium to Bonn, Cologne, Lille and Rotterdam.

In 1956 Westland began to consider adapting a turbine engine for the Whirlwind. The helicopter was fitted with a General Electric T.58 and then by the more powerful de Havilland Gnome turbine. This turbine-powered variant made its first flight in February 1959. Another new feature was its new nose which offered vastly improved visibility from the cockpit when compared to its piston-engined predecessors. In April 1960, the RAF began taking the Whirlwind Mk 10.

Westland exported over 100 of this variant to the following countries: Austria, Brazil, Canada, Cuba, France, Ghana, Iran, Jordan, Saudi Arabia, Spain and Yugoslavia. Meanwhile, in 10 years, Sikorsky built well over 1,000 S-55s in various military guises for no less than 30 operators all over the world. More than 500 others were also built under licence (the majority by Westland).

SIKORSKY-WESTLAND WHIRLWIND (1956)

NAME: Sikorsky H-19/Westland Whirlwind
(USA/Britain)
TYPE: utility helicopter
POWER PLANT: (H-19B) one 700hp Wright
R-1300-3 air-cooled radial
DIMENSIONS: rotor diameter 16.15m
(53ft 0in); fuselage length 12.88m
(42ft 3in);
height 4.06m (13ft 4in)
WEIGHTS: empty 2,381kg (5,250lb); loaded
3,583kg (7,900lb)
PERFORMANCE: maximum speed 180 km/
h (112 mph); range 579km (360 miles)
ARMAMENT: dependent on usage,
sometimes fitted with
machine-guns and rockets

Diagrams of a Whirlwind HAR 10

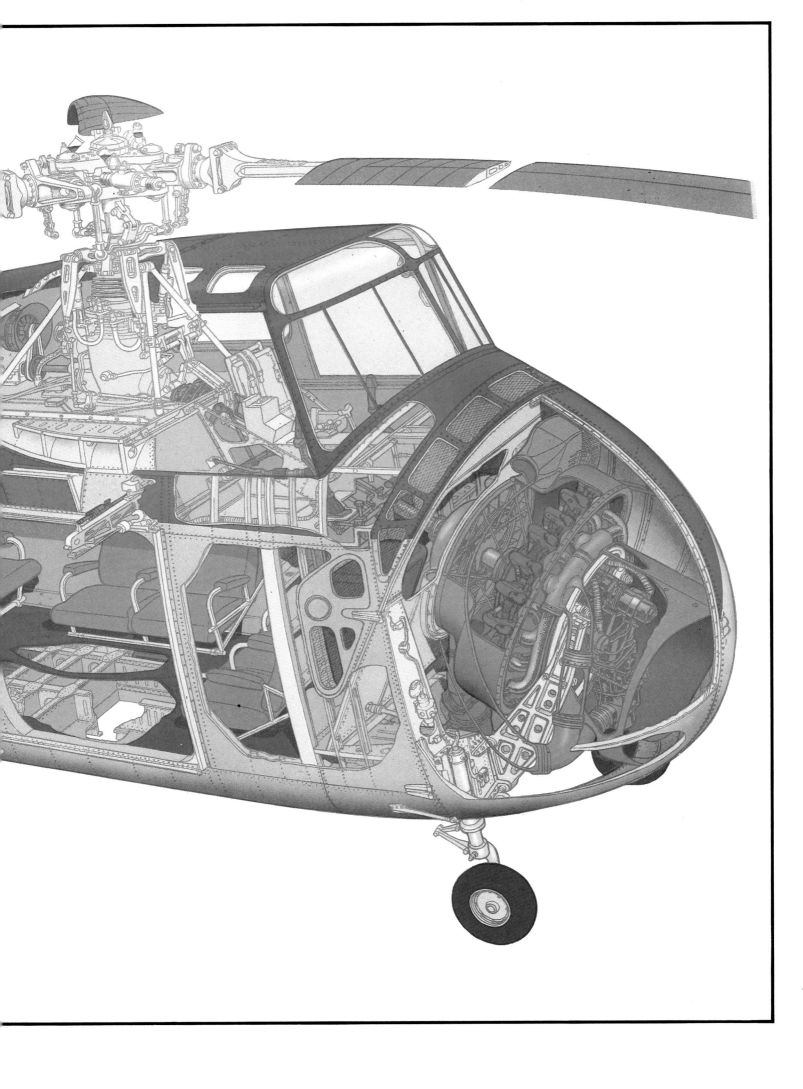

SNCASO TRIDENT (1953)

After World War II fighter designers did not know what sort of aircraft to build. The turbojet and rocket had opened up undreamed-of vistas of speed which called for exciting new shapes. They also burned fuel very quickly, making long-range escort fighters almost impossible. Some air forces looked at the opposite end of the endurance spectrum with what were variously called light fighters or target-defence interceptors. In 1944 the Germans had even used a rocket interceptor which roared off a launching ramp almost vertically. Several Allied air staffs thought this a marvellous idea, and several companies, notably Fairey in Britain, did research on vertically launched interceptors.

The French wasted little time on such projects, but were intensely interested in target-defence interceptors that could takeoff and land normally. The most remarkable of several designs was the Trident, built by SNCASO (later Ouest-Aviation, the 'west' nationalized group). In collaboration with the new rocket group SEPR work went ahead in 1948 on the S.O.9000 Trident as an interceptor, though this was later recast as a research aircraft to provide a basis of knowledge in an unknown field. The interceptor became the 'second generation' S.O.9050. Government contracts were signed for two 9000s in 1951, followed by ten S.O.9050 Trident IIs in 1954.

Few aircraft have looked more like a 'manned missile'. All Tridents had a relatively enormous, yet almost perfectly streamlined, fuselage in which were housed the pressurized cockpit, large circular tanks for rocket propellants, all three units of the landing gear and, at the tail, the SEPR rocket engine. The stubby rectangular

Far right:
The very streamlined SNCASO Trident II Target defence interceptor.

Below:
In January 1958, this Trident broke the world altitude record for aircraft taking off from the ground by attaining a height of 22,000 metres (73,000ft.).

wings carried small turbojets on their tips for use throughout each mission, the thirsty rocket being used only on takeoff and for supersonic bursts of speed. The design was bold and innovative from nose to tail.

Structurally the Trident was simple, with the fuselage built like a rocket with circular frames and heavy-gauge skin taking all the loads. The wing was said to have 'no spars', but in fact the front and rear of the main structural box did comprise upper and lower L-sections joined together to form spars. Around these were attched the upper and lower skins each comprising two sheets of light alloy forming a sandwich with a low-density balsawood core. Hardly any ribs were needed, and the skins took almost all the loads. Not least of the innovations was the tail, made up of three one-piece 'slabs' each driven by an irreversible hydraulic power unit. Conventional ailerons were fitted, outboard of the split flaps, but flight testing showed that differential use of the tailplanes gave excellent roll control and the ailerons were locked. The later Trident II had no ailerons.

SEPR experimented with various propellants before deciding on Furaline (mainly aniline) and RFNA (red fuming nitric acid). Special surface treatments were devised to inhibit attack by the concentrated acid, which was a highly dangerous liquid. Electrically controlled valves passed the two liquids to the turbopump group in the rear fuselage, which was driven by the same mixture, which is hypergolic (self-igniting on contact). A small water supply was carried to cool the pump turbine. The SEPR.481 engine had three thrust chambers, each rated at 3,307lb (1,500kg) thrust at sea level, and about 4,000lb (1,814kg) in the stratosphere. The three barrels could be fired separately or all together.

TRIDENT (1953)

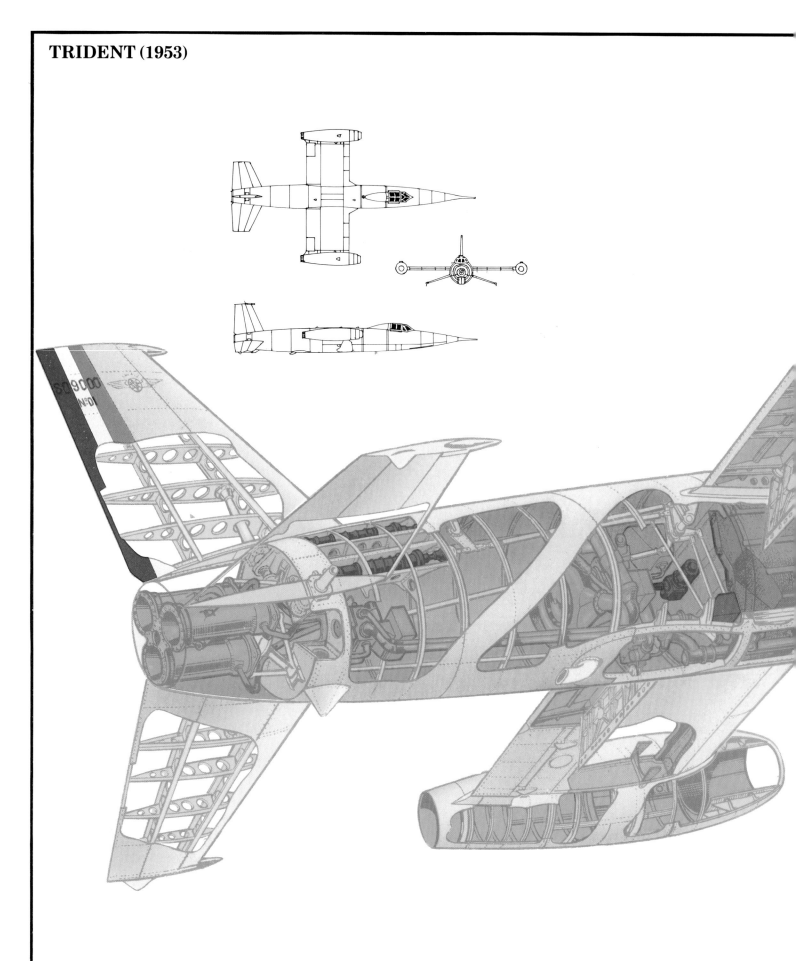

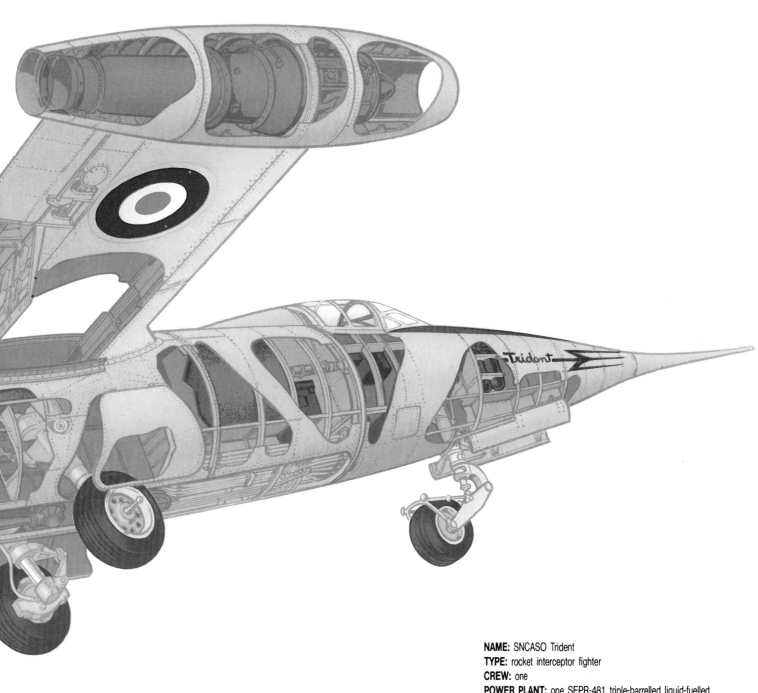

NAME: SNCASO Trident
TYPE: rocket interceptor fighter
CREW: one
POWER PLANT: one SEPR-481 triple-barrelled liquid-fuelled
    rocket motor mounted in the tail plus two 800kg
    (1,760lb) Dassault M.D.30 turbojets on wingtips
DIMENSIONS: span 6.89 (22ft 7½in); length 12.97m
    (42ft 7in); height 3.2m (10ft 6in);
    wing area 14.5m² (156.077sq ft)
WEIGHTS: empty 2,630kg (5,788lb); loaded 5,161kg
    (11,355lb)
PERFORMANCE: maximum speed Mach 2.0+, 2,124km/h
    (1,320mph) - 12,102m—21,336m (40,000ft—70,000ft)
ARMAMENT: one 150kg (330lb) Matra self-homing missile

LOCKHEED F-104 STARFIGHTER (1954)

If the preceding aircraft looked like a 'missile with a man in it', this was actually registered as a slogan by Lockheed-California Company to describe its exciting F-104 Starfighter. Planned as a day fighter for the USAF, it was schemed by 'Kelly' Johnson after he had talked to countless pilots in Korea. All called for more performance at all costs, and the famed Lockheed designer gave them just that. Even the first two prototypes, with plain inlets leading to a J65 engine, easily went supersonic without using the afterburner. The production F-104A, with the brilliant new J79 engine and variable inlets, went way beyond Mach 2, and had to be 'redlined' to prevent overheating. For anyone who wanted a fast, high-flying fighter at low cost the F-104 was hard to equal.

It had wings rather like razor blades. Thickness/chord ratio was an unprecedented 3·36 per cent, giving a maximum depth at the root of 4·2in (107mm), strictly similar to the wings of the Blériot but about 3,000 times stronger. The wing was almost solid, and the cutaway drawing shows the five massive anchorages at the root, bolted to strong fuselage frames. Technical difficulties abounded, not least being accommodating the hydraulic power units driving the ailerons in a total depth of 1in (25mm)! The answer was a 'piccolo' actuator with a row of 10 rams spaced the whole length of the aileron. Inboard were the blown flaps. Blasting engine bleed air (air allowed to escape from the main compressor) across the top of the flaps resulted in hot supersonic flow which forced the main airflow to remain 'attached' to the flaps even at large deflection angles, greatly increasing their effectiveness. Without flap blowing, the F-104 would have landed too fast for safety, despite having a hinged (drooped) leading edge.

The British Dowty company provided 'Liquid Spring' shock struts for the landing gears, which had to be extremely compact to fit inside the fuselage. The fuselage also had to house all the internal fuel, the onboard systems and the radical new M61 'Project Vulcan' six-barrel gun which fires 20mm shells at up to 100 per second and is still used in all USAF fighters. The only other weapons specified were two of the new self-homing AIM-9 Sidewinder missiles on launch rails at the wingtips, carried in place of auxiliary tanks. The needle nose housed a simple radar-ranging sight, adequate for the day fighter mission. After careful study Johnson decided to use a downward-ejecting pilot seat, to ease canopy design and eliminate the possibility of hitting the high T-tail.

From the first flight on 7 February 1954 the F-104 proved troublesome, though its performance met all expectations. Subsequent versions included the F-104B tandem trainer and F-104C fighter-bomber, but it remained a rather specialised limited-capability aircraft until, to meet a growing export market, Lockheed completely redesigned it as an all-weather multirole attack fighter (initially for Germany's Luftwaffe). The resulting F-104G Super Starfighter was a resounding success, adding 2,282 extra aircraft mainly built under licence in many countries. The cutaway drawing shows the Canadair CF-104 in which the gun was replaced by fuel. Most of the extra aircraft had Nasarr multimode radar, a strengthened structure and, after many casualties, a retrofit of a Martin-Baker seat ejecting upwards. The last version of all was the Aeritalia-built F-104S interceptor, with Sparrow radar-guided missiles. Its loaded weight of 31,000lb (14,062kg) was just twice that of the prototype.

Below:
An F104S of the Italian Air Force, built under licence by Aeritalia.

Above:
A flight of F-104Gs
of the Royal
Netherlands Air
Force.

Left:
A Starfighter with a
full complement of
external fuel tanks
accelerates down the
runway.

F-104 STARFIGHTER (1954)

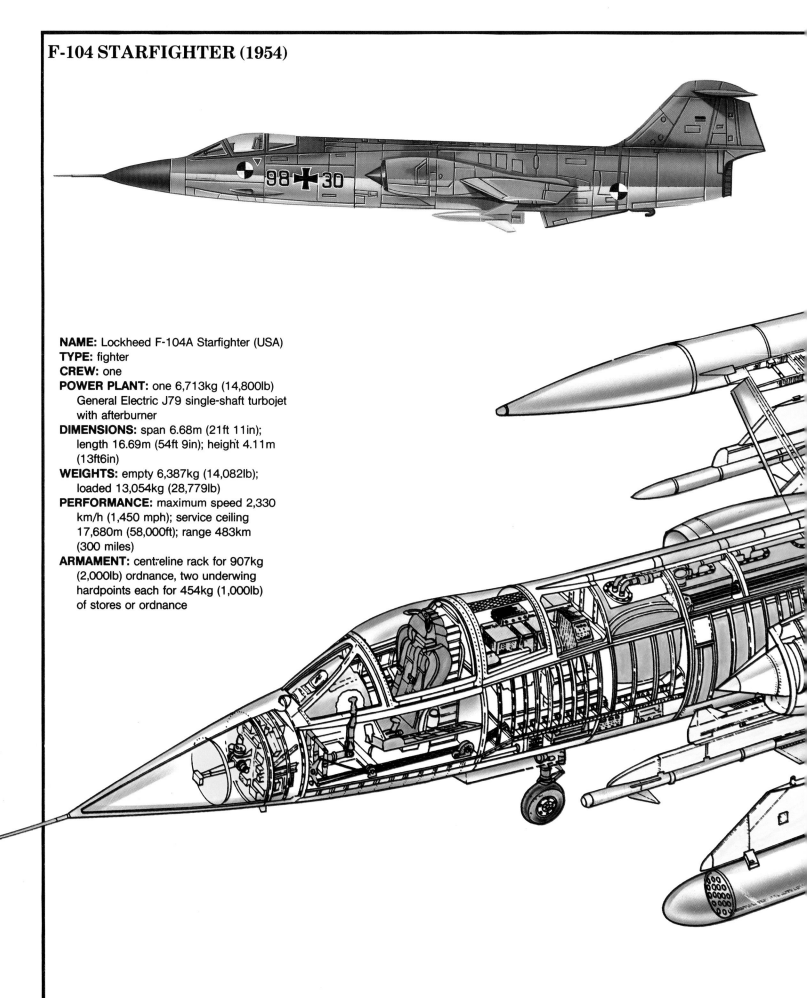

NAME: Lockheed F-104A Starfighter (USA)
TYPE: fighter
CREW: one
POWER PLANT: one 6,713kg (14,800lb)
General Electric J79 single-shaft turbojet
with afterburner
DIMENSIONS: span 6.68m (21ft 11in);
length 16.69m (54ft 9in); height 4.11m
(13ft6in)
WEIGHTS: empty 6,387kg (14,082lb);
loaded 13,054kg (28,779lb)
PERFORMANCE: maximum speed 2,330
km/h (1,450 mph); service ceiling
17,680m (58,000ft); range 483km
(300 miles)
ARMAMENT: centreline rack for 907kg
(2,000lb) ordnance, two underwing
hardpoints each for 454kg (1,000lb)
of stores or ordnance

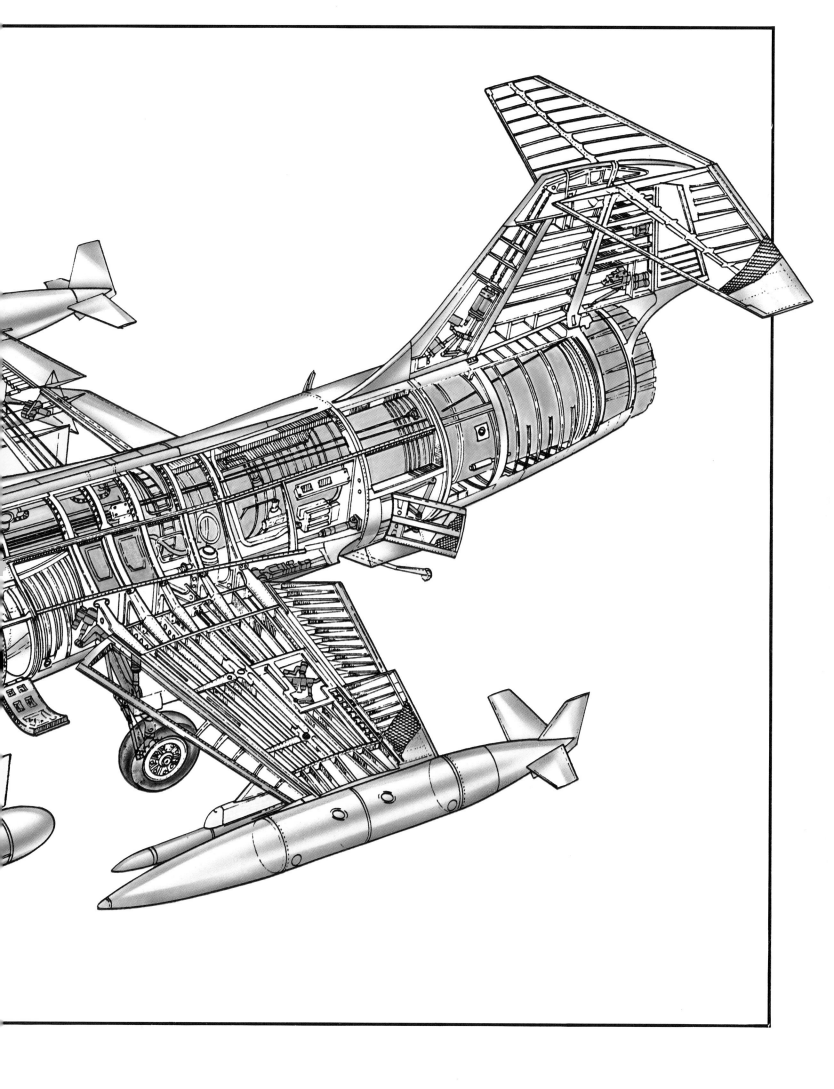

DOUGLAS A4D (A-4) SKYHAWK (1954)

One of the often-told, but true, stories of aviation is how Ed Heinemann, chief engineer of Douglas El Segundo division, told the US Navy he could meet their 1951 attack specification at just *half* the allowed weight of 30,000lb (13,608kg), and also beat their required speed of 495mph (797km/h) by a cool 100 knots! Such a thing sounds nonsense, but by sheer brilliance, and a ruthless leaving out of non-essentials, the job was done. The prototype XA4D-1, flown on 22 June 1954, turned the scales at just over 15,000lb (6,804kg) loaded. It soon set a 500km closed-circuit record at over 695mph (1,118km/h), which beat the specification by 200mph (322km/h).

Heinemann said his philosophy had been 'Take the best turbojet available, put it on a new-technology wing, add a saddle on top for the jockey and leave out the rest'. He almost accomplished this, and carried out sweeping reforms into electrics, electronics and hydraulics and also designed a streamlined range of bombs and drop tanks into the bargain, as well as the 'buddy store' which turns a combat aircraft into a tanker to refuel its friends.

The basis of this outstanding design was a wing so small it did not need to fold, and made in one piece. The upper and lower skins were machined slabs forming integrally stiffened sheets unbroken from tip to tip. The whole interior formed an integral tank. Behind this tank were attached split flaps and powered ailerons, while the entire leading edge comprised powerful slats which had never before been used on so thin a wing. The tail control surfaces were fully powered, and the tailplane had powered variable incidence for trim control. Persistent rudder 'buzz' (high-frequency flutter) was tem-

porarily cured by changing it into a single-surface design, with skin down the middle and ribs on either side. Heinemann said it embarrassed him that they never had time to redesign the rudder to look normal, and so it flew on every subsequent Skyhawk! Production was planned to terminate in 1958, but kept being extended, new models kept appearing and new customers kept asking for more, so the last one did not come off the line until 26 years later, in 1979, at No 2,960.

To avoid cutting into the wing box the main landing gear, which was long to give plenty of clearance for bulky stores, retracted straight forwards, shortening as it rotated and with the wheels pivoting through 90° to lie flat behind the leading edge, with the legs lying beneath the bottom wing skins. The nose gear also retracted forward. Large door-type airbrakes were pushed open hydraulically from each side of the rear fuselage, hinged to the same forged frame as the arrester hook. To access or change the engine the whole rear fuselage and tail could be disconnected at a double frame aligned with the central spar of the wing.

Initial production versions, designated A-4 after 1962, were powered by the 7,700lb Wright J65 (Sapphire licence) engine, and could carry up to 5,000lb (2,268kg) of underwing stores as well as two 20mm guns in the wing roots. Later versions added a long inflight refuelling probe on the right side of the nose, radar, new navigation and weapon-delivery systems and, from 1961, the more efficient J52 engine which extended range and enabled weapon load to climb to 8,200lb (3,720kg). The final versions had the 11,200lb (5,080kg) J52-408A engine, raising external weapon load to 9,155lb (4,153kg), gross weight reaching 24,500lb and with four times the mission capability.

Below:
A two-seat A-4 Skyhawk of the US Navy's Operational Test and Evaluation Force.

Left:
A United States
Navy A-4 Skyhawk.

Below:
A Malaysian Air
Force Skyhawk. Note
the external ribs on
the rudder and the
avionics hump on its
back.

DOUGLAS A4D SKYHAWK (1954)

NAME: Douglas A4D (A-4) Skyhawk (USA)
TYPE: attack bomber
CREW: one
POWER PLANT: one 3,493kg (7,700lb)
thrust Wright J65-16A single-shaft
turbojet
DIMENSIONS: (A-4B) span 8.38m
(27ft 6in); length 12.04m (39ft 6in);
eight 4.57m (15ft 4in)
WEIGHTS: empty 3,500kg (7,700lb); loaded
7,727kg (17,000lb)
PERFORMANCE: maximum speed 1,088
km/h (676 mph); service ceiling 14,935m
(49,000ft); range 1,480km (920 miles)
ARMAMENT: two 20mm Mk12 cannon;
pylons under fuselage and wing for up to
2,268kg (5,000lb) ordnance

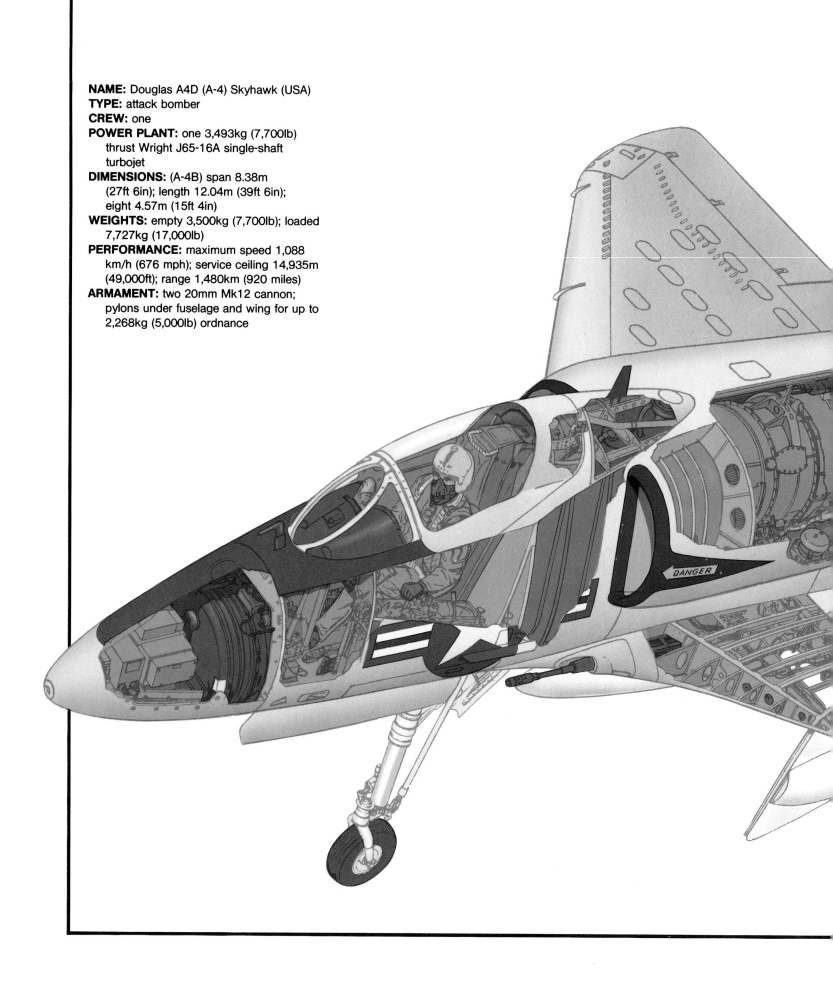

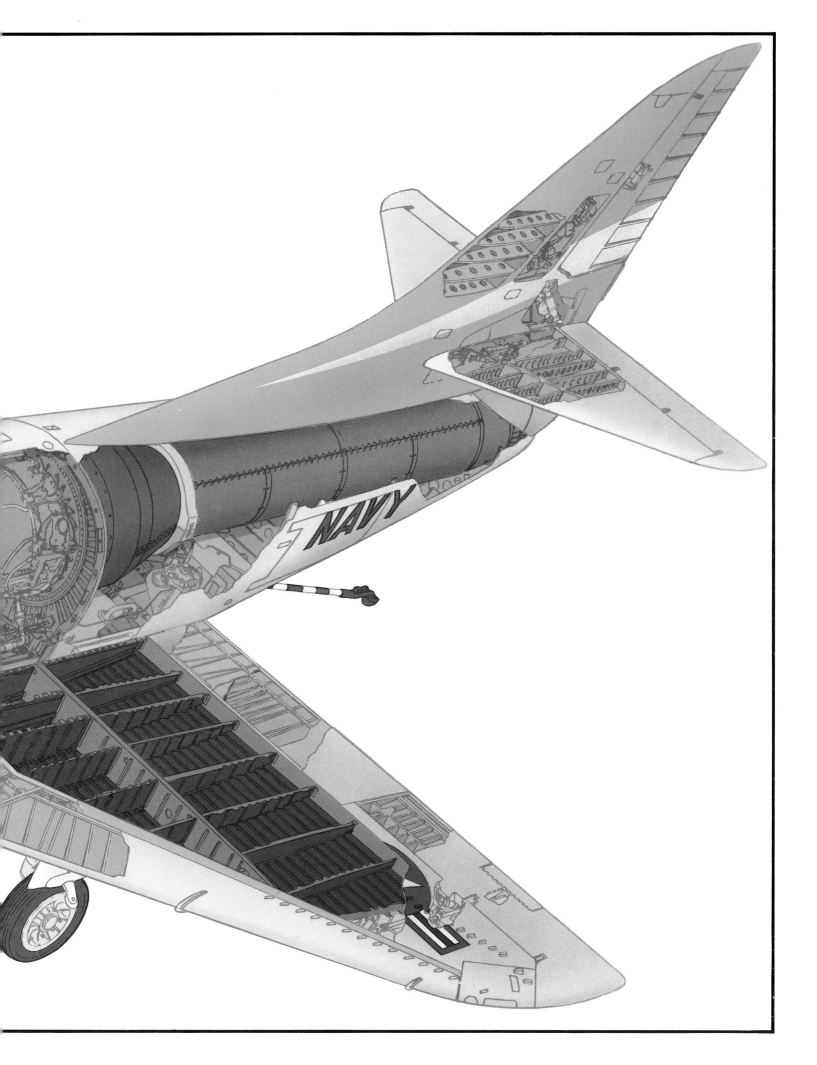

BOEING 707 (1954)

In the early 1950s Britain's pioneer Comet was entering passenger-carrying service, bringing a new realm of speed and comfort to a few air routes. The highly competitive US industry sought ways to compete. Top transport builder, Douglas, had no big jet experience. Boeing had plenty of big jet (B-47) experience, but was out of production with its not very successful Stratocruiser. There was a chance the USAF might buy a jet tanker to follow the mass-produced Boeing C-97, but it refused to make any commitment. On 20 May 1952 Boeing gambled more than the company's net worth and went ahead with the Model 367-80, the prototype of what it hoped would be both a military tanker and a commercial transport. This flew on 15 July 1954. The rest is history.

The KC-135A tanker, of which 732 were built, was very close to the 'Dash 80' prototype. The commercial 707, however, was at great cost given a fuselage 4in (100mm) wider to match 3+3 seating. Powered by four 13,000lb (5,897kg) Pratt & Whitney JT3C-6 turbojets, lightened versions of the military J57, the 707-120 weighed 247,000lb (112 tonnes) and opened jet service from New York to Paris on 26 October 1958, though it was really a 'domestic' aircraft. For the North Atlantic Boeing designed the 707-320 Intercontinental, with a significantly larger airframe, fuel increased from 14,488 to 19,635 Imp gal (65,862 to 89,261 litres), gross weight up to 295,000lb (133,812kg) and powered by 15,800lb (7,167kg) Pratt & Whitney JT4A turbojets or 17,500lb Rolls-Royce Conway turbofans. By 1962 Boeing had refined the larger version into the -320B and C with the 18,000lb (8,165kg) JT3D turbofan, and this became the standard version taking the sales total to 962, the last delivered in 1982.

Planning the 707 was a crucial blend of

innovation and tradition. The fuselage was similar to the Stratocruiser in being a 'double bubble', the cross section comprising a large (148in-diameter) circular-arc passenger section above a smaller circular-arc lower lobe for baggage, cargo, systems, bogie main landing gear and the wing. The two lobes were joined at the passenger floor, and (unlike the Stratocruiser) the external shape was almost oval, without any indentation at this level. Noting the fatigue explosions of the Comet I's fuselage great care was taken (for the first time) to design with redundant load paths, easy structural inspection and 'fail safe' construction. The passenger windows, for example, were small and numerous, and not only cut from the skin but also machined from chemically milled panels which provided a second, stronger, layer along the inside.

The wing had to be swept at 35° at the quarter-chord line, as did the tail, in order to reach the required high cruising speed of 600mph (966km/h). The wing had to be immensely strong, with giant forged and machined spars and ribs and colossal integrally stiffened skin panels, all assembled by precision bolts to form integral tankage; but this had been done already in the B-47 and B-52. Huge double-slotted flaps were fitted except behind the four engine pods. Behind the inner engines were placed all-speed ailerons. Behind the outers were conventional ailerons used only at low speeds, with flaps down. Powered spoilers above the wing augmented roll control at all speeds and also could be used symmetrically as speed brakes. Remarkably, with so very heavy and fast an aircraft, Boeing managed to use manual servo-tab control of the ailerons and tailplane/elevator, only the rudder being powered. The cutaway drawing shows the early 707-121, with multi-pipe silencers fitted to the very noisy fuel-hungry turbojets originally installed.

Below:
A Boeing 707 company demonstrator with Turbofan engines flying over rather dramatic scenery.

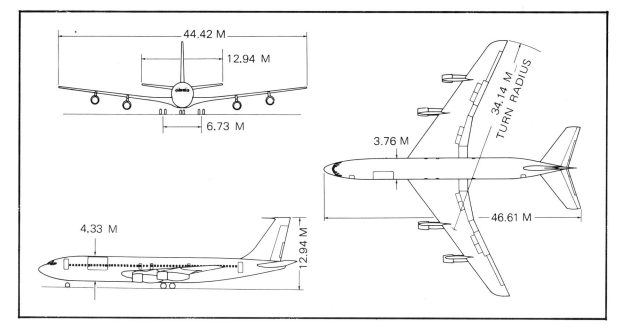

Left:
Dimensions of the
Boeing 707.

Left:
Continental Airlines
are one of the many
carriers to use the
707. This one shows
the early multi-pipe
silencers installed on
its Pratt and
Whitney turbojets.

Below:
A 707 tanker
transport refuelling a
US Navy A-7 Corsair
(far) and F-14
Tomcat (near).

BOEING 707 (1954)

NAME: Boeing 707 (USA)
TYPE: civil airliner/military transport
POWER PLANT: four 8,165kgp
(18,000lb st) Pratt & Whitney
JT3D turbofans
DIMENSIONS: span 44.42m (145ft 8.5in);
length 45.6m (152ft 11in); height 12.94m
(42ft 5.5in); wing area 283m² (3,050sqft)
WEIGHTS: basic operating
62,872-66,224kg (136,610-146,000lb);
maximum passenger payload 38,100kg
(84,000lb); maximum cargo payload
41,453kg (91,390lb); loaded 151,315kg
(333,600lb)
PERFORMANCE: maximum speed 965 km/
h (600 mph); service ceiling 11,885m
(39,000ft); range 6,920km (4,300 miles)

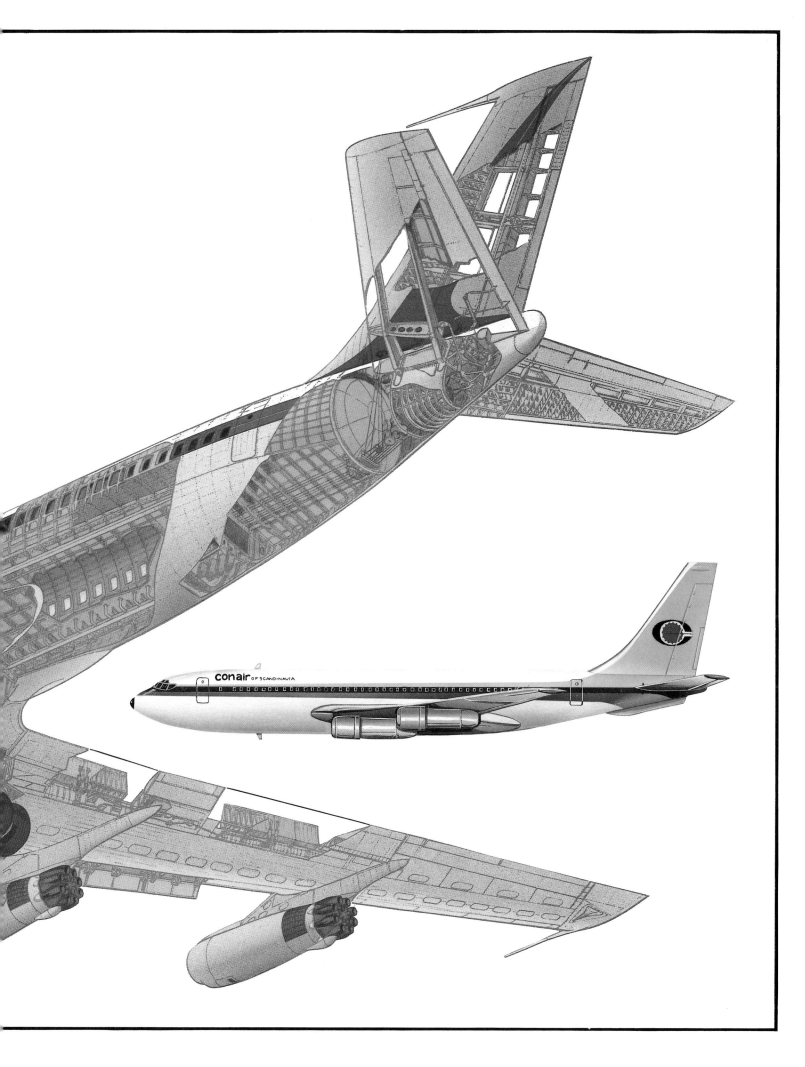

LOCKHEED C-130 HERCULES (1954)

Certainly the familiar 'Herky bird' is the first aircraft in this chronologically arranged book that is still in full production. Lockheed-Georgia Company, which builds it in the vast windowless plant outside Marietta, Georgia, says in its advertising, 'Outside it's the same; inside it keeps acting newer and newer' – a reference to the fact that almost every part has been changed in a 30-year development which among other things has pushed gross weight from 108,000 to 175,000lb (48,989 to 79,380kg) and doubled the maximum cargo load. An aside is that many planned replacements have fallen by the wayside while the C-130 line just keeps on going. Allison's T56 turboprop began at 3,750ehp and now gives 4,910ehp, and with about 7,000ehp in prospect there is plenty of development in the C-130 not yet realised.

Today the C-130 (Lockheed Model 382) looks so conventional it is hard to imagine the impact it made when new. Although the whole design was obvious, nobody had ever done it before; instead the world's military airlift was performed with aircraft which often had narrow sloping floors (with tailwheel landing gear) and side doors; if they had a rear door it could not be opened in flight unless it was removed and left on the ground! The C-130 had a cavernous unobstructed interior, at so-called truck-bed height, all on one horizontal level, with pressurization and air-conditioning. The rear doors were big enough to admit large trucks yet easily opened in the air for heavy dropping. Side doors were provided for paratroops.

Structurally the C-130 was outstanding. The slender wing was built around a main two-spar box with upper and lower skin panels each 48ft (14·6m) long and machined from solid slabs to form one of the earliest integrally stiffened structures. Almost the entire box is occupied by fuel, the space being divided into six integral tanks. Remarkably, in view of the limited airflow available from small turboprops, all leading edges are de-iced by engine bleed air. All control surfaces are metal-skinned and boosted by tandem power units in two independent hydraulic systems. This solved a lot of problems, though probably manual Flettner servos could have been used, as on the contemporary Britannia.

Takeoff and landing performance is important to an off-airfield airlifter, and the C-130 has always set a high standard (indeed a current research programme may cut field length by about half, without changing the engine power). The Fowler-type flaps have hardly changed in 30 years, with actuation by duplex hydraulic motors. The leading edge is fixed. Landing gears use low-pressure tyres suited to soft surfaces, and heated skis can be fitted. The tandem main units retract straight up into faired compartments outside the fuselage proper, the left fairing also containing a gas-turbine APU (auxiliary power unit) which drives a 40-kVA alternator and other services. The right fairing incorporates the pressure-fuelling connector, for by the early 1950s turbine transports had such large fuel capacity it took too long to refuel by the traditional 'gravity' method, as in refuelling a car (though filler caps are provided above the wing for primitive airfields).

Like all Allison turboprops the T56 (or commercial Model 501 in the L-100 commercial Hercules) has its propeller gearbox mounted in front of the power section, carried on struts. The propellers, usually Hamilton Standard, are reversible for short landings. For short takeoffs booster rockets can be attached to the rear of the landing gear fairings.

Below:
A line of the Royal Canadian Air Force's "Charlie one-thirties".

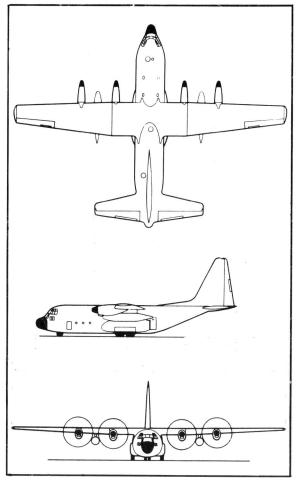

Left:
The Model 382
Hercules production
line at Lockheed's
Georgia plant.

Right:
A Royal Air Force
Transport Command
Hercules.

LOCKHEED C-130 HERCULES (1954)

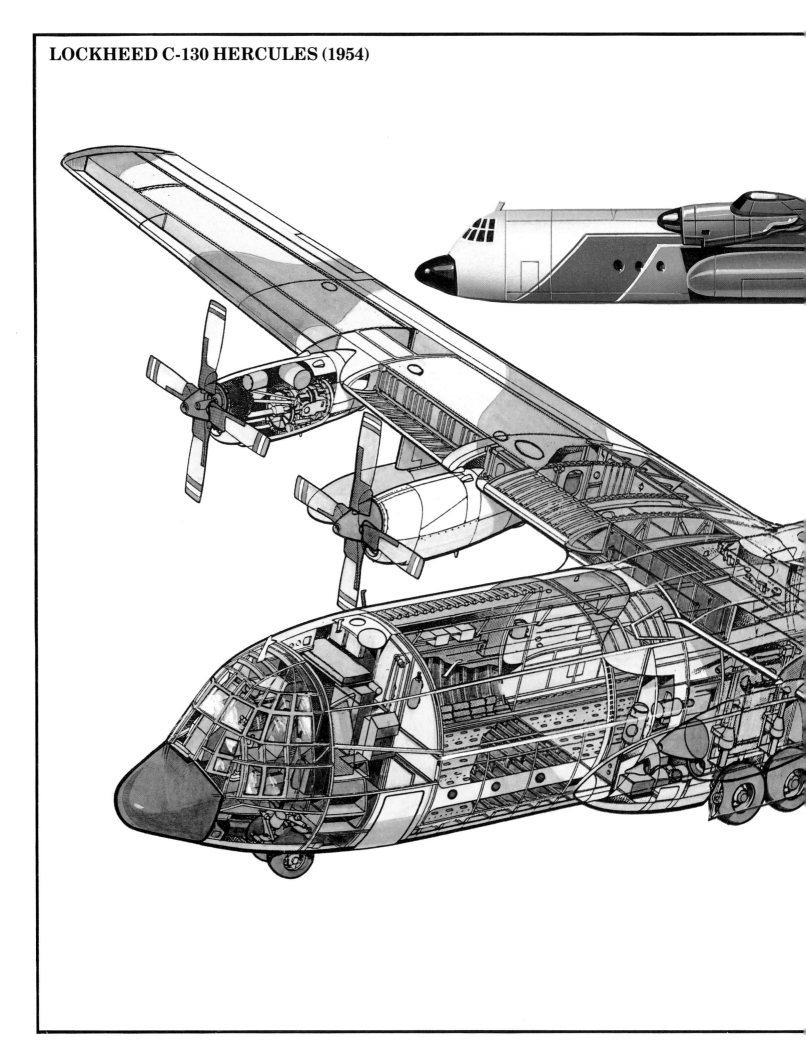

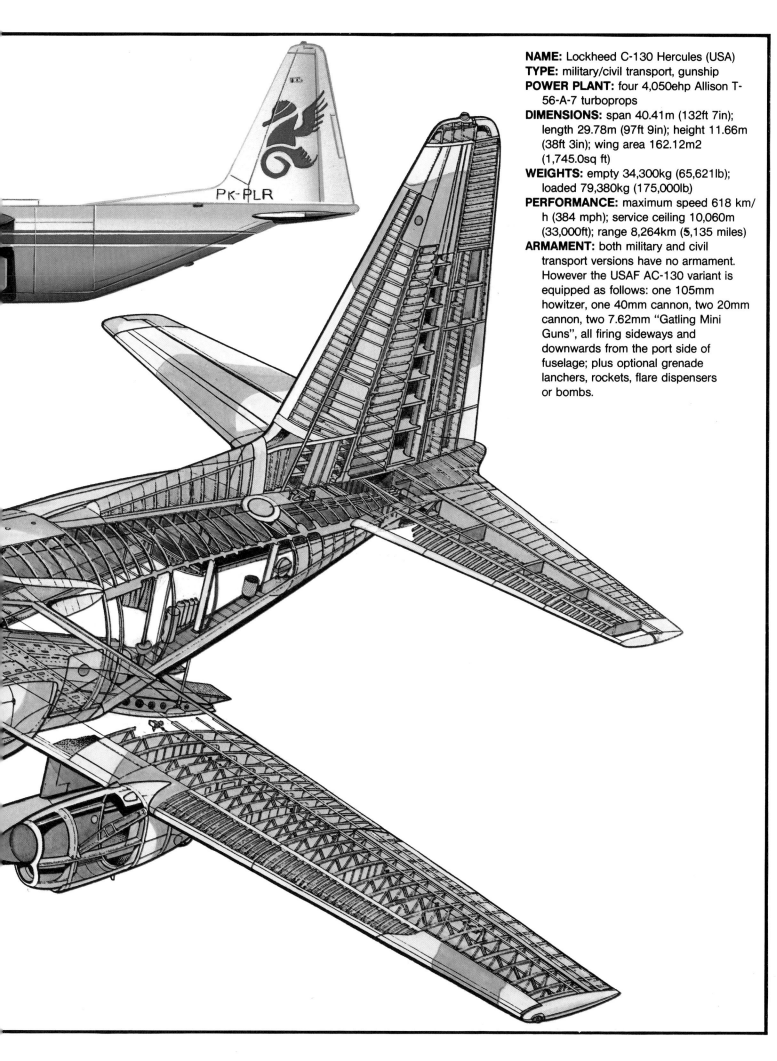

NAME: Lockheed C-130 Hercules (USA)
TYPE: military/civil transport, gunship
POWER PLANT: four 4,050ehp Allison T-56-A-7 turboprops
DIMENSIONS: span 40.41m (132ft 7in); length 29.78m (97ft 9in); height 11.66m (38ft 3in); wing area 162.12m2 (1,745.0sq ft)
WEIGHTS: empty 34,300kg (65,621lb); loaded 79,380kg (175,000lb)
PERFORMANCE: maximum speed 618 km/h (384 mph); service ceiling 10,060m (33,000ft); range 8,264km (5,135 miles)
ARMAMENT: both military and civil transport versions have no armament. However the USAF AC-130 variant is equipped as follows: one 105mm howitzer, one 40mm cannon, two 20mm cannon, two 7.62mm "Gatling Mini Guns", all firing sideways and downwards from the port side of fuselage; plus optional grenade lanchers, rockets, flare dispensers or bombs.

REPUBLIC F-105 THUNDERCHIEF (1955)

In World War II the biggest of all single-engined fighters was the Republic P-47 Thunderbolt, incidentally made in greater numbers than any other US fighter. Most of the P-47 design team worked on the F-84 Thunderjet, and in 1951 the same team began to work on a much bigger and more powerful single-jet aircraft to serve as a long-range supersonic fighter-bomber to carry heavy loads of nuclear or conventional bombs both internally and under the wings. Powered by a J57, the prototype flew on 22 October 1955, but redesign was already in hand. When the F-105B flew on 26 May 1956, reaching Mach 2·15 within three weeks, it had a beautifully curving area-ruled fuselage, larger at front and rear and narrower past the wings; and a monster after-burning J75 engine, fed by unique swept-forward inlets in the wing roots.

Though the F-105B suffered delays and cost-escalation, it was obviously a great aircraft. At first pilots called it 'the lead sled', the 'ultra hog' and 'thud', and the last name stuck. Gradually they learned that a giant fighter can also be a great warplane. Most pilots could walk under the doors of the bomb bay without stooping, and to check the inlet ducts meant jumping up and hauling up as if in a gym. The relatively small wings, swept at a sharp 45°, had conical-camber leading-edge flaps, slotted trailing-edge flaps and a row of powerful spoilers for roll control, backed up by conventional ailerons at low speeds with flaps down. The fuselage was so large that 966 Imp gal (4,392 litres) of fuel could be accommodated without putting any fuel in the wings. The tail, like the fuselage, was made of aluminium and magnesium, and the rudder and slab tailplanes were hydraulically powered like

Far right:
F-105 "Thuds" bombed up and ready to go on another sortie over Vietnam.

Below right:
An artist's impression of a flight of Thunderchiefs.

Below:
A two-seat F-105F Thunderchief gets airborne, with a few degrees of flaps and airbrakes slightly open to form divergent jet nozzle.

the low-speed ailerons. There was a ventral fin for stability at supersonic speed, the tailplane was mounted low, and the fin incorporated a ram inlet to cool the afterburner compartment.

The afterburning J75 was one of the biggest and heaviest engines used by any Western fighter. One of the most unusual features of the 'Thud' was that the entire tail of the fuselage was formed from four enormous airbrakes, made of steel and titanium, which when fully open had a tremendous effect. The strangest feature was that, in order to accelerate to supersonic speed, going into afterburner, the airbrakes had to be partly opened! This allowed the primary nozzle to be fully opened to give the required divergent final nozzle.

Most 'Thuds' (600 out of 820 production air-craft) were of the F-105D type, with completely revised avionics including Nasarr monopulse radar, doppler navigation and an advanced autopilot and flight control system. By this time the bomb bays had been sealed and used for extra fuel, but the bomb loads actually in-creased, often reaching around 14,000lb (6,350kg); a common load in Vietnam was 16 '750lb' (340kg), each of these bombs actually weighing 825lb (374kg). Many tactical missiles and 'smart' (laser guided) bombs soon enabled extremely precise attacks to be made, such as those that at last felled the great Paul Doumer bridge. Electronic-warfare systems appeared all over the 'Thud', and two-seat F-105Fs were rebuilt as Wild Weasel F-105G defence-suppres-sion aircraft bristling with countermeasures and anti-radar missiles. The final update for the F-105D single-seaters was the Thunderstick II avionic update for low-level attacks by night or in adverse weather, which added a large saddle-back fairing from cockpit to fin.

REPUBLIC F-105 THUNDERCHIEF (1955)

NAME: Republic F-105 Thunderchief (USA)
TYPE: fighter-bomber
CREW: one
POWER PLANT: one 10,660kg (23,500lb)
 Pratt & Whitney J75 two-shaft
 after-burning turbojet
DIMENSIONS: span 10.65m (34ft 11.25in);
 length 19.58m (64ft 3in); height 5.99m
 (19ft 8in)
WEIGHTS: empty 12,474kg (27,500lb);
 loaded 18,144kg (40,000lb)
PERFORMANCE: maximum speed 2,018
 km/h (1,254 mph); service ceiling
 15,850m (52,000ft); range 370km
 (230 miles)
ARMAMENT: one 20mm M-161 cannon; up
 to 3,629kg (8,000lb) of ordnance
 in internal bomb bay, plus 2,722kg
 (6,000lb) externally

DASSAULT MIRAGE III (1956)

Few aircraft have been developed through so many major improvements as the Mirage III fighter. Dassault has clouded the issue by giving the same name to many totally different aircraft, such as the Mirage F1 fighter with a high wing and separate tail, the Mirage IVA twin-engined bomber and various swing wing and VTOL aircraft, but the basic tailless delta Mirage can be traced from the Mirage I of June 1955 to today's Mirage 2000. The Mirage I was a target-defence interceptor with two very small turbojets and a rocket. Dassault wisely enlarged it into the Mirage III, flown on 17 November 1956, powered by an afterburning Atar turbojet. This in turn was refined into the prototype Mirage IIIA (shown in the cutaway drawing), of 1958, with a better Atar and completely revised structure. From this stemmed a profuse series of production Mirage IIIs and 5s of which well over 1,400 have been delivered to 21 countries.

Dassault planned the Mirage III as the smallest and simplest fighter able to reach Mach 2 while carrying basic air-combat armament. Showing greater long-term sense than other countries the French never considered outmoded guns and two 30mm DEFA cannon were installed under the inlet ducts. A large AAM (air-to-air missile) could be hung under the fuselage. Later bombs were added, but Dassault personally hated such excrescences spoiling his 'beautiful aeroplane'. Another basic design feature was low-pressure tyres for operation away from runways, but in practice this was hardly possible because of the very high landing and takeoff speeds. Though a good choice for minimum drag at supersonic speeds, the tailless delta (triangular) wing was the worst choice for takeoff and landing. Not only is it very thin and sharp-edged but the powered trailing-edge control surfaces – called elevons because they fulfil the roles of both elevators and ailerons – have to be deflected upwards, thrusting the aircraft downwards in order to raise the nose. In other aircraft the trailing-edge surfaces can be deflected down at take-off and landing to give extra lift.

Structurally the Mirage III could hardly have been simpler, though with a leading-edge sweep of just over 60° the wing comprised a triangular box, with spars at 90° to the fuselage, terminated by a spar crossing them at 60° and carrying the leading edge. The main landing gear was hinged near the main spar junction, while further forward were hinged small airbrakes above and below. The cutaway drawing shows one of these brakes fully open, and also shows the massive hinge brackets, each inside a streamlined fairing under the wing, through which twin-cylinder hydraulic power units drive the two elevons on each wing, and (inside the fuselage) the small flap section at the root.

Largely because of its long afterburner the engine occupied at least half the fuselage. The lateral inlets were fitted with half-cone centre-bodies which could be moved in or out to adjust airflow to flight Mach number. Around the ducts were flexible fuel cells, and each wing formed an

Below:
The fish-eye distortion on this view of a Mirage III gives a false impression of the dimensions of this compact French fighter.

integral tank, but total capacity was only 646 Imp gal (2,940 litres), and this was further reduced if a booster rocket motor was installed under the rear fuselage (which also required a tank in place of the 30mm ammunition). Above the jetpipe was installed a braking parachute in a cylindrical container.

The IIIA prototype had a small nose because no radar was fitted. It also had a fin and rudder of pointed triangular shape.

Right:
The delta planform shown clearly in this picture of a French Armee de l'Air Mirage III.

Below:
Four Mirage III climbing steeply aided by their optionally installed rocket boosters, at the expense of both fuel and ammunition.

DASSAULT MIRAGE III (1956)

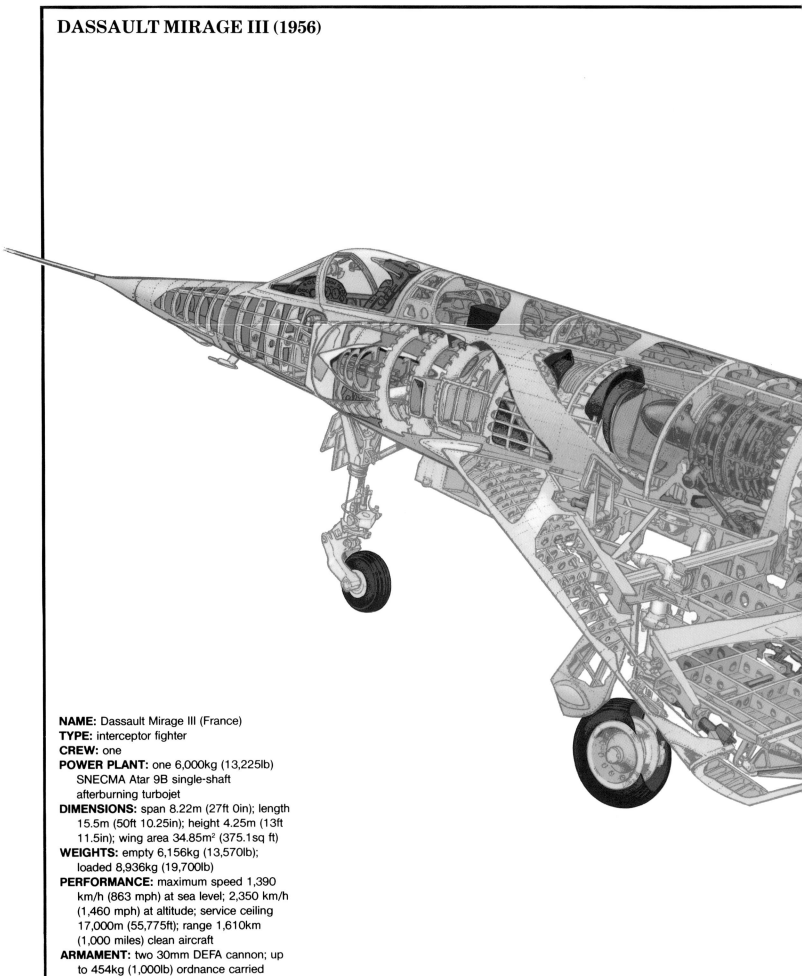

NAME: Dassault Mirage III (France)
TYPE: interceptor fighter
CREW: one
POWER PLANT: one 6,000kg (13,225lb)
   SNECMA Atar 9B single-shaft
   afterburning turbojet
DIMENSIONS: span 8.22m (27ft 0in); length
   15.5m (50ft 10.25in); height 4.25m (13ft
   11.5in); wing area 34.85m² (375.1sq ft)
WEIGHTS: empty 6,156kg (13,570lb);
   loaded 8,936kg (19,700lb)
PERFORMANCE: maximum speed 1,390
   km/h (863 mph) at sea level; 2,350 km/h
   (1,460 mph) at altitude; service ceiling
   17,000m (55,775ft); range 1,610km
   (1,000 miles) clean aircraft
ARMAMENT: two 30mm DEFA cannon; up
   to 454kg (1,000lb) ordnance carried
   externally

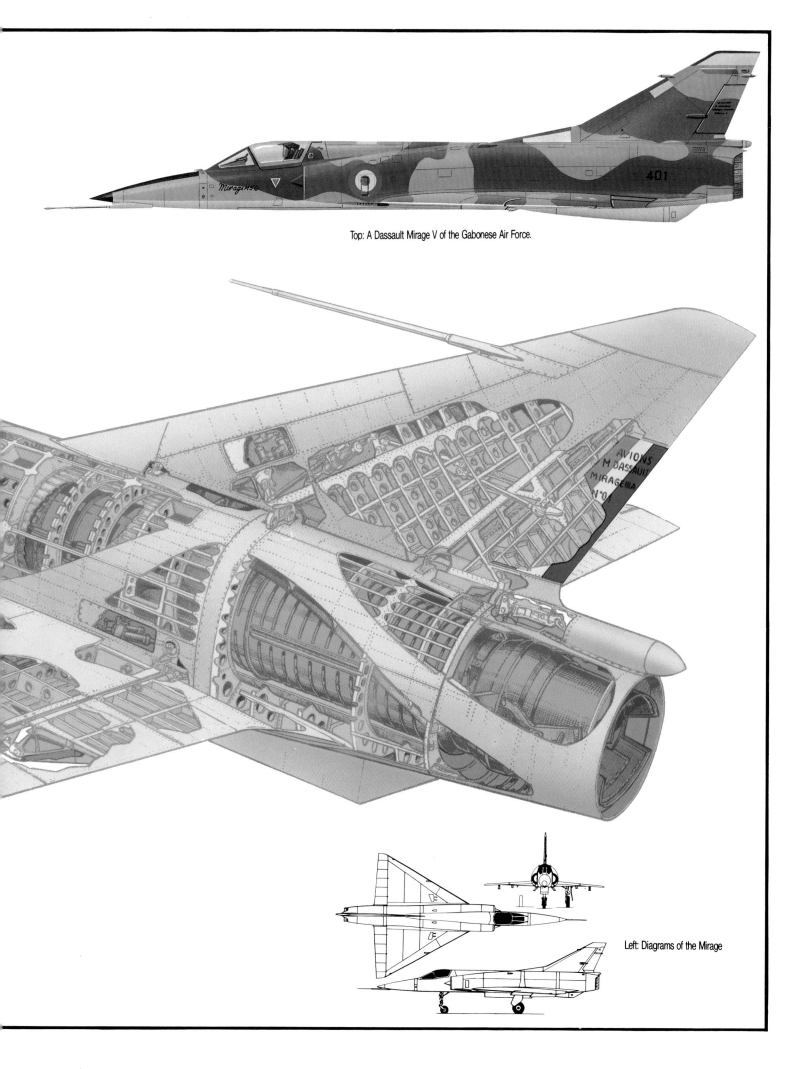

Top: A Dassault Mirage V of the Gabonese Air Force.

Left: Diagrams of the Mirage

FAIREY ROTODYNE (1957)

After World War II there was intense interest in the prospects for airline helicopters. British European Airways concluded in 1952 that to be economical a helicopter needed 30 seats. This was just right for Fairey Aviation, which in 1947 had begun studying various configurations, and in 1949 settled on a very advanced scheme for a convertiplane, or compound helicopter.

The essence of such a machine is that it is a helicopter only at takeoff and landing. In cruising flight it becomes an aeroplane, lifted by a small wing, assisted by the now freely windmilling rotor, drawn along by propellers and controlled by conventional ailerons, elevators and rudder(s). The Fairey scheme went even further, and instead of driving the rotor through a shaft used pressure jets at the tips of the blades. Compressed air from the main engines was ducted along the blades and supplied at the tips to fuel burners giving greatly increased thrust resembling small jet engines.

Named Rotodyne, the first Fairey schemes were 20-seaters with 1,000hp Mamba engines, but by April 1953, when permission was given to built a prototype, it had become a 40-seater with Napier Eland engines. These turboprops were meant to give 3,000hp but only produced 2,550 in practice, which meant that Fairey had to burn more fuel in the tip jets, which caused severe noise resembling a mighty steam freight train. The Rotodyne itself was an impressive and well-engineered machine, with a conventional stressed-skin structure. The fuselage was a lightweight unpressurized box, with a completely unobstructed interior 84in (2·13m) high and 96in (2·44m) wide. Clamshell rear doors could admit vehicles or other bulky loads, and with the promise of high cruising speeds the Rotodyne (by

Below:
A side-view of the Fairey Rotodyne.

now a 44-seater) could also be seen to have potential as a vehicle ferry, a military assault transport or a flying crane.

At all times the Eland engines drove two D.H. 14ft 6in (4·42m) propellers, which at takeoff were in neutral pitch. At the rear was a hydraulic clutch which at takeoff and landing drove a nine-stage auxiliary air compressor. The compressed air was ducted to the hub of the 90ft (27·43m) rotor and out along four tubular spars. At their ends these were joined by three pins to the broad blades, each of 79sq ft (7·34m^2) area, made mainly of stainless steel. Three pipes took the air along each blade to the tip pressure-jet, which after years of development reached an extraordinary level of power and efficiency in a very small space which had hardly any effect on the windmilling rotor in autogyro-type cruising flight. The Rotodyne was designed to climb out following an engine failure at takeoff, and engine failure in cruising flight only reduced speed from 160 to 140mph (257 to 225km/h).

The 750 Imp gal (3,410 litres) of kerosene were housed in the wings, the twin-wheel landing gear was fully retractable, and considering the totally new conception of the whole project it was remarkably 'right' from the start. Even with the under-power engines the prototype set a world rotorcraft speed record of 190·9mph (307km/h) over a 100km (62-mile) circuit, but in true British fashion the whole thing was bungled at the political level. BEA suddenly said it wanted not 44 but 66 passengers, the Treasury said no more money would be forthcoming until orders were placed and Napier never came near delivering the 4,200hp promised with the developed Eland NE1.7. Just as customers all over the world were becoming really interested Fairey were taken over by Westland, which cancelled the Rotodyne in 1962.

Right:
The Rotodyne was a
compound helicopter
that became an
aeroplane in cruising
flight, lifted by a
small wing and
drawn along
by propellers.

Below:
This view from
below reveals the
boxlike nature of
the fuselage.

FAIREY ROTODYNE (1957)

NAME: Fairey Rotodyne
TYPE: experimental rotorcraft for military and civil use
CREW: three
POWER PLANT: two 2,800shp Napier N.El.3 turboprops
DIMENSIONS: rotor diameter 27.43m (90ft 0in);
    wing span 14.17m (46ft 6in);
    fuselage length 17.88m (58ft 8in);
    height 6.76m (22ft 2in)
WEIGHTS: maximum take-off weight 17,237kg (38,000lb)
PERFORMANCE: maximum cruising speed 298km/h
    (185mph) at 1,500m (5,000ft); range 724km (450 miles)
ACCOMMODATION: 40 passengers

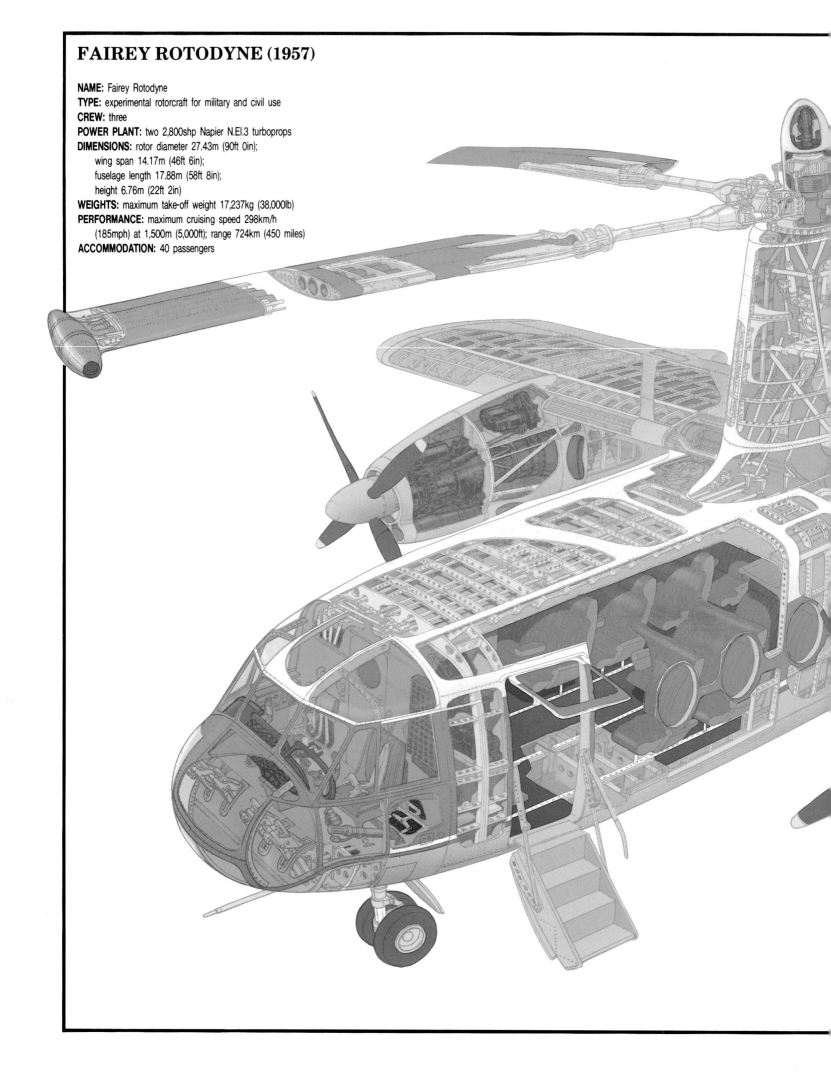

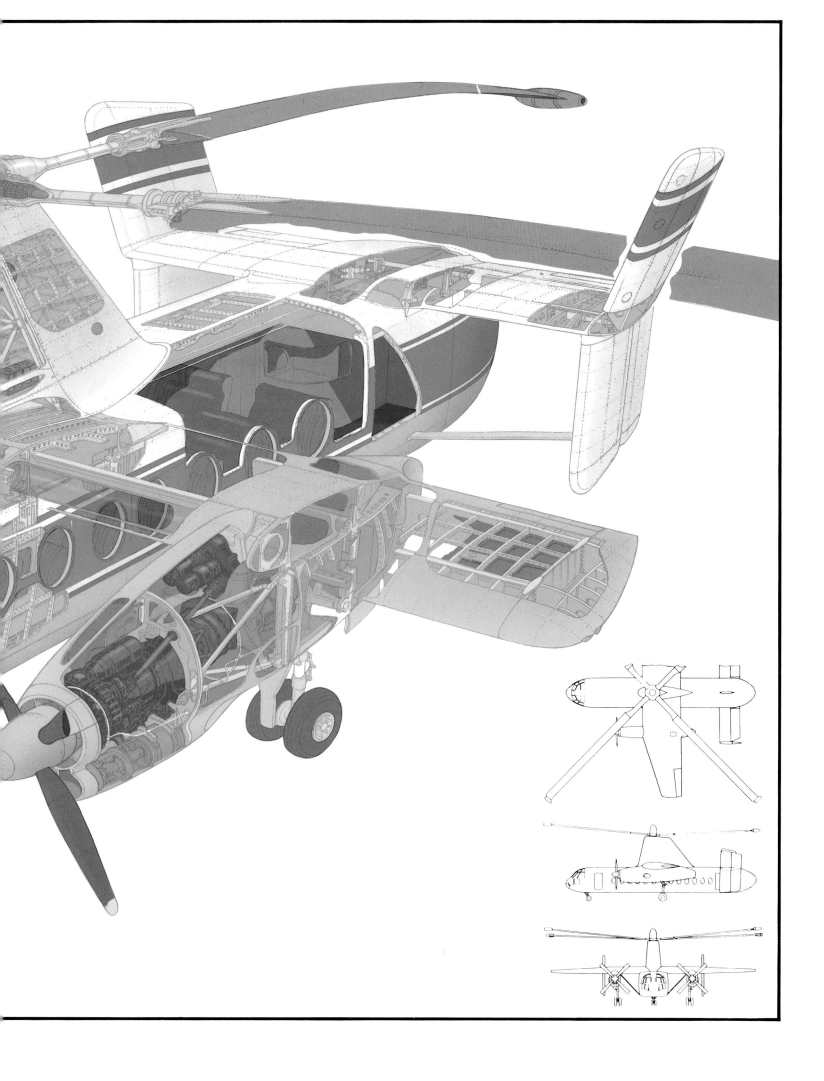

LOCKHEED L-188 ELECTRA (1957)

In 1954 American Airlines announced a competition for a short/medium-range airliner with turbine engines. At this time the British Viscount was just beginning to make a real impact on world markets, and while Boeing and Douglas were agonizing over enormous long-range jets, Lockheed entered American's competition with alacrity. It had already designed the C-130, and knew it could use four commercial versions of the same engines in a turboprop liner bigger and faster than the Viscount.

Named Electra, it easily won the contest, went into production in December 1955 and first flew on 6 December 1957, by which time a record $300 million in orders had been booked. Services began a year later, but two things happened to prevent a single Electra being sold after February 1960: a complex 'whirl mode' oscillation of the outer propellers which could reach the natural frequency of the wing, breaking the latter off at the root; and the emergence of short-haul jets, notably the 727. Jet fuel was so cheap nobody bothered about the turboprop's lower consumption until 13 years after the last Electra was built.

The Electra was designed as a superb aeroplane for both the pilot and the passenger. The pressurized fuselage had a constant cross-section – unusually, a perfect circle – over almost its entire length. The flight deck was spacious and beautifully equipped, and from it the captain could taxi out with power steering, power brakes and precise forward or negative thrust from the giant paddle-blade propellers. The takeoff was amazingly short, a full-load climb was possible with two engines on the same side shut down,

Below:
After almost fifteeen years as a passenger transport, this Electra was converted by Lockheed into an air-freighter for the Australian operator, Anset.

and it was easy to maintain height on any one engine. Huge Fowler flaps, anti-skid brakes on the very short landing gear and reverse thrust could make the landing shorter than any other transport of the era. All this with speed better than a Spitfire and extremely high operating efficiency.

Lockheed's Burbank, Los Angeles, plant had a 'Hall of Giants' containing the biggest presses and machine tools in the world. Among other things they sculpted machined planks for the Electra wings that ran in one piece from root to tip. Spar webs were divided into upper and lower halves so that no crack could travel right across, and new fatigue knowledge gained from the Comet was evident everywhere. While Boeing used mainly manual controls on the bigger and faster 707, Lockheed used duplicated hydraulic boost on ailerons, elevators and rudder of the Electra, though the tailplane was fixed. The leading edge of the wing likewise was devoid of moving surfaces, and the short field-length was due to good lift coefficient and high propeller thrust, the wing looking remarkably small. Leading edges were de-iced by bleed air, as in the C-130.

Compared with the C-130 the engines looked 'the other way up', the gearbox being below the axis of the power section and the inlet duct being above the propeller. It was trouble with the gearbox mounting struts that led to the catastrophic whirl mode crashes, which for a time resulted in a speed limit of 259mph (417km/h) indicated being imposed until the solution had been found. Fuel was housed in four integral wing tanks, the 5,506 Imp gal (25,030 litres) being pressure-filled through one socket in just over 15 minutes. In the nose was weather radar.

Above:
The large paddle-bladed propellors of the Lockheed 188 are capable of giving reverse pitch for added breaking and extra ground manoeuvrability.

Right:
A Royal New Zealand Air Force Orion. This military version of the Electra is mainly used for anti-submarine duties.

LOCKHEED L-188 ELECTRA (1957)

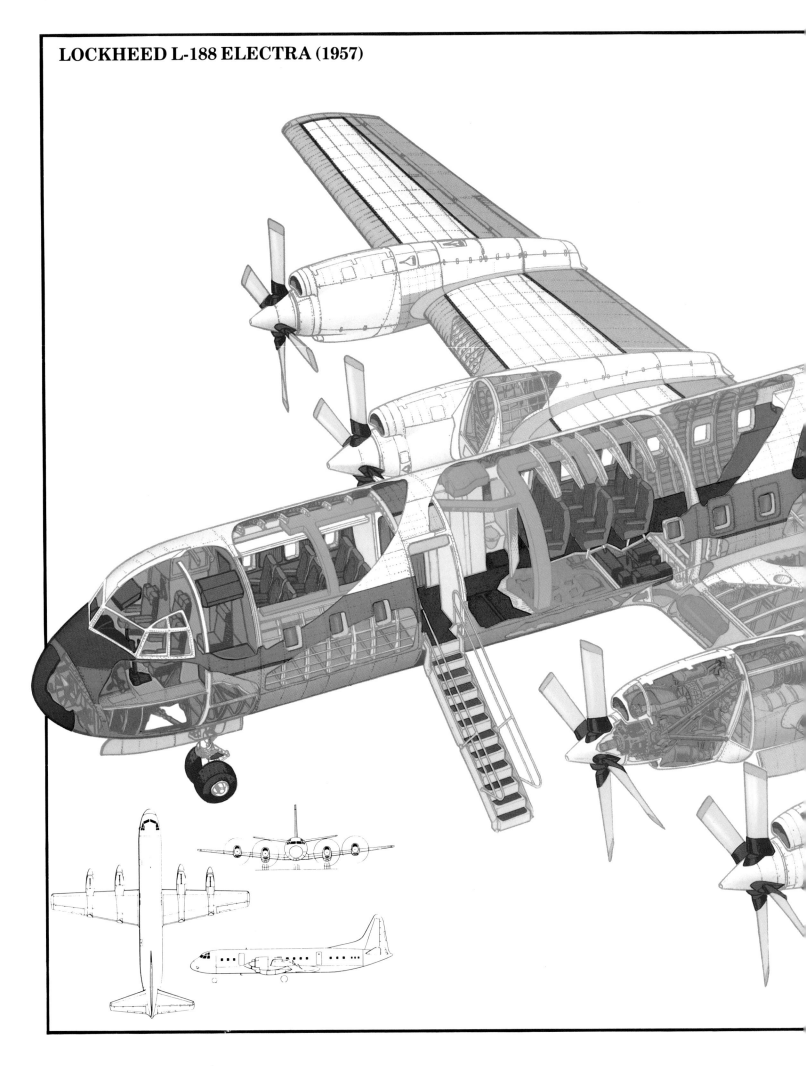

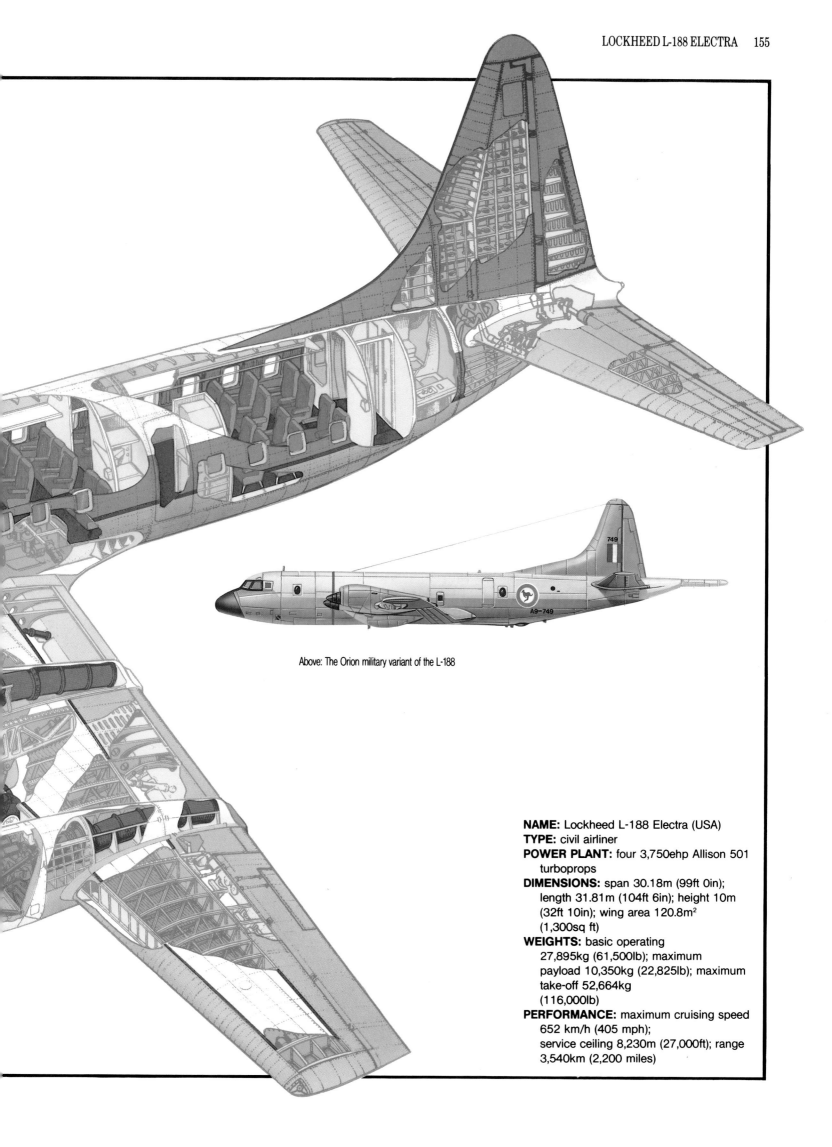

Above: The Orion military variant of the L-188

NAME: Lockheed L-188 Electra (USA)
TYPE: civil airliner
POWER PLANT: four 3,750ehp Allison 501
   turboprops
DIMENSIONS: span 30.18m (99ft 0in);
   length 31.81m (104ft 6in); height 10m
   (32ft 10in); wing area 120.8m²
   (1,300sq ft)
WEIGHTS: basic operating
   27,895kg (61,500lb); maximum
   payload 10,350kg (22,825lb); maximum
   take-off 52,664kg
   (116,000lb)
PERFORMANCE: maximum cruising speed
   652 km/h (405 mph);
   service ceiling 8,230m (27,000ft); range
   3,540km (2,200 miles)

McDONNELL F-4 PHANTOM II (1958)

For 15 years, from 1958–73, the Phantom was the yardstick against which other fighters were judged. Its production total of 5,195 handsomely exceeded that of all other non-Soviet fighters of its era. It also brought the St Louis company over $20,000 million in initial sales. It is doubtful if there has ever been a case in which so brutish and ungainly an aircraft has turned out to be such a worldbeater. Not commissioned by the US Navy, it resulted from McDonnell's keen anticipation of future requirements, and refusal to admit defeat. Planned as a multirole attack aircraft with four cannon and 11 pylons for external stores, it finally flew on 27 May 1958 as a two-seat all-weather interceptor. The guns and ten of the pylons had vanished; instead there were recesses under the broad flat-bottomed fuselage for Sparrow medium-range radar-guided missiles.

While it was being cleared for carrier-based service the original F-4A gathered a shoal of world records for speed, climb and altitude. These records were gained by regular crews flying regular aircraft, except for the high-altitude absolute speed record of 1,606·51mph (Mach 2·59) for which water was injected to cool the incoming engine air. The twin J79 engines certainly set a new high in installation technology, with fully variable inlets standing well away from the fuselage side. McDonnell had previously arranged the jetpipe(s) well short of the tail, and in the F-4 the engines were set at a pronounced down-sloping angle.

The jagged and extremely broad folding wings were fitted with very powerful blown flaps, of short span but large chord (breadth), with

ailerons occupying the rest of the inboard section. There were no movable trailing-edge surfaces on the folding outer sections, but the entire leading edge was made up of blown leading-edge flaps. These were adequate until during the Vietnam war the USAF used F-4C and F-4D Phantoms in the attack role, carrying very heavy bomb loads. Pulling tight turns at low level, some stalled and spun into the ground, and the final model, the F-4E, switched to very large leading-edge slats instead. It also had an internal gun, an M61 carried under the nose where earlier models had carried an infra-red detector.

Aerodynamically all Phantoms looked like the result of much tinkering, with a sharp dihedral on the outer wing panels only, and an even more acute anhedral on the slab tailplanes. The fin and powered rudder were remarkably broad but squat, while ahead of the ailerons were large perforated spoilers used to augment roll control. The entire aircraft was designed to the highest standards of structural strength, initially for carrier 'cat shots' and brutal arrested landings; this enabled it to be burdened by heavy offensive weapon loads never envisaged at the outset. For land use the main wheels, tyres and brakes were all enlarged and made more powerful, and the navigation and weapon-aiming avionics (aviation electronics) progressively diverged from those of the Navy versions.

All F-4s are two-seaters. The original Navy/Marines interceptor had a pilot and a backseater called a radar intercept officer, who manages the large forward-looking radar and assists the pilot to make an interception. Most land-based Phantoms have a pilot and navigator, the latter in the USAF often also being a rated pilot and having a duplicate set of flight controls.

Below:
With its after-burners alight, this USAF F-4 thunders into the sky. Upturned wingtips and anhedralled tailplane are the most distictive features of the Phantom.

Left:
Phantoms powered
by Roll-Royce Spey
engines were ordered
for the Fleet Air
Arm of the Royal
Navy.

The United States
Air Force, Navy and
Marine Corps all
operated the F-4, as
this picture shows.

Below:
A Fleet Air Arm
Phantom.
These aircraft were
handed to the Royal
Air Force when the
Navy scrapped its
large carriers.

Above:
Four American
F-4D Phantoms.

Below:
An F-4 Phantom
with Iranian
markings.

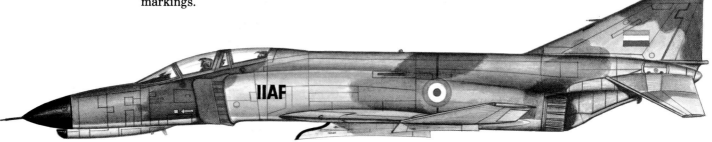

SIKORSKY S-61 SEA KING (1959)

Igor Sikorsky is credited with having built the first practical helicopter in 1939. His company developed this into the R-4, actually put to use in 1944, and subsequently the S-51, S-55 and S-58 each made tremendous advances in the helicopter state of the art. The S-61, however, transformed the helicopter in design, versatility, capability and reliability, and is still in production by licensees for military and airline customers.

Unquestionably the greatest single advance in the technology of the helicopter was the replacement of piston engines by gas turbines. Turboshaft engines dramatically increased available power, slashed weight and bulk, eliminated cooling problems, replaced special high-octane petrol (gasoline) by kerosene, reduced noise and vibration, simplified clutch and transmission problems and, above all, vastly improved reliability. Among other things they enabled designers to use them in single or even multiple installations close up against the main drive gearbox, above the fuselage. This enabled an unobtrusive cabin to be provided, evenly distributed around the centre of gravity under the main rotor. One has only to look at the tiny T58 engines of the Sea King (in 1954 launched as the first engine specifically planned for helicopters) to see how great an advance they made.

The S-61 was designed for the US Navy, primarily to carry out the ASW (anti-submarine warfare) mission. This requires the carriage of various sensors, such as radar, sonobuoys, a large sonar device dipped into the sea on a long cable, and possibly also a MAD (magnetic-anomaly detector), in order to find deeply submerged submarines. Helicopters able to carry these could not at the same time carry weapons,

such as torpedoes and depth charges, but the Sea King for the first time could do the entire hunter/killer task by itself. In turn this demanded the provision not only of a well-equipped cockpit at the front for the flight crew but also a capacious tactical compartment for the operators of the sensors. In turn this was ideal as a passenger cabin in subsequent lengthened airline versions seating (typically) 30.

Another new feature of the S-61 was that it was made amphibious, with a boat-type hull. The twin-wheel main landing gear retracted into stabilizing floats at the sides. (In another version, the S-61R, tricycle gear was used with twin nosewheels and main gears retracting into rear sponsons rather like a C-130, heavy cargo being loaded by a full-width ramp door at the rear.) All versions have all-metal stressed-skin construction, though the British licensee, Westland, introduced composite (carbon and glass fibre) blades for the main rotor. The five blades, each 30ft (9m) long, fold to the rear for stowage aboard ships, and the entire tail also folds. The tail carries a six-blade auxiliary rotor, partly to counteract the torque needed to drive the main rotor (without it the fuselage would rotate in the opposite direction to the main rotor) and also to steer the helicopter in the required direction. The tail fin and tailplane merely give stability and are fixed.

The cutaway drawing shows a British-built Westland Sea King Mk 5. This has a full range of ASW sensors including a search radar above the fuselage and a Plessey Type 195 dipping sonar which can be winched into the sea. On the right side above the large sliding cabin door is a rescue hoist with a floodlight, though there is so much equipment on board that the number of 'rescuees' could not equal the 22 of the dedicated SAR (search and rescue) version.

NAME: Sikorsky S-61 Sea King (USA)

TYPE: civil amphibious helicopter, varied military uses

POWER PLANT: two 1,250shp General Electric T-58 free-turbine turboshafts

DIMENSIONS: Main rotor diameter 18.9m (62ft 0in); overall length 22.15m (72ft 8in); height 5.13m (16ft 10in)

WEIGHTS: empty (transport versions) 4,428kg (9,763lb); loaded 9,750kg (21,500lb)

PERFORMANCE: maximum speed 267 km/h (166 mph); service ceiling 4,480m (14,700ft); range 1,005km (625 miles)

ARMAMENT: widely variable on military types

Below:
A Westland-built Sea King of the Norwegian Air Force.

Above:
Two Egyptian
Sea Kings.

Left:
A German Naval Sea
King.

MIKOYAN/GURYEVICH MiG-23 (1966?)

In 1956 S.K. Tumanskii took over the Soviet Union's Mikulin engine bureau. He began a co-operation with the MiG aircraft design team which has lasted to this day, Tumanskii producing evermore powerful jet engines which have been made in quantities which are astronomic when compared to production in other countries. Thanks to these outstanding engines, the MiG designers have produced an unrivalled succession of fighters, starting with the tailed swept-wing MiG-19 twin-jet, and going on with the MiG-21 tailed delta (one engine), MiG-23 swing-wing VG (variable geometry) aircraft with one engine, MiG-25 and 31 ultra-fast interceptors with broad fixed wings and twin engines and fins, and the MiG-29 with the same layout. Use of a fixed wing in the latest types does not mean variable geometry was a mistake. It was adopted in the MiG-23 to reconcile the conflicting requirements of short field-length, heavy fuel and bomb loads, long loiter endurance and high supersonic 'dash' speeds at all heights.

Design of the MiG-23, as the Ye-23, began in about 1961, and the first Ye-231 prototype flew in about 1966. It actually had a Lyul'ka engine, because Tumanskii's new engine was not ready. The Tumanskii R-29 is an afterburning turbojet more powerful than any engine in use in any non-Soviet fighter, and it also has good fuel economy. It is used in this family of aircraft in two versions, one configured for Mach 2·35 in the fighter versions (illustrated) with fully variable inlets and nozzle, and the other with plain inlets and a simpler nozzle matched to minimum consumption at subsonic speeds at low level. In the same way, the VG swing wings can be set to a sweep angle of 16°, 45° or 72°. Fully spread at

16°, they can extend high-lift slotted flaps along the entire trailing edge, and droop the hinged leading edges. Combined with the extremely powerful engine and optional jettisonable rocket motors, they can get a heavily loaded MiG-23 off the ground in under 2,000ft (600m). The intermediate setting is useful for air combat, and 72° is for the highest possible speeds. The wings are pivoted to a very strong carry-through box, or bridge, across the fuselage.

A key role in the MiG-23, and in the MiG-27 which is a designation of some of the attack versions, is played by the landing gear. All three units fold into the fuselage, yet they manage to combine wide track with long vertical travel, to iron out bumps in rough front-line airstrips, and low-pressure tyres for high 'flotation' on soft surfaces. The twin-wheel nose gear is fitted with power steering and has a mudguard for use in battle conditions. The fairing door over each main wheel serves the same function.

Like all modern Soviet warplanes, all operational versions of MiG-23 and MiG-27 (i.e., excluding the MiG-23U two-seat trainer) are extremely comprehensively equipped with electronics for navigation, weapon-aiming and survival. Only the interceptor versions have a large nose radar (NATO call this 'High Lark', just as they call the aircraft itself 'Flogger'), and this provides guidance signals for the semi-active homing versions of the missiles carried, the remaining missiles homing automatically on the heat emitted by target aircraft. Missiles are carried on pylons under the fixed inner wings and under the inlet ducts. In the belly is installed a pack containing either a GSh-23L twin-barrel cannon or a new gun with six barrels and higher rate of fire. Export customers have not received the latest gun missiles or radar.

MiG-23 Flogger of the Soviet Air Force parked with its wings swept back.

MiG 23 (1967)

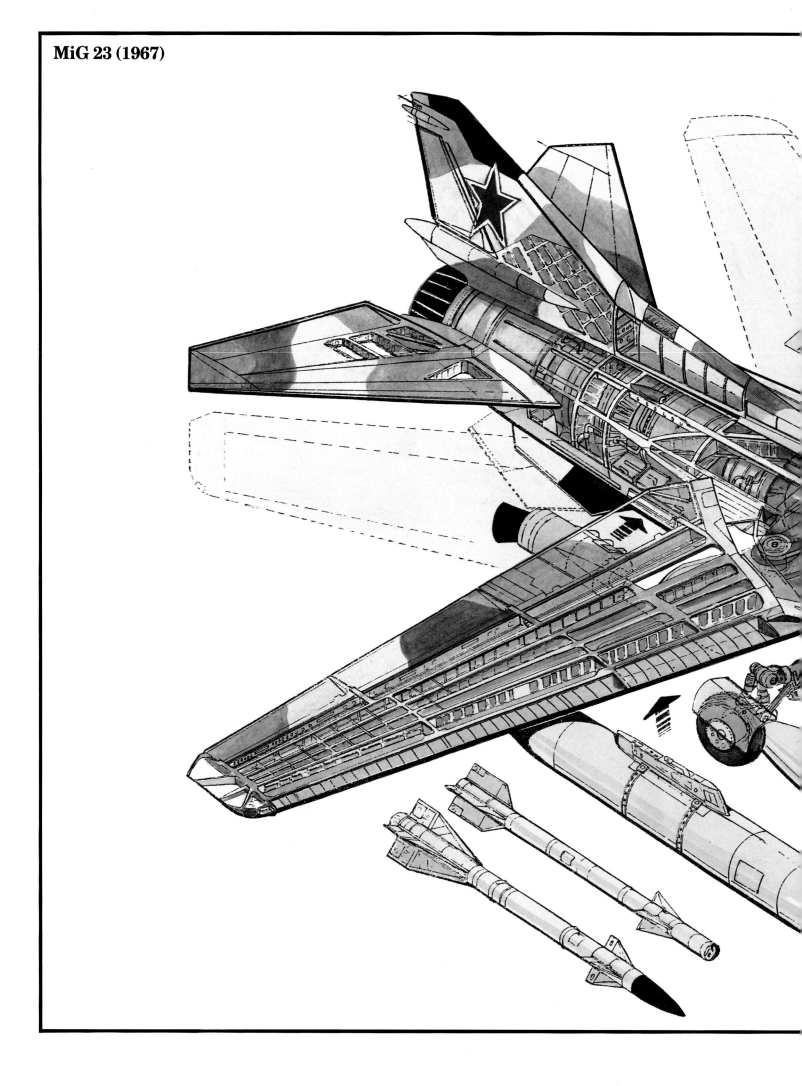

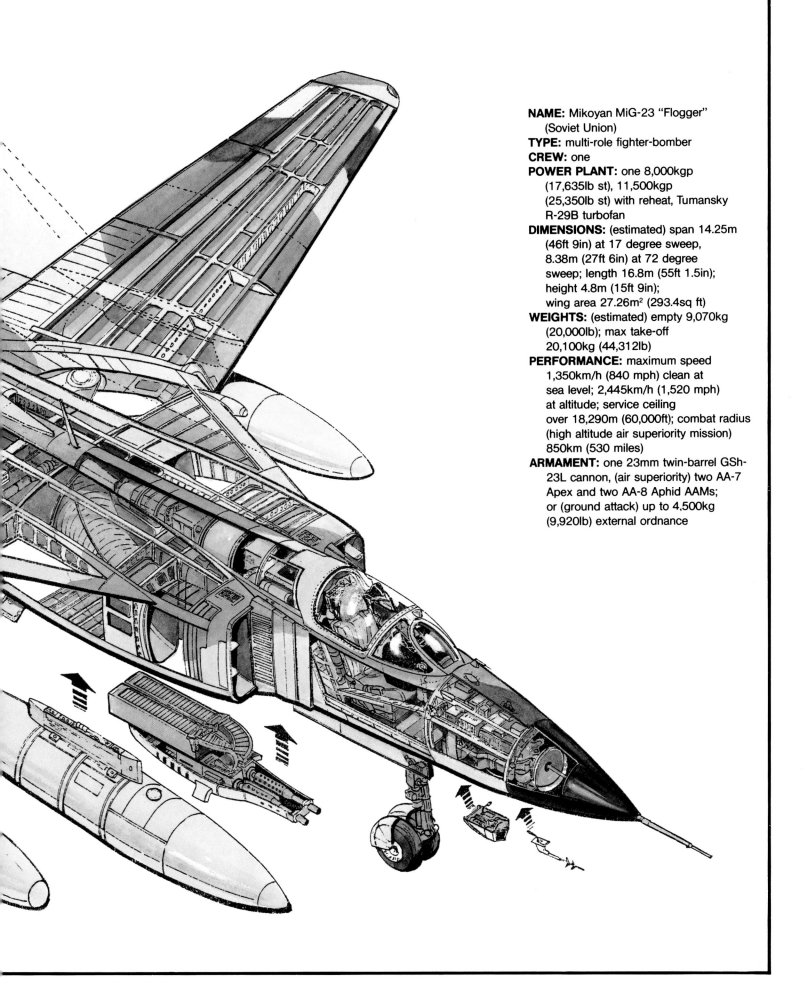

NAME: Mikoyan MiG-23 "Flogger"
(Soviet Union)
TYPE: multi-role fighter-bomber
CREW: one
POWER PLANT: one 8,000kgp
(17,635lb st), 11,500kgp
(25,350lb st) with reheat, Tumansky
R-29B turbofan
DIMENSIONS: (estimated) span 14.25m
(46ft 9in) at 17 degree sweep,
8.38m (27ft 6in) at 72 degree
sweep; length 16.8m (55ft 1.5in);
height 4.8m (15ft 9in);
wing area 27.26m² (293.4sq ft)
WEIGHTS: (estimated) empty 9,070kg
(20,000lb); max take-off
20,100kg (44,312lb)
PERFORMANCE: maximum speed
1,350km/h (840 mph) clean at
sea level; 2,445km/h (1,520 mph)
at altitude; service ceiling
over 18,290m (60,000ft); combat radius
(high altitude air superiority mission)
850km (530 miles)
ARMAMENT: one 23mm twin-barrel GSh-
23L cannon, (air superiority) two AA-7
Apex and two AA-8 Aphid AAMs;
or (ground attack) up to 4,500kg
(9,920lb) external ordnance

BAC/AEROSPATIALE CONCORDE (1969)

In the long term it is certain that supersonic air travel will become more general, but an unforeseen combination of factors – the most serious being a 3,000 per cent increase in the price of fuel – put it back. This hit the SST (supersonic transport) much harder than other airliners, because a much higher proportion of its operating expense goes on fuel. Fundamental factors stacked against the SST are that for any given passenger capacity it will be much more costly to build than a subsonic transport, will suffer much higher (at least double) the drag at cruising speed (needing engines twice as powerful) and will need a long runway. It is also likely to be noisier, and unless it has inordinate fuselage length cannot have such a spacious interior. One of the few plus factors is that, thanks to the intense compression of the air in the inlets, the efficiency of the engines is in fact greater than for any other normal type of engine (i.e., not nuclear) so far invented. This partly counteracts the need to have so much installed thrust.

Of course, like any supersonic aircraft, the engine inlets need to have variable area and profile, as do the nozzles. These are extras not found on ordinary airliners, and they introduce masses of complex electronics. Yet the Concorde, the only SST currently in operation, has proved to be one of the most reliable commercial transports ever. It was planned in the 1950s, and went ahead in November 1962 in a 50/50 programme between Britain and France. The design had to be repeatedly enlarged, to carry much more fuel to fly the North Atlantic with up to 130 passengers. Even so, only 16 production aircraft were built, which made the project very unrewarding financially. Despite the difficulties, one of the operators, British Airways, consistently makes a genuine operating profit, while achieving a utilization per aircraft much less than half the 3,500 hours per year assumed when Concorde was designed.

From the start Concorde had to be a new shape, a very slender tailless delta with a wing having a curved form called an ogive. Wing chord at the root is well over 90ft (27·7m), far greater than the span. The control surfaces comprise three elevons on each wing, used as ailerons (to control roll) and elevators (for pitch). These elevons are of honycomb-filled sandwich construction, and like the two-section rudder are of aluminium. Most other parts of the airframe get too hot at over Mach 2, and have to be of special alloys. Almost the whole wing is of RR.58 alloy (called AU2GN in France), much of the big engine nacelles are of titanium, and the sharp inlets are steel.

By chance, the British Olympus turbojet happened to be almost exactly right for Concorde, though it had to grow with the enlarged aircraft. Short afterburners at the rear blast through unique variable nozzles which not only match the jet to the Mach number but also squeeze the jet to an oval shape on takeoff to reduce noise and, on landing, swing right over to become thrust reversers. Almost all available wing com-

Air France (below) and British Airways (bottom) - the only two airlines to operate the Concorde.

partments form integral tanks with a capacity of 26,350 Imp gal (119,786 litres). The fuel is used to soak up the large amounts of unwanted heat generated in flight.

One of the many unusual features is the 'droop snoot' nose. To give the pilots a good view ahead on takeoff and landing the entire nose can be hydraulically hinged downwards, while a transparent vizor in front of the cockpit windscreen is retracted downwards. After takeoff the nose is raised and later, after climbing away, the vizor is also raised to give perfect streamlining.

Left:
Concorde number 3,
a French built
example, on a route
proving flight from
Paris to South
America.

Left:
The "droop snoot"
nose in the cruising
position, it is
lowered to give the
crew better visibility
for landing and
take-off.

BAC/AEROSPACE CONCORDE (1969)

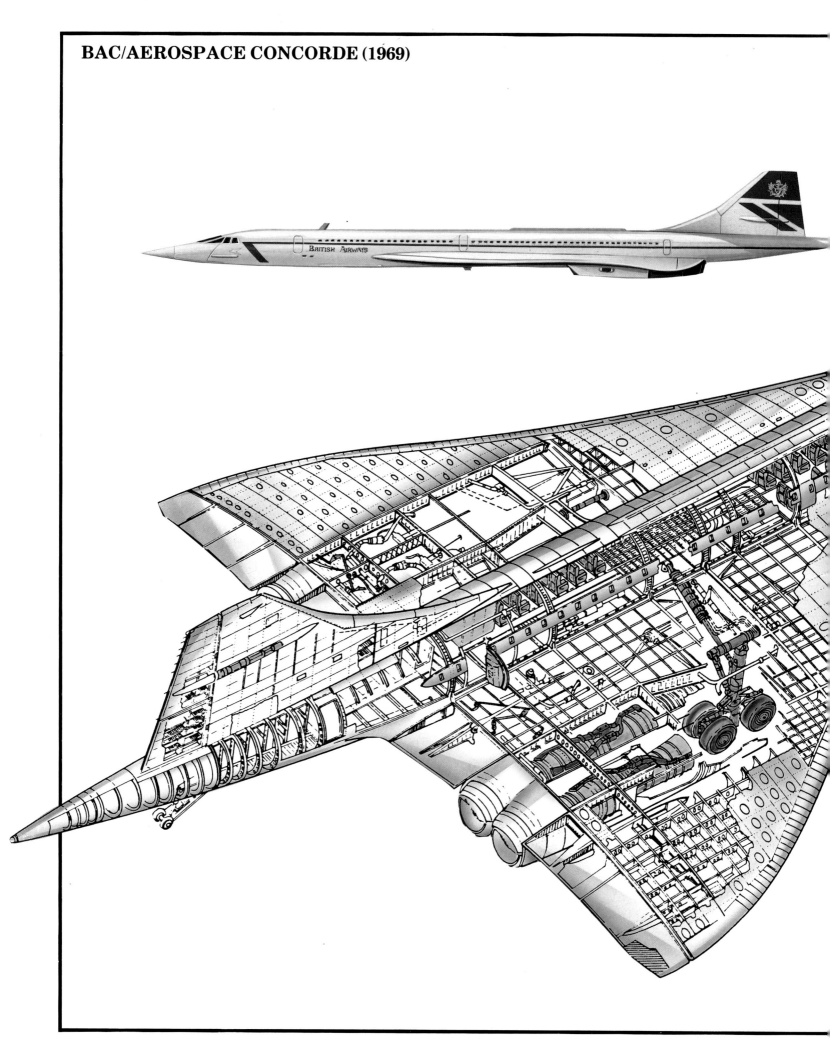

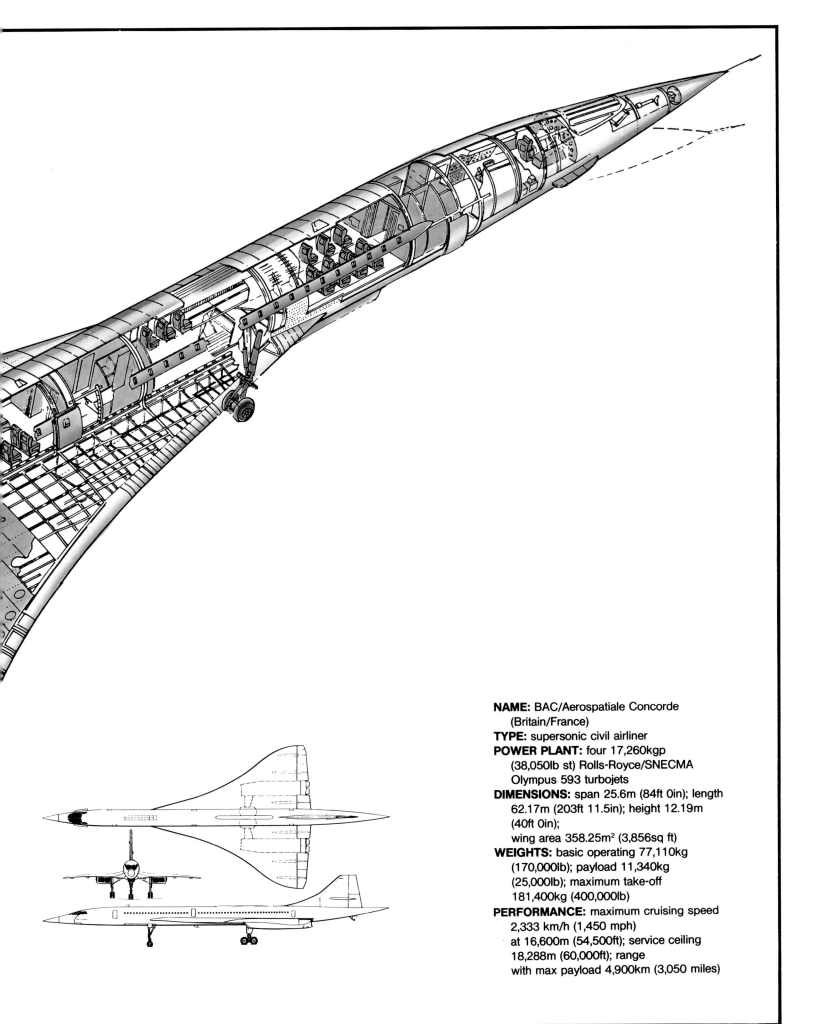

NAME: BAC/Aerospatiale Concorde
(Britain/France)
TYPE: supersonic civil airliner
POWER PLANT: four 17,260kgp
(38,050lb st) Rolls-Royce/SNECMA
Olympus 593 turbojets
DIMENSIONS: span 25.6m (84ft 0in); length
62.17m (203ft 11.5in); height 12.19m
(40ft 0in);
wing area 358.25m² (3,856sq ft)
WEIGHTS: basic operating 77,110kg
(170,000lb); payload 11,340kg
(25,000lb); maximum take-off
181,400kg (400,000lb)
PERFORMANCE: maximum cruising speed
2,333 km/h (1,450 mph)
at 16,600m (54,500ft); service ceiling
18,288m (60,000ft); range
with max payload 4,900km (3,050 miles)

BOEING 747 (1969)

In August 1965, the Boeing Commercial Airplane Company made a firm commitment to go ahead with a serious study of a new civilian aircraft. After talks with the world's major airlines, a basic concept was agreed upon that the aircraft would weigh at least 700,000lb (317,520kg) and be capable of transporting twice the payload of any airliner then in service.

Boeing finally came up with a completely new design. The airframe would have a fuselage with a nose to tail length of 231ft 4in (70.51m), a circular cross-section 19ft 5in (5.81m) wide, and a height for the main cabin of 8ft 4in (2.45m). There was an upper deck for the main compartment and a forward lounge section with a spiral staircase leading to this area. The final decision to proceed with the production of a prototype 747 was taken at a meeting of the Boeing Board of Directors in March 1966.

At this time, there was one important factor that stood out most clearly in everyone's minds: there were no orders for the aircraft despite the fact that many airlines had been involved in the design of the plane. However, this was to change a month later when Pan American Airways announced an order for 25 of the gigantic craft of which two were to delivered in an all-cargo configuration. The order was valued at $525,000,000 and was, at the time, the largest single order for one aircraft type ever received in the history of aviation. By July 1966, orders had been received from BOAC, Japan Air Lines, Lufthansa and TWA.

Production was soon underway and the first 747-100 was rolled out on 30 September 1968 at the company's new factory at Everett. Incred-

A size comparison can be drawn between the standard 747 and the SP or Special Performance variant.

ibly, only 30 months had passed since the whole project was started. The prototype took to the air for its inaugural flight on 9 February 1969. The first 747 to be delivered was to Pan American World Airways, the launch customer. Airframe number six (N733PA) landed at Kennedy International Airport, New York on 13 December 1969.

Even before the first flight, Boeing had announced plans at the end of 1968 to build the 747B (later to become the 200 series). It was to be a longer-range aircraft with still more power and an increased take-off weight of 775,000lb (351,540kg). The first example made its inaugural flight on 11 October 1970, and this type eventually replaced the Series 100 as the standard production aircraft.

Boeing released details of a new, extended life 747 shortly after the first 747B flew which was aimed at the high-capacity domestic market of Japan. The potential sales market for this 747SR (Short Range) was very good. Pratt and Whitney engines were used, and the aircraft was designed around the idea that its take-off weight would be restricted to under 600,000lb (272,160kg). The need for less fuel per take-off was offset by the need for a higher number of take-offs and landings per flight hour. Therefore certain vital areas of the airframe were strengthened to give a much improved resistance to fatigue.

Five 747 models were available by the end of 1972: the SR; the 747-100 (the original passenger variant); the Series 200 (the new standard aircraft); the 747-200F, which was the dedicated freight version; and the 747-200C, which was a convertible passenger and cargo aircraft.

In August 1973, Boeing announced a new

The 747 production line at the Boeing Plant at Everett, near Seattle in Washington State. The rudder of the main aircraft in the picture, line number 672, already carries the British Airways logo.

addition to the '747 family'. The 747SP (Special Performance) had a very long range although the fuselage was 48ft (14,63m) smaller than the 747-100. The passenger capacity was lower, but the wing and inertial fuel tanks were almost identical to the standard type. Horizontal and vertical tails were enlarged to compensate for the shorter lever arm. The prototype's inaugural flight was on 4 July 1975, and full certification was given on 4 February 1976. The first aircraft was ordered by South African Airlines and demonstrated the aircraft's capabilities by flying the 10,290 miles (16,560km) from Paine Field, Washington to Capetown, South Africa non-stop. The aircraft landed with well over two hours of fuel remaining.

Various military variants of the 747 have been proposed but most have never been taken up. One variant that Boeing did sell to the United States Air Force was the E4A/B Advanced Airborne National Command Post programme. These aircraft are based on specially modified 747-200B airframes, and are capable of flying continuously for up to 72 hours in the most

menacing national emergencies.

An unusual role for the 747 came when NASA purchased a greatly modified ex-American Airlines Series 100 in 1974 to give a 'piggy back' to the prototype Space Shuttle.

On 12 June 1980 Boeing announced its intentions to 'stretch' its 747. The Series 300 would accommodate more than 500 passengers, and be able to fly 6,500 miles (10,463km) non-stop. An extended upper deck on a strengthened fuselage and more fuel efficient engines were also features. Swissair became the launch customer for the Series 300, and the prototype made its inaugural flight in October 1982. Swissair received the first aircraft on 28 March 1983.

In May 1985, Boeing announced the 747-400. This variant has improved fuel efficient engines, a modern two-crew digital flight deck, a greater variety of interior configurations, and increased range. This Series 400 has an increased wingspan as well as a 6ft (1.83 metre) winglet added to each wing. Its inaugural flight was on 29 April 1988, and deliveries began at the end of the year.

BOEING 747 (1969)

NAME: Boeing 747 (USA)

TYPE: civil airliner

POWER PLANT: (747-200) four 19,730kgp (43,500lb st)
Pratt & Whitney JT9D-3 turbofans

DIMENSIONS: span 59.64m (195ft 8in); length 70.51m
(231ft 4in); height 19.33m (63ft 5in); wing area 511m²
(5,500sq ft)

WEIGHTS: basic operating 166,876kg (367,900lb); maximum
payload 71,940kg (158,600lb); maximum take-off
356,070kg (785,000lb)

PERFORMANCE: maximum speed 978 km/h (608 mph) at
9,150m (30,000ft); service ceiling 13,705m (45,000ft);
range (max fuel) 11,410km (7,090 miles), (max payload)
8,023km (4,985 miles)

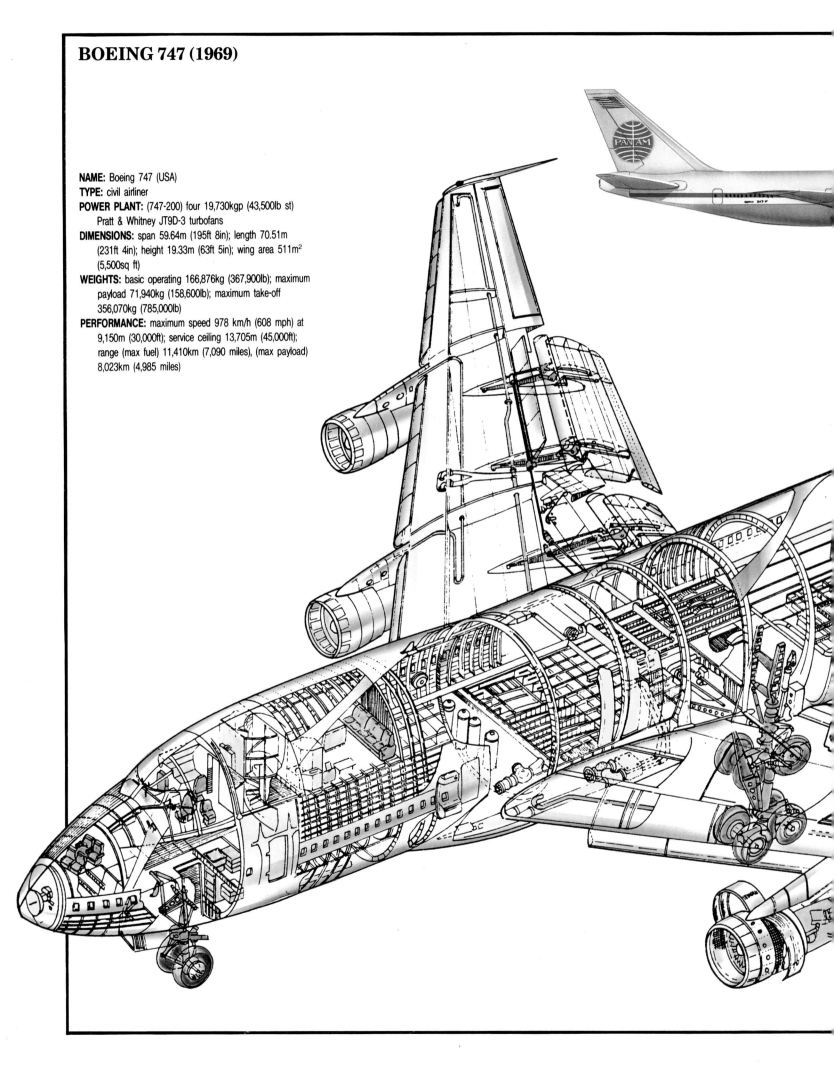

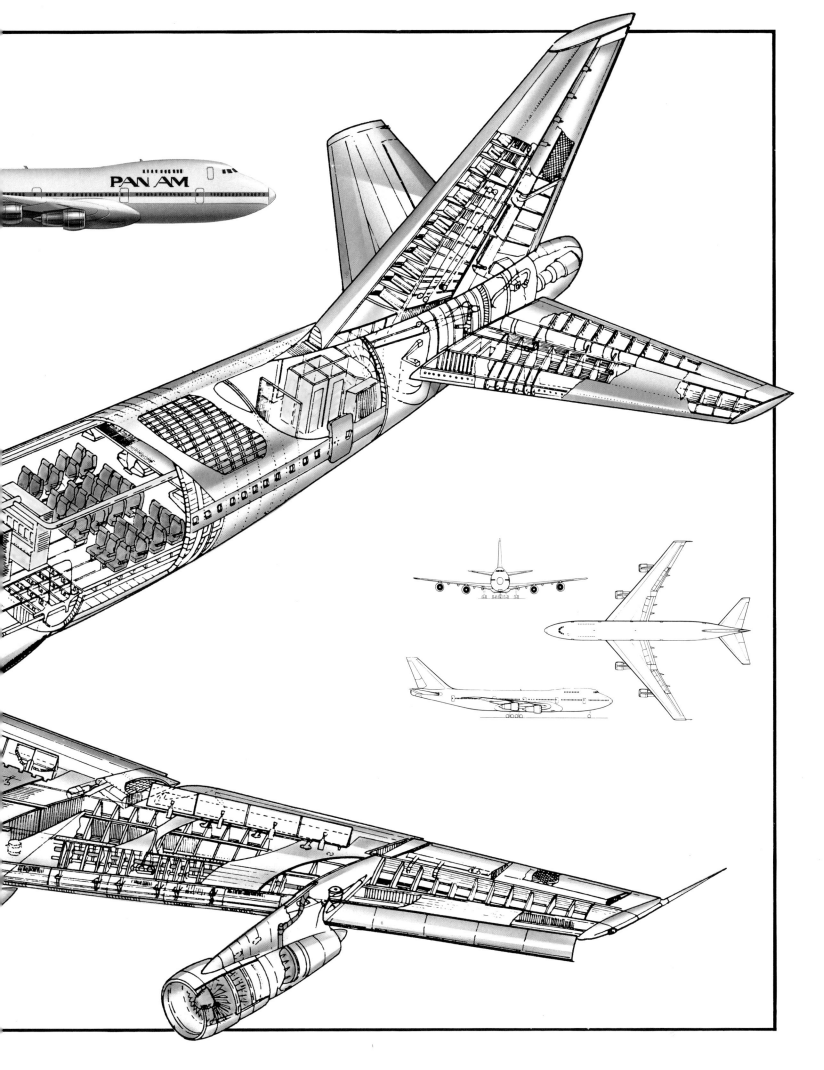

FAIRCHILD REPUBLIC A-10A THUNDER-BOLT II (1972)

During World War II, the Soviet Union built 36,163 Il-2 Stormoviks, a greater number than for any other aircraft type. Today's A-10A is its exact counterpart, an aircraft so armoured as to be capable of surviving over a hostile force, and so heavily armed as to have the capability of knocking out the heaviest battle tanks. Both aircraft suffered the disadvantage of being rather slow and unwieldy; both ran a fair risk of being shot down, and the A-10 has already demonstrated that it can suffer appreciable attrition merely by hitting the ground during its extremely low-level operations. Today, survival means not only armour but also getting 'down among the weeds', and flying manually within a few feet of the ground has always been hazardous.

In 1967 the USAF issued a requirement for an 'AX', a close-support aircraft. Such a job had previously been done by ordinary fighter and attack aircraft, but the AX was to be based up with the forward troops, operating from dirt strips, and to carry a devastating gun, more powerful than any previously seen, to punch through tank armour. It was to be able to fly home after taking terrific punishment from weapons up to 23mm calibre, and it was to be able to carry massive loads of attack weapons and still use short airstrips. Beating the rival A-9A, the A-10A flew on 10 May 1972, and 713 production Thunderbolt IIs were delivered.

A single-seater, it was deliberately made 'austere' in equipment, and it has never had full night or adverse-weather capability despite the fact that its major scene of operations would probably be Europe. The entire cockpit is protected by a 'bathtub' of titanium armour. Most of the front fuselage is occupied by the mighty

Below:
A heavily armed
A-10 waits on an
airfield. This aircraft
can carry up to
7,250kg (16,000lb)
in external ordnance.

GAU-8/A gun and its drum of 1,174 enormous rounds of ammunition, far more powerful than ordinary ammunition of 30mm calibre, the armour-piercing projectiles having dense cores of depleted uranium. Under the wings and fuselage are 11 pylons for up to 16,000lb (7,258kg) of weapons or tanks, including almost all types of tactical bomb, missile, cluster dispenser and EW (electronic-warfare) equipment.

The cool-jet turbofan engines were placed at the back so that residual jet heat might be largely shielded from the ground by the wings and tail, and sustained flight is possible with one pod shot completely away. Likewise the twin-finned tail can control the aircraft with either half shot off. All fuel tanks are protected against fire or explosion, and if the main landing gears cannot be extended a landing can be made without serious damage on the partly projecting wheels. The airframe is conventional all-metal stressed skin, but particularly robust and with everything possible duplicated, so that if No 1 is shot through there is always a No 2 still working.

Provision is made for an inflight-refuelling receptacle able to accept either a tanker boom or a clip-on probe. Equipment for navigation and communication is excellent, an inertial navigation system being retrofitted in all A-10As and with secure voice radio contact possible with friendly ground troops. Under the nose is carried a Pave Penny laser designator for guiding 'smart' weapons, but the vital radars, FLIR (forward-looking infra-red) and similar sensors needed for round-the-clock operation have not been provided for. It is hoped this omission will be rectified by adding either one or two LAN-TIRN (low-altitude navigation targeting infra-red for night) pods, such as are also being added to the F-16 fighter described later.

Left:
A flight of A-10A
Thunderbolt II
ground attack
aircraft.

Bottom:
An A-10 executes a
tight banking turn.

NAME: Fairchild Republic A-10A
    Thunderbolt II (USA)
TYPE: close air support
CREW: one
POWER PLANT: two 4,112kgp
    (9,065lb st) General Electric
    TF34-GE-100 turbofans
DIMENSIONS: span 17.53m
    (57ft 6in);
    length 16.25m (53ft 4in);
    height 4.47m (14ft 8in);
    wing area 47.01m² (506sq ft)
WEIGHTS: empty 9,006kg
    (19,856lb);
    loaded 22,221kg (46,786lb)
PERFORMANCE: maximum speed
    697 km/h (433 mph)
    at sea level; service ceiling
    10,575m (34,700ft);
    typical combat radius with
    bomb load 463km (288 miles)
ARMAMENT: one 30mm seven-
    barrel GAU-8 rotary cannon;
    up to a maximum of 7,250kg
    (16,000lb) external ordnance

AIRBUS A300B (1972)

One of the most amazing demonstrations of the world airline industry's inability to believe its own assessments occurred when Airbus Industrie was formed in 1970. Existence of giant turbofan engines, originally created for American 'widebody' transports, made it possible to extend the new technology down the range scale to the true mass market, at sectors below 1,000 miles (1,600km) where many millions travel each week. A short-haul widebody would enable the traffic to be carried in greater comfort, with fewer aircraft movements and with less than 1 per cent as much noise. The first A300B flew on 28 October 1972 and showed itself to be a superb aircraft. But instead of forming a queue, the customers just kept buying noisy fuel-hungry narrow-body jets. Three years after the first flight, and over a year after first service by Air France, total sales were just 21.

Even as late as 1979, American rivals were still keeping customers away by explaining that the Airbus was 'designed by a committee, a useless machine, sold only with government subsidies'. Gradually the airlines realised what was obvious from the start: the A300B was by a colossal margin the best short-haul mass-carrier of people and cargo in the world. Another 200 sales came with a rush, the smaller A310 was launched and by 1985 orders and options topped 500. Boeing has now produced an exact rival in the 767, but this emerged into a world in which, for the first time since 1945, most customers were already flying the non-American product.

The A300B and its partner A310 have beautifully streamlined fuselages with a circular section of 18ft 6in (5·64m) diameter. Above the floor it is possible to seat passengers nine-abreast in great comfort, or seven-abreast in luxury, with two aisles for easy movement of people and service carts. Under the floor are holds tailored to the same standard container for cargo and baggage as carried by the other wide-bodies (the 767 cannot carry these), and it is possible to make a healthy profit without any passengers! Special cargo versions carry cargo above the floor as well, loaded via giant doors and positioned by computer control.

At the front is the most modern airline cockpit now flying, with coloured TV-type displays instead of circular instruments, and configured for just two pilots (no radio officer, navigator or engineer). Automatic systems monitor every part of the aircraft, telling the pilots of any malfunction (an extremely rare occurrence) and automatically taking corrective action. At first some people doubted the wisdom of carrying up to 345 people on just two engines. In practice the Airbus has the best safety record of any airliner in history. Several million hours have been flown with not one accident.

French cabin staff tend to tell passengers they are in a French aeroplane, but in fact it is the result of collaboration in many countries. The superb main wing box, with deep 'supercritical' section and full of fuel, is made at Chester, England. The leading slats and trailing flaps come from Amsterdam but are attached to Britain's wing in Hamburg. Complete wings then fly to Toulouse, France, where they are fixed to fuselage sections made in Germany and a nose made in Toulouse. Spain supplies the tailplane and doors. The USA supplies the mighty engines, though with much European participation. Right in the tail is an APU (auxiliary power unit) from Arizona. Furnishings and equipment come from all the chief Western manufacturing nations, but everything fits – often with microscopic precision.

Below:
An Eastern Airlines Airbus accelerates down the runway.

NAME: Airbus A300
(International Consortium -
Britain, France, Germany
and Spain)

TYPE: medium-haul civil airliner

POWER PLANT: (A300-600) two
25,400 kgp (56,000lb st)
Pratt & Whitney JT9D-7R4H1
or General Electric
CF6-80C2 turbofans

DIMENSIONS: span 44.84m
(147ft 1.25in); length 54.08m
(177ft 5in);
height 16.53m (54ft 3in);
wing area 260m² (2,799sq ft)

WEIGHTS: empty 87,728kg
(193,410lb);
maximum take-off 165,000kg
(363,760lb)

PERFORMANCE:
maximum cruise speed
891km/h (518 mph); range
maximum payload
5,200km (3,430 miles)

Right:
Thai Airways
International also
use the Airbus.

Below:
A lateral view of an
Eastern Airlines
Airbus.

McDONNELL DOUGLAS F/A-18 HORNET (1974)

The history of the F/A-18 Hornet is unique. In 1974 Northrop flew two YF-17 lightweight fighters to compete against the YF-16. The YF-17 was adopted by the US Navy as the basis for an NACF (Navy air-combat fighter), lighter and cheaper than the F-14, but it had to be developed with a partner, McDonnell Douglas. Northrop tried to market a simpler land-based F-18L but without success, and after a giant lawsuit it was accepted that the Hornet had become a McDonnell Douglas product! Northrop is associate contractor responsible for the centre and rear fuselage sections.

Today's Hornet is much heavier than the YF-17. It has a wider fuselage, housing twice as much fuel, new turbofan engines, a much bigger and stronger landing gear, a larger wing, bigger nose with Hughes APG-65 multimode radar and a totally new cockpit which has become the model for all subsequent Western fighters. All traditional instruments have been replaced by three giant square MFD's (multifunction displays) like colour TVs, on which the pilot, by pressing 'menu buttons', can call up any information, numbers, pictures, maps or target displays he needs. Like the F-16, the Hotas (hands on throttle and stick) enable the pilot to do everything necessary in combat without letting go of these two items, and his wide-angle HUD (head-up display) gives a fantastic picture of the scene ahead plus all necessary steering or shooting information.

Structurally the Hornet is conventional, with a mix of light alloy, graphite/epoxy (carbon fibre), steel and titanium. The giant canopy is in two parts, the forward section hinging up for access behind the cockpit panel. The thin unswept wing has powerful variable-camber leading and trailing flaps which, like the large tailerons (tailplane/ailerons, used for roll control

NAME: McDonnell Douglas F/A-18 Hornet (USA)

TYPE: fighter

CREW: one

POWER PLANT: Two 4,810kgp (10,600lb st) dry and 7,167kgp (15,800lb st) reheat General Electric F404-GE-400 turbofans

DIMENSIONS: span 11.43m (31ft 6in); length 17.07m (56ft 0in); height 4.67m (15ft 4in); wing area 36.79m² (396sq ft)

WEIGHTS: empty 12,700kg (28,000lb); loaded 25,400kg (56,000lb)

PERFORMANCE: maximum speed 1,915 km/h (1,190 mph); service ceiling 19,200m (63,000ft); range 770km (480 miles)

ARMAMENT: one 20mm M-61A-1 rotary cannon and (air to air) two AIM-7E/F Sparrow and two AIM-9G/H Sidewinder AAMs, or (attack) up to 7,711kg (17,000lb) of ordnance

A naval Hornet drops a string of mark 83 bombs.

as well as pitch), are of honeycomb sandwich construction. Enormous wing root strakes projecting past the cockpit give good control at previously impossible angles approaching 90°, during which the twin outward-canted vertical tails really pay off. At takeoff the rudders are both automatically turned inward to push down the tail and raise the nose. Between them is the giant airbrake.

The outer wings fold for carrier operations, and the whole fixed wing box inboard forms an integral tank which, with the fuselage cells, provides for 11,000lb (4,990kg) of internal fuel. In the nose is a neat retractable inflight-refuelling probe, and three 275 Imp gal (1,249 litre) drop tanks can be carried. The F404 engines, which have proved most satisfactory, are fed by plain inlets because, like the F-16 but unlike the Mirage 2000, extreme Mach numbers were considered of little importance. The landing gear, folding into the marvellously-engineered fuselage, is probably the strongest of its size ever made. The nose unit incorporates the catapult towbar, which would fling the aircraft off the deck at 200 knots even if the wheelbrakes were clamped on! A remarkable achievement is the outstanding reliability of the delicate radar immediately under the muzzle of the gun. The gun and ammunition can be replaced in the RF-18 by a multisensor reconnaissance package which gives a bulged underside to the nose. Up to 17,000lb (7,711kg) of weapons can be carried, including large radar-guided Sparrow air-to-air missiles attached in low-drag locations beside the inlet ducts. Like most modern fighters, the Hornet has a computer-controlled digital FBW (fly-by-wire) flight control system which, together with the comprehensive sensors and other aids, makes the Hornet the most versatile and formidable single-seat aircraft (in the Western World at least).

GENERAL DYNAMICS F-16 FIGHTING FALCON (1974)

Since 1916 there has always been one type of fighter that was generally regarded as the world's best, or most exciting. Since the F-16 matured in the late 1970s, it has occupied this niche, despite plenty of competition of which the Mig-29 is certainly the toughest. Indeed, the Indian Air Force is confident its new Mig-29s will outfight the F-16s of neighbouring Pakistan. Be that as it may, the F-16 turned out to be a very much better multirole warplane than anyone except its designers expected it to be. Planned as a mere technology demonstrator to investigate whether a fighter much lighter and cheaper than the sacrosanct F-15 could be of any value, it matured as a superlative air-combat aircraft which, especially in updated F-16C form, has outstanding capability in the air-to-ground mission.

GD Fort Worth cleverly designed the F-16 around the same F100 engine as used in the F-15 (but using only one instead of two). This greatly eased its adoption by the US Air Force, reduced the price of F100 engines and almost eliminated powerplant problems. But, for various reasons, future F-16s are now being bought with the more powerful General Electric F110 engine, which, especially when carrying a heavy bombload, gives higher performance. The engine is fed via a plain inlet just ahead of the nosewheel; no attempt was made to attain the highest possible Mach number and there was no justification in fitting expensive variable geometry.

Likewise, the wings have a fixed sweep angle (Fort Worth having previously built the variable-geometry F-111), but a flight-control computer automatically varies the camber of the wing by adjusting the angles of the leading-edge manoeuvre flaps and the trailing-edge flaperons (which serve as flaps and ailerons). All these are

An F-16 Fighting Falcon. This lightweight fighter can perform other roles and is in service with many air forces.

light-alloy honeycomb sandwich structures. The main wing has 11 spars but only five ribs, one-piece upper and lower machined skins, and is 'blended' into the fuselage in smooth curves which gives more fuel volume and reduced weight. The blend fairing on the left side houses the single gun. Almost the whole structure of the tail surfaces is graphite/epoxy (carbon fibre) composite, which gives enormous strength for weights less than half that of aluminium. Aft of the wing on each side are long box fairings which carry the tailplanes and whose rear section splits open to form the airbrakes. Ahead of the wing root is a very sharply-swept vortex-control extension running as far forward as the front of the cockpit, which improves stability and lift at extreme nose-up angles of attack.

These sharp strakes help the F-16 to be probably the most manoeuvrable fighter in the Western world at present. The pilot lies backwards in a reclining ejection seat under a vast frameless canopy of moulded polycarbonate material, with a perfect view in all directions except directly down to the rear. His left hand rests on the throttle and his right forearm lies along the right side of the cockpit on a padded rest, his hand holding the small controller. This does not move significantly but senses any force imparted to it, and via an electronic FBW (fly-by-wire) system the aircraft responds almost before the pilot has decided what manoeuvre to make. Thanks to the tremendous engine thrust, the F-16 can make a sustained turn at 9g, a brutal figure which only a very fit pilot can withstand. Despite this, it can carry tremendous external loads of missiles or bombs, and (especially with LANTIRN pods and other updates) can deliver them with pinpoint accuracy at night or in adverse weather. Manufactured in large numbers the F-16 is a worldwide best-seller.

GENERAL DYNAMICS F-16 FIGHTING FALCON (1974)

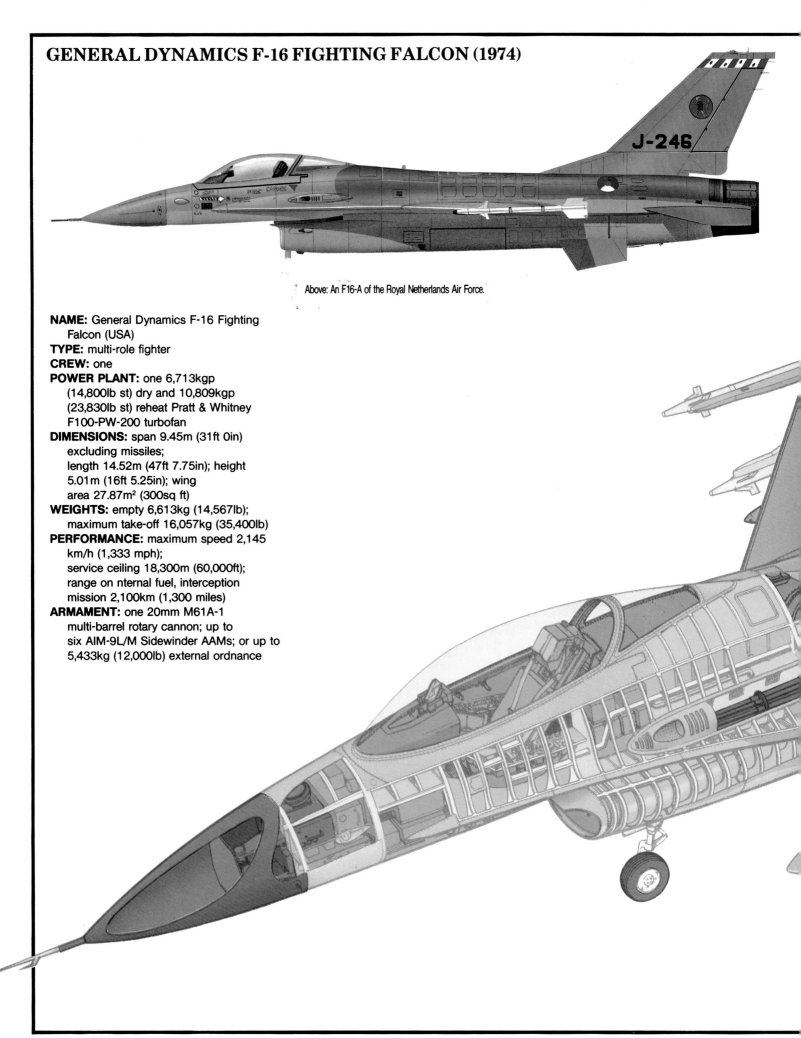

Above: An F16-A of the Royal Netherlands Air Force.

NAME: General Dynamics F-16 Fighting
   Falcon (USA)
TYPE: multi-role fighter
CREW: one
POWER PLANT: one 6,713kgp
   (14,800lb st) dry and 10,809kgp
   (23,830lb st) reheat Pratt & Whitney
   F100-PW-200 turbofan
DIMENSIONS: span 9.45m (31ft 0in)
   excluding missiles;
   length 14.52m (47ft 7.75in); height
   5.01m (16ft 5.25in); wing
   area 27.87m² (300sq ft)
WEIGHTS: empty 6,613kg (14,567lb);
   maximum take-off 16,057kg (35,400lb)
PERFORMANCE: maximum speed 2,145
   km/h (1,333 mph);
   service ceiling 18,300m (60,000ft);
   range on nternal fuel, interception
   mission 2,100km (1,300 miles)
ARMAMENT: one 20mm M61A-1
   multi-barrel rotary cannon; up to
   six AIM-9L/M Sidewinder AAMs; or up to
   5,433kg (12,000lb) external ordnance

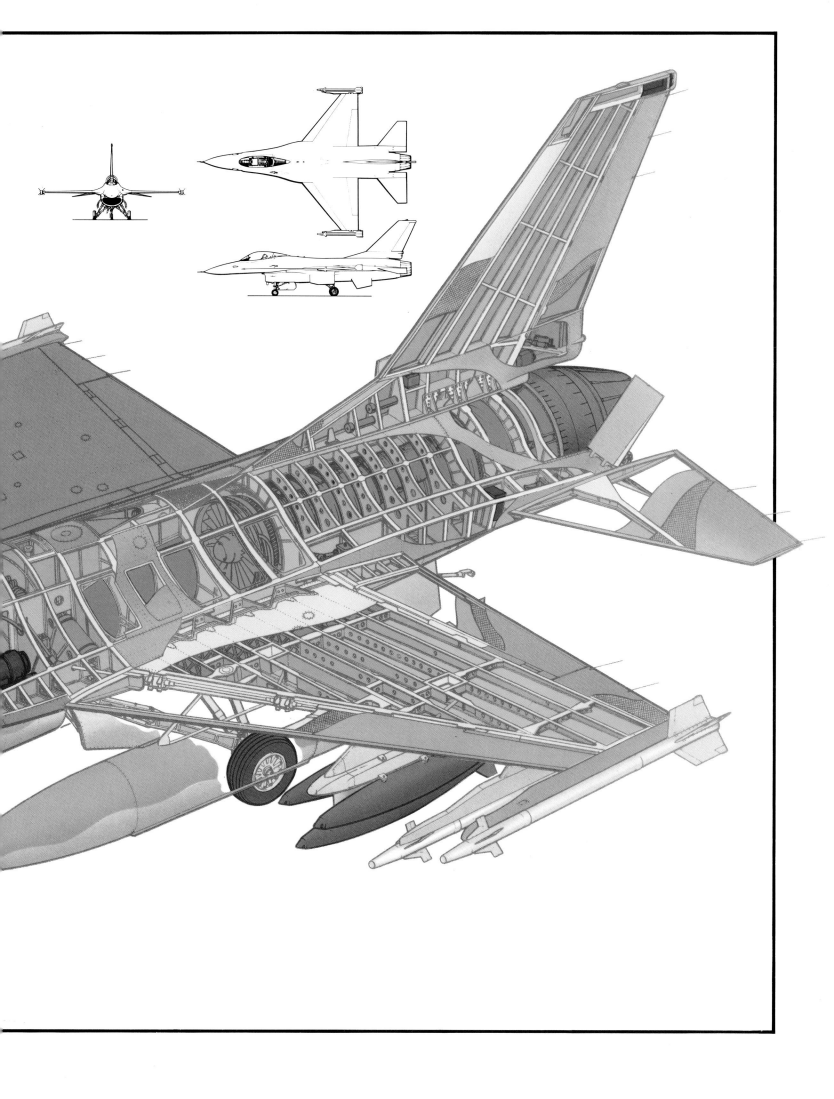

BRITISH AEROSPACE HARRIER (1966) AND SEA HARRIER (1978)

Procurement of combat aircraft is dictated far more by fashion than by common sense or urgent need. In the mid-1950s the NATO nations, aware of the vulnerability of their airfields, planned tactical aircraft that could operate from any reasonably level strip of ground. In the early 1960s jet-lift VTOL (vertical takeoff and landing) was all the rage, opening the way to true dispersal and flexible operation of airpower; but everything was cancelled. Perhaps because the successful jet-lift technology was British, the Americans – who dictate the fashion – decreed that henceforth all tactical airpower should be incapable of operating except from good runways. Alone, Britain pressed on with the Harrier. Today, almost frantic effort is being applied to nonsensical schemes aimed at keeping aircraft in operation after their runways have been blasted, overlooking the fact that neither the aircraft nor their pilots would survive anyway.

The reason for the 25 years of disinterest in jet-lift aircraft is that they suffer supposed 'penalties' of a few percentage points in comparison with machines which blast off down a mile of concrete. In fact in almost all real-life situations it is the long-runway aircraft which suffer the penalties, because they have to fly from bases which are far from the battlefront. In contrast, the Harriers and Sea Harriers in the Falklands campaign actually operated from a small flat area almost beside the forward troops, and where wooded cover is available they would be very hard to find. It all stems from the unique Rolls-Royce Pegasus engine, basically a conventional turbofan but one whose output issues from four nozzles, two at the front for fan air and two at the rear for hot jet gas. The four nozzles can be rotated together to point downwards, to lift the aircraft vertically, to the rear to propel it at the speed of sound, or diagonally forwards to slow it violently in the air. Viffing (from VIFF, vectoring in forward flight) enables these nimble aircraft to make previously impossible flight manoeuvres. Coupled with their small size, odd shape and smokeless engine this makes all Harriers tough opponents in a dogfight.

Harriers are actually used in the STOVL mode, of short takeoff (with a heavy weapon load) and vertical landing. They burn less than half as much fuel as any comparable long-runway aircraft on a similar mission, and the margin goes up in bad weather in which the Harrier can 'stop and then land, instead of landing and then hoping to stop'. All have all-metal airframes (except for the new joint BAe/McDonnell Douglas Harrier II which has a carbon fibre wing), the overall size being small and compact. Tandem landing gears are used, with small outriggers near the wingtips. The wing is one piece, dropped on the fuselage from above, and all movable surfaces are bonded honeycomb sandwich structures for lightness and rigidity. All flight controls are fully powered, and the control circuits also operate special heat-resistant valves at the nose, tail and wingtips. As the engine nozzes gradually rotate down

Below:
BAe's Harrier T52 demonstrating the skyhook principle. This idea enables a robot arm with a space stabilized head, which could be fitted to a small ship, to capture a hovering Sea Harrier.

to the lift position, as speed dies away towards the hover, valves progressively open to supply engine bleed air to these reaction-control jets. At the hover, when conventional controls are useless, full control is exercised by the supersonic air jets from the reaction-control nozzles.

Under the belly are two 30mm guns, and up to 8,000lb (3,628kg) of weapons (including the guns) can be carried on pylons under the fuselage and wings. Compared with the Harrier, the Sea Harrier has a larger nose with radar, a raised cockpit, and equipment intended for air combat as a primary role. All Harriers are receiving various updates, future Sea Harrier rework being extensive.

Right:
A Sea Harrier FRS.1
accelerates along the
deck of HMS
Hermes.

Below:
Two FRS.1s - the
nearest armed with
four sidewinder
AIM- 9Ls and two
30mm Aden guns in
the pods under the
fuselage. It also
carries two 190
gallon drop tanks.

SEA HARRIER FRS Mk.1 (1979)

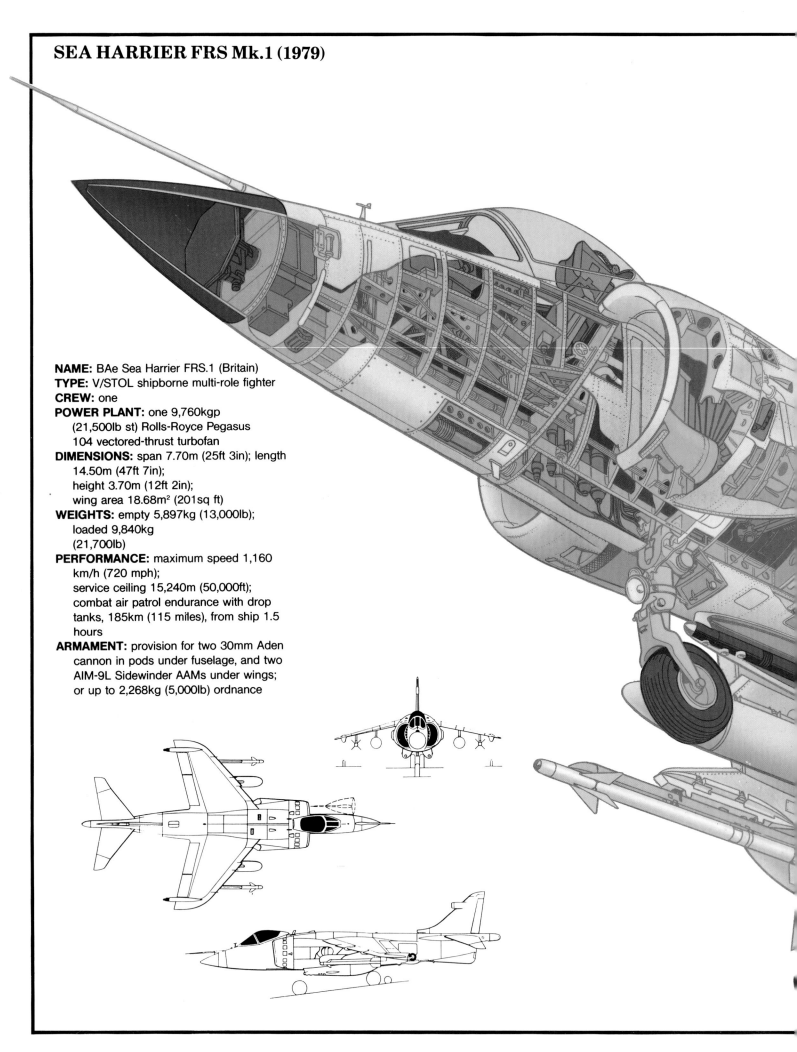

NAME: BAe Sea Harrier FRS.1 (Britain)
TYPE: V/STOL shipborne multi-role fighter
CREW: one
POWER PLANT: one 9,760kgp
(21,500lb st) Rolls-Royce Pegasus
104 vectored-thrust turbofan
DIMENSIONS: span 7.70m (25ft 3in); length
14.50m (47ft 7in);
height 3.70m (12ft 2in);
wing area 18.68m² (201sq ft)
WEIGHTS: empty 5,897kg (13,000lb);
loaded 9,840kg
(21,700lb)
PERFORMANCE: maximum speed 1,160
km/h (720 mph);
service ceiling 15,240m (50,000ft);
combat air patrol endurance with drop
tanks, 185km (115 miles), from ship 1.5
hours
ARMAMENT: provision for two 30mm Aden
cannon in pods under fuselage, and two
AIM-9L Sidewinder AAMs under wings;
or up to 2,268kg (5,000lb) ordnance

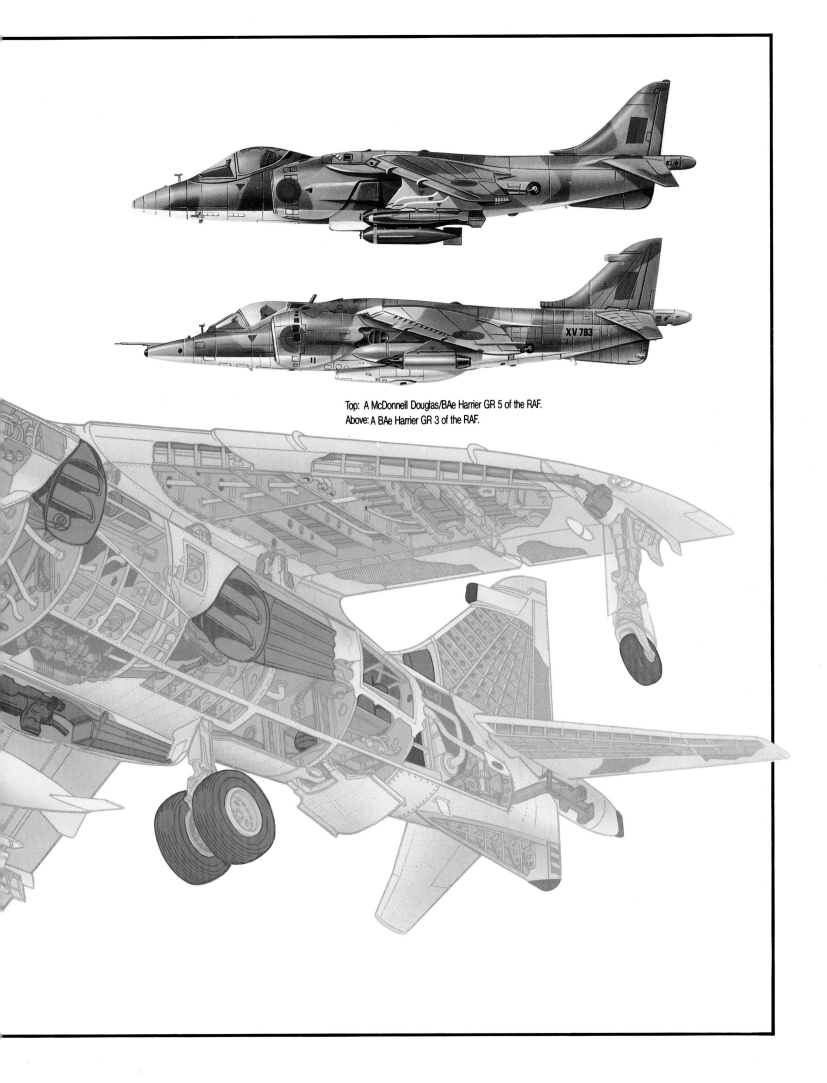

Top: A McDonnell Douglas/BAe Harrier GR 5 of the RAF.
Above: A BAe Harrier GR 3 of the RAF.

GRUMMAN X-29A (1984)

On 22 December 1981, Grumman received an $80 million contract from the Defense Advanced Research Projects Agency to design, build and test two forward swept-wing aircraft that were to be designated the X-29. To cut costs, the forward fuselage was taken from a Northrop F-5 light fighter, the main gears from an F-16, and many others were purchased 'ready-made'.

The amazing wing was totally unique: swept forward on a quarter-chord line at nearly 34 degrees; yet it was very thin, stiff and strong, with carbon fibres arranged in different directions so that no catastrophic divergence could occur. Further new features included the canard foreplanes, the long rear inbound section of each wing, which terminated with a trailing-edge flap that was somewhat like an elevator.

The most interesting feature of all is a fast-acting computerized control section which (over 40 times a second) corrects the flight of what is basically a very highly unstable aircraft. Computer models and analyses reduced the wind-tunnel testing on the X-29 by over 10 per cent by comparison to other aircraft. A radio-controlled scale model was built and flown in 1977, and this confirmed the computer results. As the programme quickly progressed, a one-eighth scale model was tested in a wind-tunnel subsonically, transonically and supersonically at angles of attack which were as high as 90 degrees. Data on the model's force, movement and pressure were acquired from a half-scale model.

Various structural element tests were done to test materials and structural combinations during the development of the X-29. The flight vehicle was then subjected to full-scale testing.

The first of two X-29s undergoing system testing at Grumman's Bethpage Plant, prior to ground and then flight testing.

The aircraft was installed in a test fixture and simulated aerodynamic loads were imposed on the wings, fuselage and control surfaces by using hydraulic jacks. These tests confirmed that all structural design strength and aeroelastic tailoring characteristics of the X-29 were met, and in some cases exceeded.

Next followed tests on the aircraft itself as well as on a laboratory model that was housed in Grumman's establishment in New York. All of the X-29's digital and analog flight control systems underwent the most extensive testing. Simulators allowed the pilots to experience real flight conditions. A hybrid simulation computer used a mathematical model of the aircraft's flight control system.

Another development aid was the total in-flight simulator. Full flight controls of the X-29 were fitted into a separate cockpit which extended from the nose of a United States Air Force C-131B aircraft. With the assistance of this simulator, pilots were able to gain the experience of hands-on control responses they so desperately needed, using the fly-by-wire control systems.

Other ground tests were performed, including the testing on the X-29's actuators and other components. All of these tests were monitored by the aircraft's hydraulic test stand. By this time, the X-29 was one of the most thoroughly tested aircraft before it had even left the ground! Few inaugural flights have been awaited with such eagerness as that of the radical and potentially testing X-29 (designated the 82-0003).

On 14 December 1984, Grumman's chief test pilot, Charles A, 'Chuck' Sewell, made the aircraft's inaugural flight at NASA's Dryden Research Center in California. Everything went better than expected and before long other pilots were taking the X-29 into the air. By now the aircraft was being tested to its limits by being made to fly at supersonic speeds. In 1988 the second prototype (82-0049) made its debut.

Grumman's Forward Swept Wing, Advanced Technology Demonstrator: the X-29. This development project was funded by DARPA (Defense Advanced Research Projects Agency), administered by the US Air Force, with flight testing controlled by NASA.

GRUMMAN X-29A (1984)

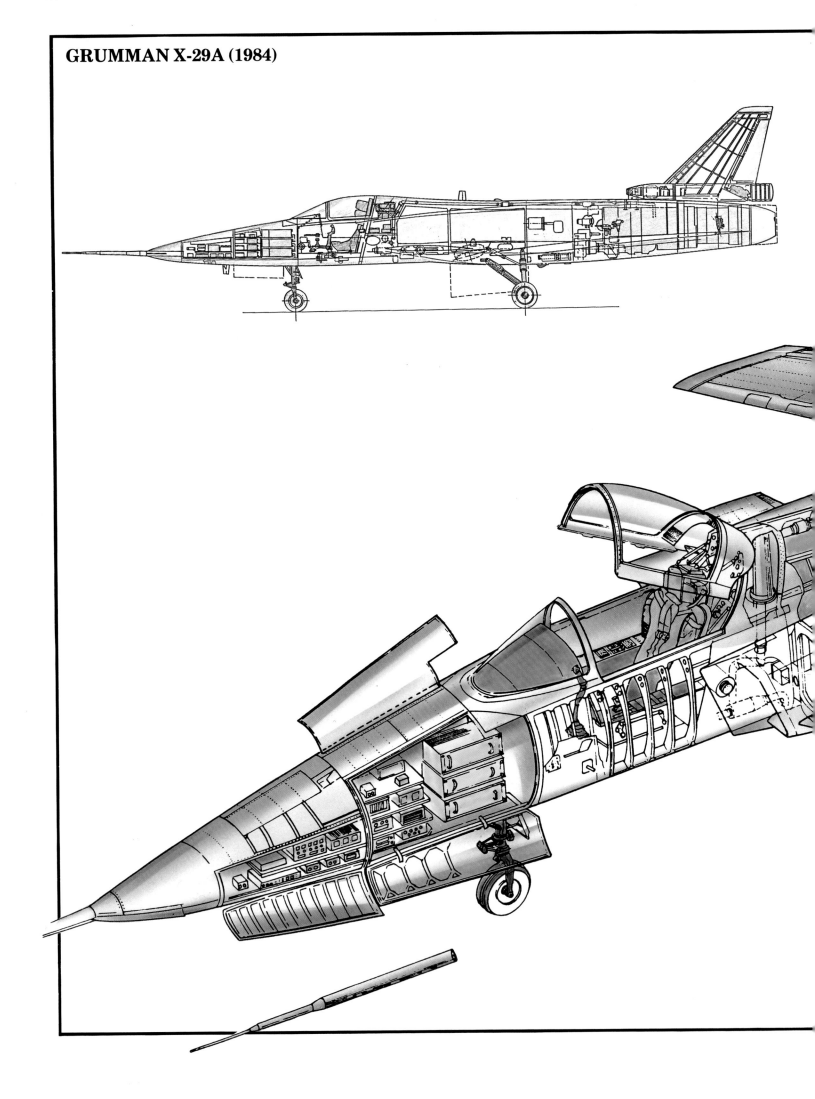

NAME: Grumman X-29A (USA)
TYPE: advanced technology, forward swept
  wing demonstrator
CREW: one
POWER PLANT: one 4,810kgp
  (10,600lb st) dry and
  7,167kgp (15,800lb st)
  reheat General Electric
  404-GE-400 turbofan
DIMENSIONS: span 8.23m (27ft 0in); length
  14.63m (48ft 0in);
  height 4.27m (14ft 0in);
  wing area 17.54m² (189sq ft)
WEIGHTS: empty 6,078kg (13,400lb);
loaded 7,893kg (17,400lb)
PERFORMANCE: (estimated) maximum
  speed 1,700 km/h (1,056
  mph) at 10,975m (36,000ft)

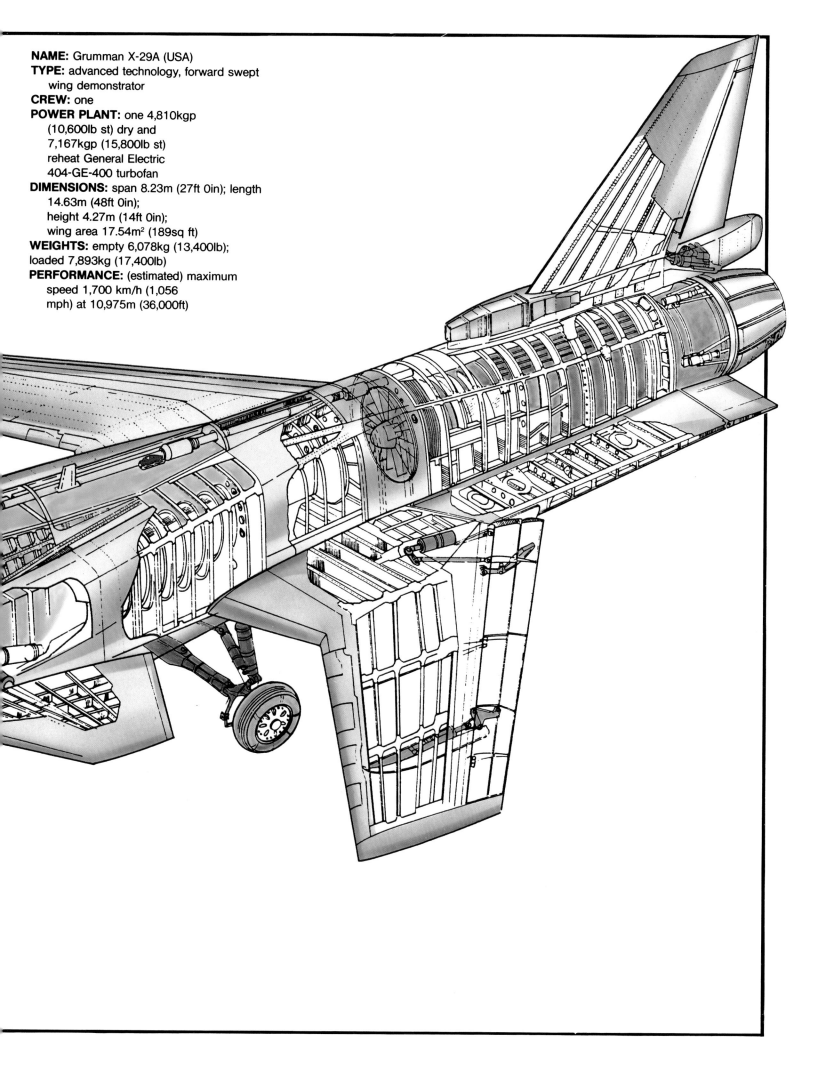

NORTHROP B-2 (1989)

Before the November 1988 roll-out of the USAF's new 'stealth' bomber the only clue to the aircraft's configuration was a sketch released the previous April. Greeted at the time with widespread scepticism, it showed a flying wing design with an unlikely-looking zig-zag trailing edge, a bulged centre section housing the crew compartment and flanked by delicately scalloped engine air intakes. As it turned out, the artist's impression was remarkably accurate, and since the B-2's first flight on 17 July 1989 much more has been revealed.

Such openness is in marked contrast to the secrecy that surrounded the bomber's development. The Advanced Technology Bomber programme, as it was known, got under way in 1978, when it was decided that the USAF needed a means of attacking targets such as Soviet mobile ICBM launchers that could not be targeted by any other weapon in the US strategic arsenal.

In 1981 a Lockheed/Rockwell submission was rejected in favour of a Northrop/Boeing proposal. Northrop as prime contractor was awarded a development contract in October 1981, and in November 1987 an initial $2 billion production contract followed. Boeing Advanced Systems manufactures the aft centre section and outboard sections, as well as the fuel system, weapons delivery system and landing gear. Another subcontractor, LTV, builds the intermediate sections, including the areas around the engines and landing gear. Northrop makes the forward centre section, including the cockpit, and carries out integration and final assembly of the aircraft.

No doubt the USAF would have preferred to maintain the almost impenetrable security blanket that had cloaked the development programme since its inception. However, at a time of increasing pressure on the US defence budget, the B-2's $530 million price tag made it one of the Pentagon's most controversial programmes, and secrecy has been sacrificed in the cause of public relations.

One of the most surprising revelations was the publication in October 1989 of detailed figures comparing the ranges of the B-2 and its predecessor in Strategic Air Command, the Rockwell B-1B. These predicted that with a 37,300lb (16,919kg) weapon load made up of eight Short Range Attack Missiles (SRAMs) and eight B83 nuclear bombs, plus more than 160,000lb (72,576kg) of fuel carried internally for a take-off weight of 371,000lb (168,421kg), the B-2 will have an unrefuelled range of 6,300nm at high altitude, or 4,400nm if the flight profile includes a low-level sector of 1,000nm. With lighter B61 bombs the respective figures are 6,600nm and 4,500nm.

Of course, the B-2 is equipped for air-to-air refuelling, a capability that was demonstrated during the prototype's sixth test flight in November 1989. The significance of the unrefuelled ranges is that they are as much as a quarter higher than those of the B-1B, which carries much more fuel, so that for nuclear strike missions against the Soviet Union the new bomber would need less than half the in-flight refuelling support required by its predecessor. Alternatively, on a conventional mission, the USAF calculates that three or four B-2s supported by just one or two tankers could have achieved the same results as the 100-plus tactical fighters and support aircraft used for the 1986 raid on Libya, with greater surprise and less risk of life.

Fuel efficiency on its own is not enough, though. The whole point of the B-2, and the only justification for its enormous cost, is that it is expected to be able to penetrate Soviet air defences, find its targets, deliver its weapons, and make it home again in one piece. To make maximum use of its long range it needs to be able to do so without resorting to low-level flight, which is where the low-observable or 'stealth' technology that governs every aspect of the bomber's shape, structure and general arrangement comes in.

Radar is the most important sensor used to detect hostile aircraft. The B-2's leading edges are designed to reflect radar energy in only two directions, focused in narrow beams and diluted by their coating of radar-absorbent material (RAM). Much of the aircraft's skin probably consists of honeycomb radar-absorbent structure (RAS), and the General Electric F118 engines are buried deep inside the wings, below and behind intricately-shaped intakes further shielded by RAM. Apart from the planform outline, there are no straight lines to be seen on the B-2, and surfaces are everywhere curved rather than flat.

As well as hiding the engines from radar, their buried location helps mask their noise and infra-red signatures. The B-2 is also said to be able to suppress its contrails while cruising at altitude, and in one of the three operational modes—'go to war'—that can be selected by a master switch, (the others are for takeoff and landing) all radio-frequency emitters are silenced. The most important emitter is the Hughes APQ-118 radar, whose transmitting elements are mounted in the underside of the leading edge. This is said to have unique features and performance characteristics specifically developed to avoid giving away the bomber's position while it uses its radar to search for targets.

Naturally, no flat surfaces means no vertical tail, and it is the need to compensate for the absence of conventional fin and rudder that accounts for that startling trailing edge. The outboard trailing edges carry drag rudders, which are usually kept open and which deflect to 45 degrees up and down on the landing approach. Inboard of each drag rudder is an elevon, with a further pair of elevons on the next leg of the zig-zag; the latter are used for primary flight control, supplemented by the outboard pair for low-speed flight. Finally, a beaver-tail control surface in the centre combines with the elevons to counteract the effects of gusts in low-level flight.

The control surfaces are large, accounting for some 15 per cent of the B-2's total wing area of more than 5,000 sq.ft (464.5m^2), and they are controlled by a quadruple-redundant fly-by-wire system using a 4,000psi hydraulic system for rapid actuation. The complex flight control system is able to take care of the aerodynamic problems resulting from the flying wing configuration, and as far as the pilots are concerned the bomber is very stable.

Although the flying wing has disadvantages in terms of control and stability, these appear to have been overcome by the General Electric flight control system, allowing its advantages to be exploited. Among the advantages are the fact that handling characteristics and thrust requirements remain virtually unchanged by changes in gross weight, allowing the crew to use a single take-off speed whatever the gross weight.

Meanwhile, despite an apparently successful initial flight test programme and the programme's survival after the first rounds of Congressional attempts to cancel it, there are still two question marks over the B-2. One is whether such an expensive warplane can continue to survive in an era of arms control and general budget cuts. The other is whether it would be able to survive the wartime operational scenario for which it was designed.

The USAF itself has identified more than 40 techniques that might enable a stealth aircraft to be detected, from acoustic systems to space-based radars. Nevertheless, the Air Force maintains that even though simple detection might be possible, effective defence against the B-2 is another matter. That would require the ability to detect it consistently at all altitudes, and to track it long enough and accurately enough for fighters to intercept it or for air-defence missiles to be guided within lethal range and detonated close enough to secure a kill. Invisible the B-2 may not be, the USAF admits, but it is survivability that counts.

To thunderous applause, the B-2 was unveiled to a select group of people in November 1988.

NORTHROP B-2 (1989)

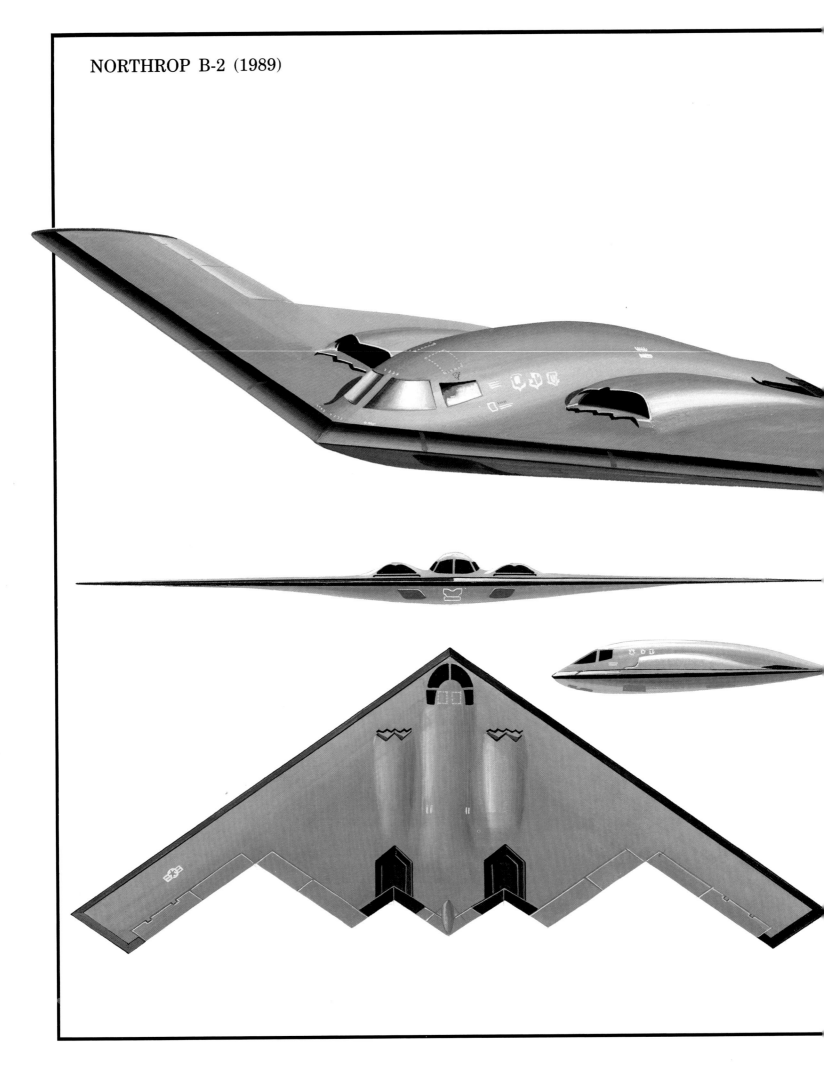

NAME: Northrop B-2 'Stealth'
TYPE: Long-range, low-detectability bomber
CREW: Two/three
POWER PLANT: Four 8,620kgp (19,000 lb s.t.)
  General Electric F118-GE-100 turbofans
DIMENSIONS: Span 52.43m (172ft); length 21.03m
  (69 ft)
WEIGHTS: MTOW 136,080kg (300,000 lb)
PERFORMANCE: Maximum speed 1,012km/h (546
  knots) at 15,240m (50,000 ft); range 11,110+km
  (6,000+naut. miles) unrefuelled
ARMAMENT: Up to sixteen SRAM II, AGM-129 or B83
  nuclear bombs stowed internally and carried on
  rotary dispenser within three weapons bays.
  Note: data on empty weight and operational ceiling
  remain classified

INDEX

Page numbers in **bold** refer to main entries including double-page illustrations: those in *italics* refer to photographic illustrations.